수능 영어 독해
번호별 완벽 대비

수능 트레이닝

유형편

수능 소개 및 머리말

○ 수능 영어 시험 알아보기

　이 시험은 학생들의 영어 실력을 평가하기 위해 고안되었으며, 주로 독해, 어휘, 문법, 듣기 영역을 포함합니다. 시험은 총 45문항으로 구성되며, 모두 객관식입니다. 듣기 평가 17문제를 제외하면 독해 문제는 총 28개이며, 45분 동안 28개의 독해 지문을 읽고 답을 찾아야 합니다.

　수능 영어 절대평가는 2018학년도부터 도입된 평가 방식으로, 학생들의 영어 실력을 상대평가가 아닌 절대평가로 평가하는 제도입니다. 절대평가는 모든 응시자의 점수를 기준으로 등급을 부여하는 것이 아니라, 일정 점수 이상을 획득하면 해당 점수에 맞는 등급을 받는 방식입니다. 100점 만점을 기준으로 1등급부터 9등급까지 9개의 등급으로 나뉘며, 이 제도의 도입 배경은 학생들이 영어에 과도한 시간과 노력을 투자하지 않도록 하고, 다른 과목의 학습에 더 많은 시간을 할애할 수 있도록 유도하기 위함입니다. 그러나 절대평가 도입 이후에도 영어의 중요성은 여전히 높으며, 특히 최상위 대학에 지원하려는 학생들에게는 1등급을 받는 것이 매우 중요합니다. 수능 독해의 번호별 유형과 [수능 트레이닝 유형편] UNIT 구성표는 아래와 같습니다.

○ 기출 유형별 UNIT 구성 - 수능 트레이닝 유형편

번호	유형	문제 수	수능 트레이닝 유형편 UNIT	페이지
18	목적 파악하기	1	UNIT 01	10
19	분위기, 심경 파악하기	1	UNIT 02	16
20	주장 파악하기	1	UNIT 03	24
21	함축 의미 파악하기	1	UNIT 05	38
22	요지 파악하기	1	UNIT 03	24
23	주제 파악하기	1	UNIT 04	30
24	제목 파악하기	1	UNIT 04	30
25	도표 내용 파악하기	1	UNIT 06	46
26 27 28	내용 일치/불일치 파악하기	3	UNIT 07	52
29	어법 적합성 판단하기	1	UNIT 08	60
30	어휘 적합성 판단하기	1	UNIT 09	68
31 32 33 34	빈칸 추론하기	4	UNIT 10	76
35	무관한 문장 파악하기	1	UNIT 11	84
36 37	글의 순서 파악하기	2	UNIT 12	90
38 39	주어진 문장 위치 파악하기	2	UNIT 13	96
40	요약문 완성하기	1	UNIT 14	104
41 42 43 44 45	장문 독해	5	UNIT 15	112

　수능 영어를 번호별로 유형 공략하는 수능 트레이닝 시리즈는 실제 기출 출제 순서에 맞춰 번호별로 문제를 풀어보고, 수능 유형에 익숙해지도록 돕는 **유형 학습 기본서 & 실전서 시리즈** 입니다.

책의 구성과 특징

1 번호별 문제 공략하기

유닛별 기출 유형의 정답률과 난이도를
파악하고, 해당 유형에 대한 학습 전략을
제시합니다.

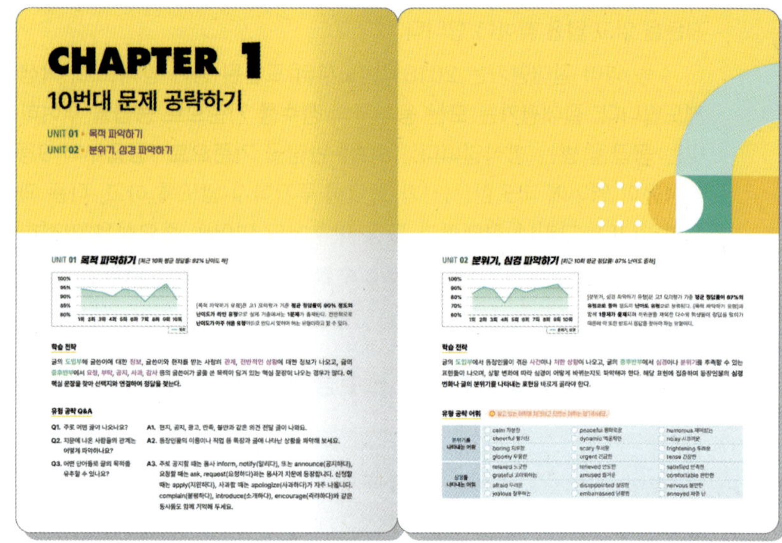

2 예제

실제 기출을 분석하여 중학생 또는 수능을
시작하는 모든 초보 학습자의 난이도에 맞춰
새로 쓴 실전 연습용 예제를 제공합니다.
우리말로 다시 정리해 보며 문해력을 향상시킬
수 있는 *READING BOOSTER* 코너
(지문 한눈에 보기, 정답 적중하기)도 함께
제공합니다. 지문에 나온 어휘 중
주요 중·고등 필수 어휘는
반드시 학습하도록 합니다.

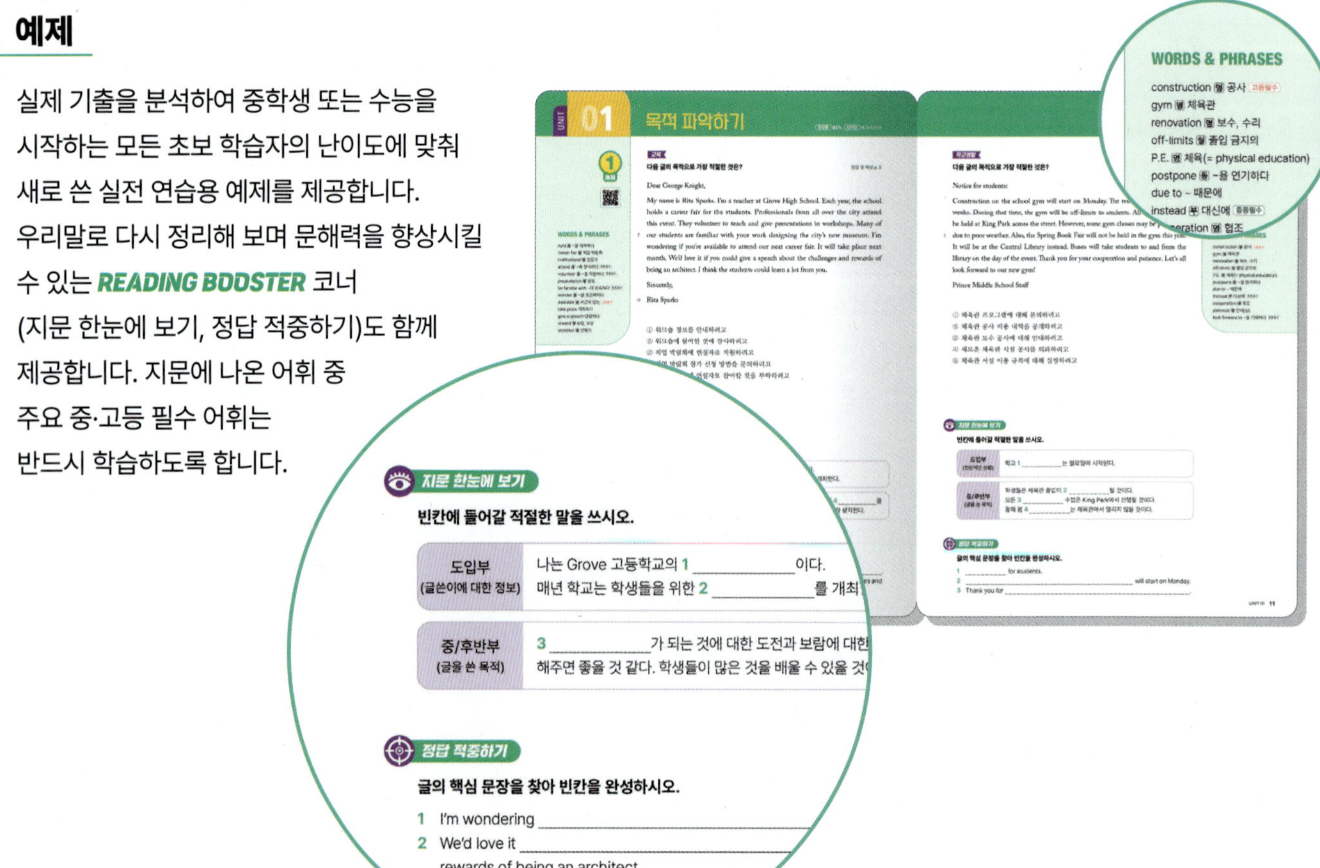

 **연습문제**

유닛별로 2개의 연습문제가 제시되며, 문제를 풀어 본 후
다양한 *GRAPHIC ORGANIZER*(FLOWCHART, MAPPING, BREAKDOWN)를 통해 지문을 정리합니다.
또한, 지문을 다시 학습할 수 있도록 *COMPREHENSION CHECK-UP*을 추가로
풀어볼 수 있습니다. 주요 표현을 다시 써보는 *PARAPHRASING DRILL*과
주요 어법을 학습하는 *TRANSLATION DRILL* 코너도 함께 제공합니다.

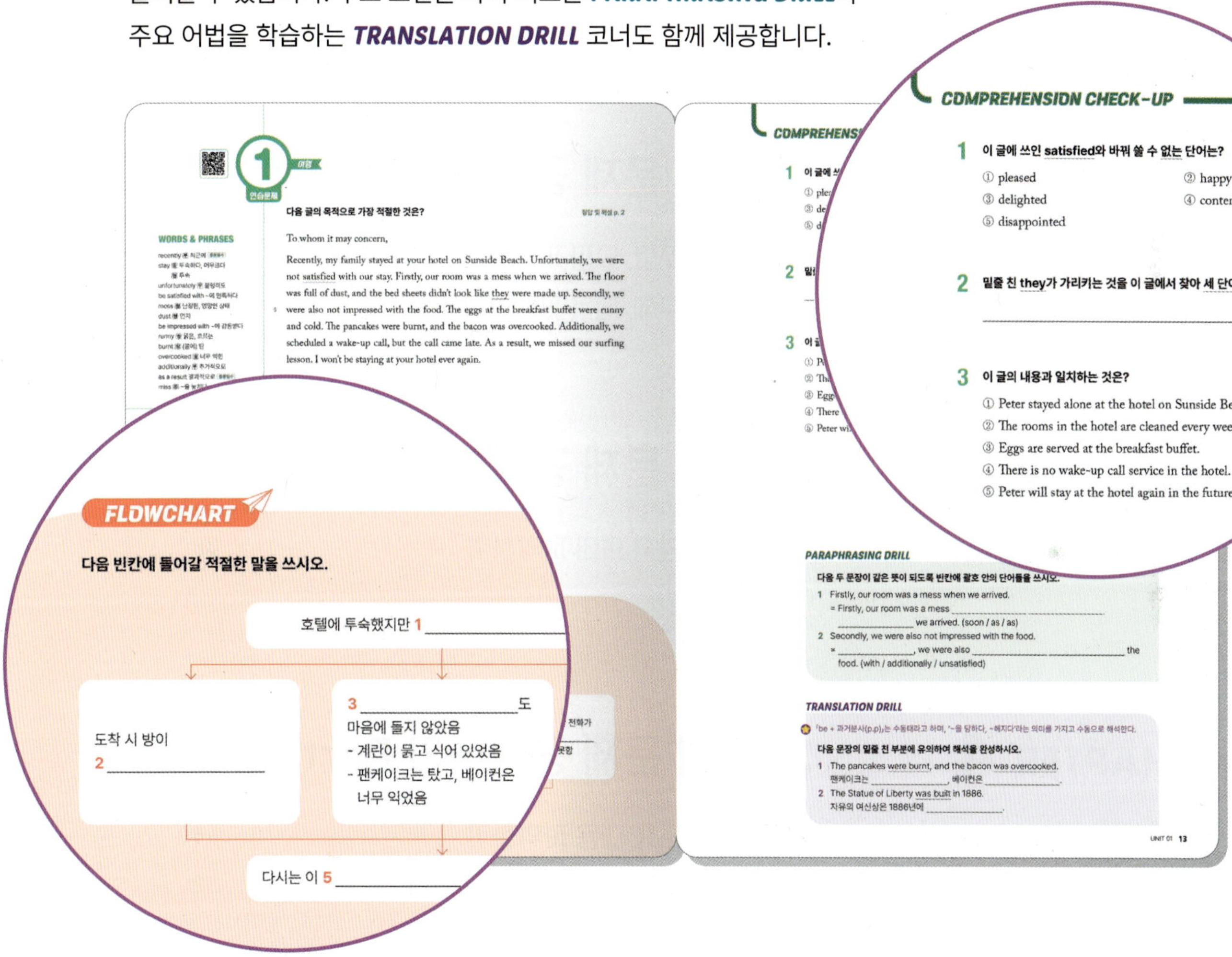

 **수업과 자습에 꼭 필요한 다양한 부가자료**

Audio, 지문 첨삭 해설, Word List, Word Test, Midterm Test, Final Test,
직독 직해 Worksheet, 구문 영작 Worksheet, Background Knowledge 부가자료 제공

CONTENTS

CHAPTER 1
10번대 문제 공략하기

UNIT 01 ● 목적 파악하기
UNIT 02 ● 분위기, 심경 파악하기

UNIT 01 목적 파악하기 [최근 10회 평균 정답률: 92% 난이도 하]

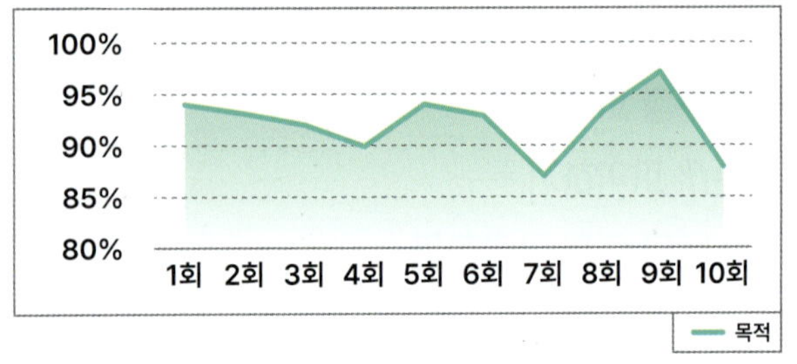

[목적 파악하기 유형]은 고1 모의평가 기준 **평균 정답률이 90% 정도의 난이도가 하인 유형**으로 실제 기출에서는 **1문제**가 출제된다. 전반적으로 **난이도가 아주 쉬운 유형**이므로 반드시 맞혀야 하는 유형이라고 할 수 있다.

학습 전략

글의 도입부에 글쓴이에 대한 정보, 글쓴이와 편지를 받는 사람의 관계, 전반적인 상황에 대한 정보가 나오고, 글의 중후반부에서 요청, 부탁, 공지, 사과, 감사 등의 글쓴이가 글을 쓴 목적이 담겨 있는 핵심 문장이 나오는 경우가 많다. 이 핵심 문장을 찾아 선택지와 연결하여 정답을 찾는다.

유형 공략 Q&A

Q1. 주로 어떤 글이 나오나요?

A1. 편지, 공지, 광고, 만족, 불만과 같은 의견 전달 글이 나와요.

Q2. 지문에 나온 사람들의 관계는 어떻게 파악하나요?

A2. 등장인물의 이름이나 직업 등 특징과 글에 나타난 상황을 파악해 보세요.

Q3. 어떤 단어들로 글의 목적을 유추할 수 있나요?

A3. 주로 공지할 때는 동사 inform, notify(알리다), 또는 announce(공지하다), 요청할 때는 ask, request(요청하다)라는 동사가 지문에 등장합니다. 신청할 때는 apply(지원하다), 사과할 때는 apologize(사과하다)가 자주 나옵니다. complain(불평하다), introduce(소개하다), encourage(격려하다)와 같은 동사들도 함께 기억해 두세요.

 분위기, 심경 파악하기 *[최근 10회 평균 정답률: 87% 난이도 중하]*

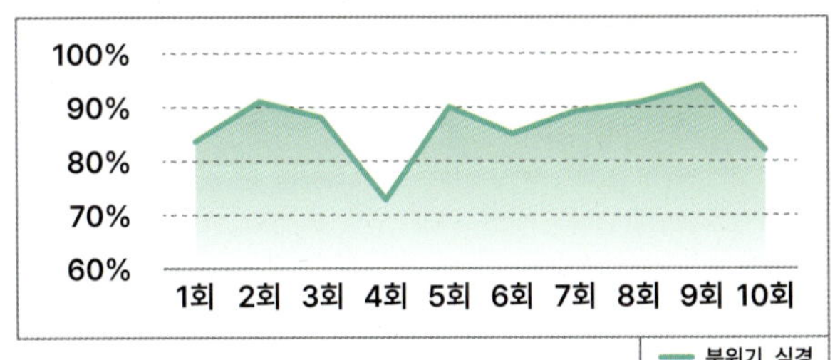

[분위기, 심경 파악하기 유형]은 고1 모의평가 기준 **평균 정답률이 87%의 유형으로 중하** 정도의 **난이도 유형**으로 분류된다. [목적 파악하기 유형]과 함께 **1문제가 출제**되며 하위권을 제외한 다수의 학생들이 정답을 맞히기 때문에 이 또한 반드시 정답을 찾아야 하는 유형이다.

학습 전략

글의 도입부에서 등장인물이 겪은 사건이나 처한 상황이 나오고, 글의 중후반부에서 심경이나 분위기를 추측할 수 있는 표현들이 나오며, 상황 변화에 따라 심경이 어떻게 바뀌는지도 파악해야 한다. 해당 표현에 집중하여 등장인물의 **심경 변화나 글의 분위기를 나타내는 표현**을 바르게 골라야 한다.

유형 공략 어휘 ⭐ 알고 있는 어휘에 체크하고 모르는 어휘는 암기하세요.

분위기를 나타내는 어휘	☐ calm 차분한 ☐ cheerful 활기찬	☐ peaceful 평화로운 ☐ dynamic 역동적인	☐ humorous 재미있는 ☐ noisy 시끄러운
	☐ boring 지루한 ☐ gloomy 우울한	☐ scary 무서운 ☐ urgent 긴급한	☐ frightening 두려운 ☐ tense 긴장한
심경을 나타내는 어휘	☐ relaxed 느긋한 ☐ grateful 고마워하는	☐ relieved 안도한 ☐ amused 즐거운	☐ satisfied 만족한 ☐ comfortable 편안한
	☐ afraid 두려운 ☐ jealous 질투하는	☐ disappointed 실망한 ☐ embarrassed 당황한	☐ nervous 불안한 ☐ annoyed 짜증 난

목적 파악하기

정답률 92% 난이도 ★☆☆☆☆

WORDS & PHRASES

hold 통 ~을 개최하다
career fair 명 직업 박람회
professional 명 전문가
attend 통 ~에 참석하다 중등필수
volunteer 통 ~을 자원하다 중등필수
presentation 명 발표
be familiar with ~에 친숙하다 중등필수
wonder 통 ~을 궁금해하다
available 형 시간이 있는 고등필수
take place 개최되다
give a speech 연설하다
reward 명 보람, 보상
architect 명 건축가

교육

다음 글의 목적으로 가장 적절한 것은?

정답 및 해설 p. 2

Dear George Knight,

My name is Rita Sparks. I'm a teacher at Grove High School. Each year, the school holds a career fair for the students. Professionals from all over the city attend this event. They volunteer to teach and give presentations in workshops. Many of
5 our students are familiar with your work designing the city's new museum. I'm wondering if you're available to attend our next career fair. It will take place next month. We'd love it if you could give a speech about the challenges and rewards of being an architect. I think the students could learn a lot from you.

Sincerely,

10 Rita Sparks

① 워크숍 정보를 안내하려고
② 워크숍에 참여한 것에 감사하려고
③ 직업 박람회에 연설자로 지원하려고
④ 직업 박람회 참가 신청 방법을 문의하려고
⑤ 직업 박람회에 연설자로 참여할 것을 부탁하려고

👁 지문 한눈에 보기

빈칸에 들어갈 적절한 말을 쓰시오.

도입부 (글쓴이에 대한 정보)	나는 Grove 고등학교의 **1** ____________ 이다. 매년 학교는 학생들을 위한 **2** ____________ 를 개최한다.
중/후반부 (글을 쓴 목적)	**3** ____________ 가 되는 것에 대한 도전과 보람에 대한 **4** ____________ 을 해주면 좋을 것 같다. 학생들이 많은 것을 배울 수 있을 것이라 생각한다.

🎯 정답 적중하기

글의 핵심 문장을 찾아 빈칸을 완성하시오.

1 I'm wondering ____.
2 We'd love it ________________________________ about the challenges and rewards of being an architect.

다음 글의 목적으로 가장 적절한 것은?

정답 및 해설 p. 2

Notice for students:

Construction on the school gym will start on Monday. The renovation will take six
weeks. During that time, the gym will be off-limits to students. All P.E. classes will
be held at King Park across the street. However, some gym classes may be postponed
5 due to poor weather. Also, the Spring Book Fair will not be held in the gym this year.
It will be at the Central Library instead. Buses will take students to and from the
library on the day of the event. Thank you for your cooperation and patience. Let's all
look forward to our new gym!

Prince Middle School Staff

① 체육관 프로그램에 대해 문의하려고
② 체육관 공사 비용 내역을 공개하려고
③ 체육관 보수 공사에 대해 안내하려고
④ 새로운 체육관 시설 공사를 의뢰하려고
⑤ 체육관 시설 이용 규칙에 대해 설명하려고

WORDS & PHRASES

construction 명 공사 [고등필수]
gym 명 체육관
renovation 명 보수, 수리
off-limits 형 출입 금지의
P.E. 명 체육(= physical education)
postpone 동 ~을 연기하다
due to ~ 때문에
instead 부 대신에 [중등필수]
cooperation 명 협조
patience 명 인내(심)
look forward to ~을 기대하다 [중등필수]

지문 한눈에 보기

빈칸에 들어갈 적절한 말을 쓰시오.

도입부 (전반적인 상황)	학교 **1** ______________ 는 월요일에 시작된다.
중/후반부 (글을 쓴 목적)	학생들은 체육관 출입이 **2** ____________ 될 것이다. 모든 **3** ____________ 수업은 King Park에서 진행될 것이다. 올해 봄 **4** ____________ 는 체육관에서 열리지 않을 것이다.

정답 적중하기

글의 핵심 문장을 찾아 빈칸을 완성하시오.

1 ____________ for students.

2 ____ will start on Monday.

3 Thank you for ____ .

다음 글의 목적으로 가장 적절한 것은? 정답 및 해설 p. 2

WORDS & PHRASES

recently (부) 최근에 (중등필수)
stay (동) 투숙하다, 머무르다
　　　(명) 투숙
unfortunately (부) 불행히도
be satisfied with ~에 만족하다
mess (명) 난장판, 영망인 상태
dust (명) 먼지
be impressed with ~에 감동받다
runny (형) 묽은, 흐르는
burnt (형) (불에) 탄
overcooked (형) 너무 익힌
additionally (부) 추가적으로
as a result 결과적으로 (중등필수)
miss (동) ~을 놓치다

To whom it may concern,

Recently, my family stayed at your hotel on Sunside Beach. Unfortunately, we were not <u>satisfied</u> with our stay. Firstly, our room was a mess when we arrived. The floor was full of dust, and the bed sheets didn't look like <u>they</u> were made up. Secondly, we were also not impressed with the food. The eggs at the breakfast buffet were runny and cold. The pancakes were burnt, and the bacon was overcooked. Additionally, we scheduled a wake-up call, but the call came late. As a result, we missed our surfing lesson. I won't be staying at your hotel ever again.

Sincerely,

Peter Black

① 모닝콜 서비스를 요청하려고
② 새로 지은 호텔을 홍보하려고
③ 객실 서비스에 대해 문의하려고
④ 새로운 상품의 가입을 안내하려고
⑤ 불만족스러운 서비스에 대해 항의하려고

FLOWCHART

다음 빈칸에 들어갈 적절한 말을 쓰시오.

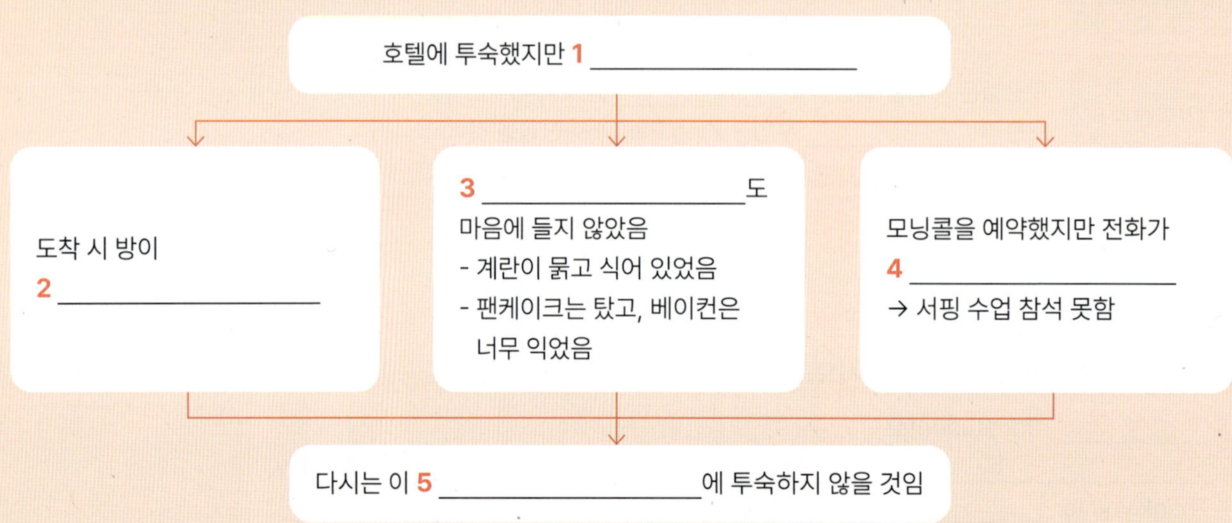

1 이 글에 쓰인 **satisfied**와 바꿔 쓸 수 없는 단어는?

① pleased   ② happy

③ delighted   ④ content

⑤ disappointed

2 밑줄 친 **they**가 가리키는 것을 이 글에서 찾아 세 단어로 쓰시오.

____

3 이 글의 내용과 일치하는 것은?

① Peter stayed alone at the hotel on Sunside Beach.

② The rooms in the hotel are cleaned every week.

③ Eggs are served at the breakfast buffet.

④ There is no wake-up call service in the hotel.

⑤ Peter will stay at the hotel again in the future.

PARAPHRASING DRILL

다음 두 문장이 같은 뜻이 되도록 빈칸에 괄호 안의 단어들을 쓰시오.

1 Firstly, our room was a mess when we arrived.

= Firstly, our room was a mess ______________ ______________ ______________ we arrived. (soon / as / as)

2 Secondly, we were also not impressed with the food.

= ______________, we were also ______________ ______________ the food. (with / additionally / unsatisfied)

TRANSLATION DRILL

⭐ 「be + 과거분사(p.p)」는 수동태라고 하며, '~을 당하다, ~해지다'라는 의미를 가지고 수동으로 해석한다.

다음 문장의 밑줄 친 부분에 유의하여 해석을 완성하시오.

1 The pancakes were burnt, and the bacon was overcooked.

팬케이크는 ______________, 베이컨은 ______________.

2 The Statue of Liberty was built in 1886.

자유의 여신상은 1886년에 ______________.

다음 글의 목적으로 가장 적절한 것은?

정답 및 해설 p. 3

WORDS & PHRASES

attention 몡 주목
lover 몡 애호가
improve 통 ~을 향상시키다 고등필수
offer 통 ~을 제공하다
a variety of 다양한
instructor 몡 강사
talented 혱 재능 있는
knowledgeable 혱 지식이 풍부한
sign up for ~에 등록하다
sculpt 통 조각하다
photography 몡 사진 촬영(술)
pottery 몡 도자기
knitting 몡 뜨개질
semester 몡 학기
receive 통 ~을 받다 중등필수
information 몡 정보 중등필수

Attention art lovers!

Are you interested in improving your art skills? Bright Studios is now offering a variety of courses. Our instructors are both talented and knowledgeable. They are ready to guide you along your art journey. Beginners can <u>sign up</u> for the Art Basics course. You will learn how to sketch and paint. If you're interested in sculpting, take Sculpting Level 1, 2, or 3. We also offer photography, pottery, and knitting classes. The next semester begins in early January. Classes will be held twice a week over seven weeks. Sign up by December 28th and receive a 10% discount! Visit our website for more information: www.brightstudios.com.

① 미술 대회 불참을 통보하려고
② 미술 수업 과정을 홍보하려고
③ 단체 등록 특별 할인을 요청하려고
④ 미술 전시회 일정 변경을 공지하려고
⑤ 수업 단계 변경 가능 여부를 확인하려고

MAPPING

다음 빈칸에 들어갈 적절한 말을 <보기>에서 찾아 쓰시오.

보기

| signing up | sketch | levels | twice | knowledge |

Instructors
Having talent and **1** ________________

Next Semester
Starting from early January, taking classes
4 ________________ a week for 7 weeks

Beginners
Learning skills to
2 ________________ and paint

Bright Studios Art Courses

Discount
Offering 10% off when
5 ________________ by December 28th

Other Classes
Different **3** ________________ of sculpting, also photography, pottery, knitting classes

1 이 글에 쓰인 **sign up**과 뜻이 비슷한 단어는?

① solve　　　　　　　② select

③ trigger　　　　　　④ register

⑤ abandon

2 다음 빈칸에 들어갈 말로 가장 적절한 것은?

> Art lovers can ________________________________.

① sign up for an advanced class only

② learn only sketches in basic classes

③ take various sculpting classes

④ attend classes once a week

⑤ get a 20% discount by December 28th

3 이 글을 읽고 다음 질문에 대한 답을 두 단어로 쓰시오.

> **Q:** When does the next semester begin?

→ ________________________________

PARAPHRASING DRILL

다음 문장들이 같은 뜻이 되도록 빈칸에 들어갈 적절한 말을 <보기>에서 찾아 쓰시오.

> **보기**
>
> lead　　　prepared　　　throughout

They are ready to guide you along your art journey.

= They are ______________ to guide you along your art journey.

= They are ready to ______________ you along your art journey.

= They are ready to guide you ______________ your art journey.

TRANSLATION DRILL

⭐ 「how + to부정사」는 '~하는 방법'이라고 해석한다.

다음 문장의 밑줄 친 부분에 유의하여 해석을 완성하시오.

1 You will learn how to sketch and paint.

당신은 ______________________을 배울 것이다.

2 Can you show me how to use this software?

이 소프트웨어를 ______________을 보여줄 수 있나요?

WORDS & PHRASES

autumn 명 가을
village 명 마을 중등필수
celebrate 동 ~을 기념하다
harvest 동 수확하다 명 수확 고등필수
crop 명 농작물 고등필수
pumpkin 명 호박
villager 명 마을 사람
gather 동 모이다 중등필수
bonfire 명 모닥불
feast 명 진수성찬, 잔치
elder 명 원로, 연장자
ancestor 명 조상
beat 동 ~을 치다, 두드리다
join in ~에 합류[동참]하다

문화

다음 글의 상황에 나타난 분위기로 가장 적절한 것은?   정답 및 해설 p. 4

Every autumn, Kabelo's village celebrated the harvest. Kabelo was small for a nine-year-old, but he worked hard to help his village all summer. Together, they grew crops, such as potatoes, pumpkins, and corn. Harvesting the crops was hard work, but finally, the job was done. The villagers gathered around a large bonfire. They prepared
5 a delicious feast with the food they grew. After the feast, the village elders sat around the fire and told stories of their brave ancestors. Then the drummers began to beat their drums, and the singers joined in. Kabelo watched young boys and girls twirl around the fire. It looked like so much fun, so he joined them. Together, they danced and danced under the stars. Kabelo hoped every harvest could be that wonderful.

* twirl 빙글빙글 돌다

① festive
② scary
③ boring
④ relaxing
⑤ urgent

👁 지문 한눈에 보기

빈칸에 들어갈 적절한 말을 쓰시오.

도입부 (인물의 상황)	매년 가을, Kabelo의 마을은 **1** ______________을 기념했다. 마을 사람들은 감자, 호박, **2** ______________와 같은 농작물을 키웠다.

중/후반부 (분위기 추측)	수확 후에는 재배한 음식으로 **3** ______________을 준비했다. 드럼 연주자는 드럼을 쳤고, 가수들도 합류했다. 소년, 소녀들은 **4** ______________ 주변에서 빙글빙글 돌며 춤을 추었다.

🎯 정답 적중하기

글의 핵심 문장을 찾아 빈칸을 완성하시오.

1 Kabelo's village ________________ the harvest.
2 Then the drummers began to ____________________________, and the singers joined in.
3 It looked like ____________________________, so he joined them.

다음 글에 드러난 Thomas의 심경 변화로 가장 적절한 것은? 정답 및 해설 p. 4

Thomas' palms were clammy as he approached a cluster of students in the hallway. They all huddled around a notice taped to the wall. The drama teacher had posted the audition results. Last week, Thomas had tried out for the lead role in *The Littlest Lion*. Now, he would finally know if he made the cut. Sweat broke out on Thomas'
5 forehead as he pushed through the crowd. He read the list of names on the paper. There was his own name right next to the words *Lead Role*. The students patted Thomas on the back and cheered his name. Thomas had never felt so wonderful and finally his dream came true!

① fascinated → tragic
② concerned → relaxed
③ hopeless → thankful
④ discouraged → relieved
⑤ nervous → delighted

WORDS & PHRASES

palm 명 손바닥
clammy 형 축축한
approach 통 다가가다, 접근하다 중등필수
cluster 명 무리
hallway 명 복도
huddle 통 옹기종기 모이다
notice 명 안내문
post 통 게시하다 중등필수
try out for (오디션 등에) 지원하다
lead role 명 주연, 주인공 역할
make the cut 최종 명단에 들다,
　　　　　 본선에 진출하다
sweat 명 땀
break out (땀, 여드름 등이) 나다
forehead 명 이마
crowd 명 군중 중등필수
pat 통 토닥거리다
cheer 통 환호하다

 **지문 한눈에 보기**

빈칸에 들어갈 적절한 말을 쓰시오.

도입부 (인물의 상황)	복도에 있는 학생들에게 다가갈 때 Thomas의 손바닥은 **1** ＿＿＿＿＿＿＿했다. 연극 선생님이 벽에 오디션 결과 **2** ＿＿＿＿＿＿＿을 붙여 놓으셨다.
중/후반부 (심경 변화 추측)	**3** '＿＿＿＿＿＿'이라는 말 바로 옆에 그의 이름이 있었다. 학생들은 Thomas의 등을 두드리며 그의 이름을 **4** ＿＿＿＿＿＿했다. Thomas는 이렇게 멋지게 느낀 적이 없었고, 마침내 그의 꿈이 이루어졌다.

정답 적중하기

글의 핵심 문장을 찾아 빈칸을 완성하시오.

1 Thomas' palms were ＿＿＿＿＿＿＿＿＿＿＿＿＿＿＿＿＿＿ a cluster of students in the hallway.
2 ＿＿＿＿＿＿＿＿＿＿＿＿＿＿＿＿＿ on Thomas' forehead as he pushed through the crowd.
3 Thomas had ＿＿＿＿＿＿＿＿＿＿＿＿＿＿＿＿ and finally his dream came true!

다음 글의 상황에 나타난 분위기로 가장 적절한 것은?

정답 및 해설 p. 4

WORDS & PHRASES

stare 통 응시하다 (중등필수)
alive 형 (살아 움직이는 것들이) 가득한
hoot 통 (부엉이 등의 새가) 울다
howl 통 긴 울음소리를 내다
in the distance 먼 곳에
scratch 통 긁다
shake-shook-shaken 통 흔들리다
as if 마치 ~인 것처럼 (중등필수)
brush 통 ~을 스치다
coyote 명 코요테
frozen 형 얼어붙은
utter 통 (입으로 소리를) 내다
fade 통 (서서히) 사라지다
lie-lay-lain 통 눕다, 누워 있다 (중등필수)
disappear 통 (완전히) 사라지다 (중등필수)

Anna woke up and stared into the pitch black of her tent. It was the middle of the night at Glenview Campground and the forest was alive with noise. Owls hooted and wolves howled in the distance. Anna listened to each sound <u>carefully</u>. One sound was getting closer and closer. Something was scratching the ground near the door to Anna's tent. The tent shook as if something large had just brushed up against it. Perhaps it was a coyote or maybe it was a bear. Anna wanted to scream and wake her parents, but fear kept her frozen. She couldn't utter a single sound. Soon, the scratching faded and then appeared again. All night, Anna lay awake, listening for the scratching. She waited for whatever it was to disappear.

* pitch black 칠흑같이 어두컴컴한 곳

① hilarious and fun
② festive and exciting
③ strange and frightening
④ calm and relaxing
⑤ quiet and dull

다음 빈칸에 들어갈 적절한 말을 쓰시오.

Anna는 한밤중 **1** ________________이 가득한 숲에서 캠핑을 함
부엉이들이 울고, 늑대들이 울부짖음

↓

한 소리가 점점 텐트에 **2** ________________
텐트는 거대한 어떤 것에 스친 것처럼 흔들렸음

↓

부모님을 깨우고 싶었지만 **3** ________________이 그녀를 얼어붙게 함
소리를 전혀 낼 수 없었음

↓

긁는 소리가 계속되어, 밤새 누운 채로 **4** ________________

1 이 글에 쓰인 **carefully**와 뜻이 비슷한 단어는?

① hardly　　　　　　　　② closely

③ politely　　　　　　　　④ steadily

⑤ passively

2 이 글을 읽고 다음 질문에 답할 때 빈칸에 들어갈 말을 한 단어로 쓰시오.

> **Q:** Why did Anna wake up in the middle of the night?

→ It is because there was full of ________________ in the forest.

3 이 글의 내용과 일치하지 <u>않는</u> 것은?

① Anna could hear the distant animal howl.

② One of the sounds was getting closer and closer.

③ Something was scratching the ground near Anna's tent.

④ Large coyotes and bears tried to tear Anna's tent apart.

⑤ Anna couldn't say even a single word due to fear.

PARAPHRASING DRILL

다음 두 문장이 같은 뜻이 되도록 빈칸에 괄호 안의 단어들을 쓰시오.

1 The tent shook as if something large had just brushed up against it.
= The tent ________________ ________________ ________________
something large had just brushed up against it. (though / trembled / as)

2 Anna wanted to scream and wake her parents, but fear kept her frozen.
= Anna ________________ ________________ ________________ ________________ ________________
and wake her parents, but fear kept her frozen. (desire / shout / to / had / a)

TRANSLATION DRILL

⭐ 「get + 비교급 + and + 비교급」은 '점점 더 ~하게 되다'로 해석하고, 비교급을 두 번 반복해 줌으로써 의미를 강조한다.

다음 문장의 밑줄 친 부분에 유의하여 해석을 완성하시오.

1 One sound was <u>getting closer and closer</u>.
한 소리는 ________________________ 있었다.

2 The birds were <u>getting higher and higher</u> in the sky.
그 새들은 하늘로 ________________________ 있었다.

다음 글에 드러난 Jenny의 심경 변화로 가장 적절한 것은? 정답 및 해설 p. 5

WORDS & PHRASES

win a prize 상을 받다
after all 결국
solar system 몡 태양계
expect 통 예상하다 중등필수
blow-blew-blown 통 (바람이) 불다
carry 통 ~을 옮기다
suddenly 분 갑자기
crash 통 충돌하다
planet 몡 행성
tumble 통 굴러 떨어지다
sidewalk 몡 인도, (포장된) 보도
crack 통 갈라지다, 금이 가다
ruin 통 망치다, 망가지다 고등필수
urge 몡 충동
dig into 뒤지다, 파헤치다
pull out ~을 꺼내다
glue 몡 접착제
chance 몡 기회, 가능성

Jenny knew she would win a prize at the science fair. After all, she had spent three weeks building her model of the solar system. But the model was heavier than Jenny expected. A strong wind blew in as she carried it to school. Suddenly, the model crashed to the ground. The planets tumbled across the sidewalk, and some cracked in
5 half. "It's ruined!" Jenny said as she fought the <u>urge</u> to kick something. Then, Jenny's best friend, Mindy ran over. She dug into her bag, pulled out a bottle of glue, and said, "Let's fix it together." Jenny smiled and began picking up the cracked planets. There was still a chance she would win a prize.

① thankful → nervous
② frustrated → hopeful
③ embarrassed → relaxed
④ fascinated → annoyed
⑤ amused → guilty

다음 빈칸에 들어갈 적절한 말을 영어로 쓰시오.

> Jenny thought that she could **1** __________ a prize.

↓

> Due to a strong wind, Jenny's model suddenly tumbled and some planets **2** __________ in half.

↓

> Mindy, her best friend, tried to help her **3** __________ the planets with the glue.

↓

> Jenny felt like there was still a **4** __________ she would win a prize.

1 이 글에 쓰인 **urge**와 뜻이 비슷한 단어는?

① peace
② advice
③ support
④ desire
⑤ suggestion

2 다음 빈칸에 들어갈 말로 가장 적절한 것은?

> What Jenny made for the science fair was heavier than she ___________________.

① saw
② told
③ completed
④ participated
⑤ anticipated

3 밑줄 친 **It**이 가리키는 것을 이 글에서 찾아 두 단어로 쓰시오.

____

PARAPHRASING DRILL

다음 문장들이 같은 뜻이 되도록 빈칸에 들어갈 적절한 말을 <보기>에서 찾아 쓰시오.

> • 보기 •
>
> down   rolled   split

The planets tumbled across the sidewalk, and some cracked in half.

= The planets ________________ across the sidewalk, and some cracked in half.

= The planets tumbled ________________ the sidewalk, and some cracked in half.

= The planets tumbled across the sidewalk, and some ________________ in half.

TRANSLATION DRILL

⭐ 「spend + (시간) + (in) + 동명사」는 '~하는 데 (시간)을 보내다'라고 해석한다. 이때 동명사 앞의 in은 생략 가능하다.

다음 문장의 밑줄 친 부분에 유의하여 해석을 완성하시오.

1 She had spent three weeks building her model.
그녀는 그녀의 모형을 ________________________________.

2 He spent four hours repairing the broken fence in the backyard.
그는 뒷마당에 있는 부서진 울타리를 ________________________________.

CHAPTER 2
20번대 문제 공략하기 Part 1

UNIT 03 • 주장, 요지 파악하기
UNIT 04 • 주제, 제목 파악하기

UNIT 03 주장, 요지 파악하기 [최근 10회 평균 정답률: 주장 85% 난이도 중하 / 요지 80% 난이도 중하]

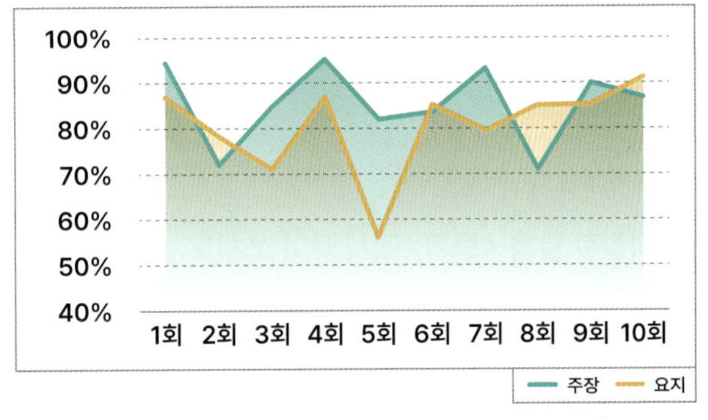

[주장, 요지 파악하기 유형]은 **평균 정답률**이 **80%** 정도로 **중하의 난이도**로 출제되는 유형이다. 정답률이 높은 유형이나 그래프를 통해 알 수 있듯이, 가끔 킬러 문항으로 바뀌어 낮은 정답률을 보이는 경우도 있다. 주제, 제목 유형과 함께 **각각 1문제**가 출제되며 선택지가 한글로 제시된다는 점이 주제, 제목 유형과는 다르다. 30번대에 포진한 킬러 문항을 틀릴 수 있기 때문에 20번대 해당 유형들은 반드시 정답을 맞혀야 한다.

학습 전략

주장과 요지 유형 모두 중심 소재를 먼저 파악하고, 그 소재에 대한 글쓴이의 의견을 정확하게 파악해야 한다. 또한 선택지의 내용을 명확하게 이해해야 한다. 멋진 말을 써 놓았거나 일반적인 사실을 말한 경우, 그리고 지문 내용의 일부만 요약한 경우 오답을 이끌기 위한 함정일 수 있다. 글쓴이의 의견을 전체적으로 잘 요약한 선택지를 골라야 한다.

유형 공략 어휘 ⭐ 알고 있는 어휘에 체크하고 모르는 어휘는 암기하세요.

당위성을 나타내는 어휘	☐ should, must, have to ~ 해야 한다	☐ need to ~할 필요가 있다
	☐ had better ~하는 것이 낫다	☐ it is important(necessary) ~ ~하는 것이 중요하다(필요하다)
대조를 나타내는 어휘	☐ however 하지만	☐ on the other hand 반면에
양보를 나타내는 어휘	☐ although, even though 비록 ~일지라도	☐ nevertheless 그럼에도 불구하고
강조를 나태내는 어휘	☐ in short 요약하면	☐ above all 무엇보다
	☐ as a matter of a fact 사실	☐ in other words 다시 말해

UNIT 04 *주제, 제목 파악하기* *[최근 10회 평균 정답률: 주제 72% 난이도 중 / 제목 69% 난이도 중]*

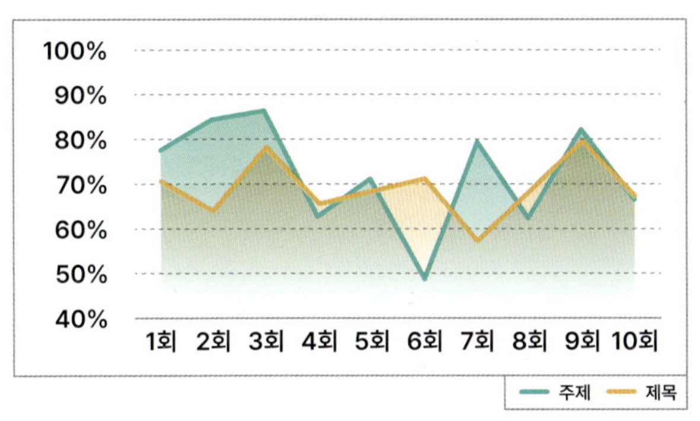

[주제, 제목 파악하기 유형]은 **평균 정답률이 60~70%** 정도로 **고득점을 가르는 핵심 유형**이다. 기출에서 **각각 1문제**가 출제되며 **고득점을 위해 반드시 맞혀야 하는 유형**이지만, 실력을 쌓지 않으면 쉽게 맞힐 수 없는 유형이다. 전체적인 내용 이해를 통해 지문의 핵심을 파악하는 것이 중요하다.

학습 전략

중심 내용을 파악하는 것이 [주제, 제목 파악하기] 유형의 기본이며, 아래와 같이 지문 구조에 대해 알고 중심 내용을 찾는 연습을 꾸준히 해야 한다. 제목 유형의 경우 주제 유형과 같이 접근하되 그 내용을 핵심적이고 함축적으로 **요약한 문장**을 제목으로 골라야 한다.

■ 주제문을 제시하는 방식

❶
- 주제문
- 뒷받침 문장, 예시

❷
- 문제점 제기, 예시 또는 소재 소개
- 주제문

❸
- 일반적 의견이나 경향
- 반론하는 주제문
- 뒷받침 문장

❹
- 주제문
- 예시나 근거를 나타내는 뒷받침 문장
- 주제문

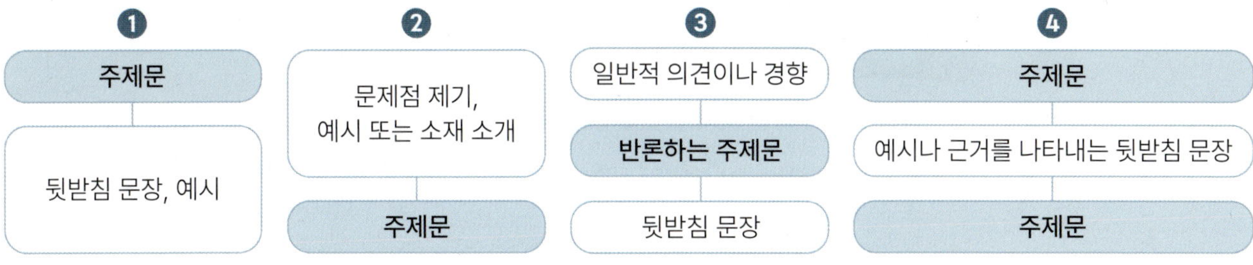

WORDS & PHRASES

fairy 명 요정
godmother 명 대모
flick 명 휙 움직임, 튕기기
wand 명 지팡이
spell 명 (마법) 주문
exist 동 존재하다 중등필수
reality 명 현실
negative 형 부정적인
get stuck on ~에 집착하다
helpless 형 무력한
rather 부 차라리, 오히려
positive 형 긍정적인
envision 동 마음에 그리다, 상상하다
solve 동 ~을 해결하다 중등필수
achieve 동 ~을 성취하다 중등필수
statement 명 진술
motivate 동 동기부여하다
come true 이루어지다

심리

다음 글에서 필자가 주장하는 바로 가장 적절한 것은? 정답 및 해설 p. 6

Do you ever wish you could have a fairy godmother like Cinderella did? In fairy tales, you could get what you want with a flick of a wand or a magic spell. However, magic does not truly exist. In reality, a pen may be as powerful as a wand. If there's something you want to change about your life, try writing about it. But don't focus
5 on your negative feelings. Don't get stuck on feeling helpless. Rather, try to focus on the positive. Try to envision your life once your problem has been solved. List all the goals you hope to achieve. For example, you might write, "I will make the soccer team this year." You might also write, "I will pass all of my exams." These statements will motivate you to make your dreams come true.

① 무기력함을 벗어나기 위해서는 성취하고자 하는 목표를 가져라.
② 내가 원하는 삶을 살고자 한다면 매일 자기 전에 상상하라.
③ 자기 삶에 변화를 원한다면 긍정적인 내용의 글을 써 보라.
④ 마법과 같은 말로 사람을 설득할 수 있도록 노력하라.
⑤ 꿈을 이루기 위해서는 스스로 동기부여를 하라.

👁 지문 한눈에 보기

빈칸에 들어갈 적절한 말을 쓰시오.

도입부 (일반적인 사실)	현실에서는 마법 지팡이나 **1** ＿＿＿＿＿은 존재하지 않는다.

중반부 (반론/주제문)	삶에 대해서 **2** ＿＿＿＿ 것이 있다면, 그것에 대해 펜으로 써 보라. 단, 부정적인 감정이 아닌 **3** ＿＿＿＿ 것에 집중하려 노력하라.

후반부 (뒷받침 문장)	성취하기를 원하는 모든 목표를 목록으로 만들면, 당신의 꿈을 이루도록 **4** ＿＿＿＿를 부여할 것이다.

🎯 정답 적중하기

글의 핵심 문장을 찾아 빈칸을 완성하시오.

1 In fairy tales, you could get ＿＿＿＿＿ you want with a flick of a wand or a magic spell.
2 In reality, a pen may be as ＿＿＿＿＿ as a wand.
3 If there's something you want to change about your life, try ＿＿＿＿＿ about it.

다음 글의 요지로 가장 적절한 것은?

정답 및 해설 p. 6

The car, the light bulb, the airplane and the ball-point pen. These are just a few of the inventions that have changed the way humans live. How do inventors come up with their inventions? Most of the time, they identify a need. For example, in the past, travel was limited and time-consuming. People needed a faster and more efficient
5 way to get around, and cars provided that. Likewise, inventors must constantly look at the world around them and find problems. Then, they must come up with ideas that solve these problems. This is a lengthy process, however. Most initial ideas are not all that useful, and the inventors require a lot of testing and improvements. In some cases, this can take years or even decades. But with that patience, inventors can
10 help change the world.

① 우수한 발명품은 뜻밖의 경험으로 인해 만들어진다.
② 발명가는 가장 효율적인 방법으로 발명을 해야 한다.
③ 모든 사람에게 가장 중요한 덕목은 바로 인내심이다.
④ 좋은 아이디어는 대부분 발명 초기에 발견되는 경향이 있다.
⑤ 발명가들은 인내심을 가지고 세상을 바꾸는 발명품을 만들어 낸다.

WORDS & PHRASES

light bulb 명 전구
invention 명 발명 [중등필수]
come up with ~을 생각해 내다
identify 동 ~을 찾아내다, 알아내다
need 명 필요
limited 형 제한적인
time-consuming 형 시간이 많이 걸리는
efficient 형 효율적인 [고등필수]
get around 돌아다니다
provide 동 ~을 제공하다
likewise 부 이와 같이, 마찬가지로
constantly 부 끊임없이
lengthy 형 긴
process 명 과정
initial 형 초기의
require 동 ~이 필요하다 [중등필수]
improvement 명 개선
decade 명 십 년
patience 명 인내(심)

지문 한눈에 보기

빈칸에 들어갈 적절한 말을 쓰시오.

도입부 (구체적인 사례)	발명가들은 어떻게 발명품을 생각해 낼까? - 1 _____________한 것이 무엇인지 알아낸다. 사람들이 돌아다닐 수 있는 더 빠르고 2 _____________ 방법을 위해 자동차를 발명했다. - 끊임없이 주변을 바라보고 3 _____________을 파악한다. - 해결책을 생각한다. - 초기 아이디어를 테스트하고 개선한다.
후반부 (주제문)	4 _____________으로 발명가들은 세상을 바꾸는 것을 돕는다.

정답 적중하기

글의 핵심 문장을 찾아 빈칸을 완성하시오.

1 How do inventors _____________ their inventions?
2 Most of the time, they _____________ a need.
3 But with that patience, inventors can _____________ the world.

다음 글에서 필자가 주장하는 바로 가장 적절한 것은?

정답 및 해설 p. 6

WORDS & PHRASES

sight 몡 시야
phrase 몡 문구
refer to ~을 의미하다
directly 뷔 직접적으로
affect 동 ~에 영향을 주다 [중등필수]
when it comes to ~에 관한 한
billion 몡 십억
pollute 동 ~을 오염시키다 [중등필수]
on a daily basis 매일
consider *A B A*를 *B*로 여기다, 간주하다
take steps 조치를 취하다
continue 동 계속하다 [중등필수]
environmental 형 환경의
campaign 몡 캠페인
raise 동 ~을 높이다 [중등필수]
awareness 몡 인식
work 동 작동하다
expose 동 노출시키다
eventually 뷔 결국
ignore 동 ~을 무시하다 [고등필수]

"Out of sight, out of mind." Have you ever heard this phrase? It refers to the fact that many people will not think about a problem they cannot see. This means they only think about things that directly <u>affect</u> them. This is true when it comes to our planet, too. Every year, humans make billions of tons of trash. This trash pollutes our land and water. However, most people do not see this trash on a daily basis. So, they do not consider it a big problem. They do not take steps to change their ways, either. In fact, many people continue to produce the same amount of trash. However, environmental campaigns have done much to raise awareness. These work by exposing people to facts and images. Eventually, they can't ignore the problem anymore.

① 모든 사람들이 쓰레기 문제에 대해 이미 잘 알고 있다.
② 보이지 않는 문제를 전달하는 방식은 달라야 한다.
③ 인간은 스스로 환경 오염 문제를 해결할 수 없다.
④ 생태계 파괴의 주된 원인을 찾는 과정을 정립할 필요가 있다.
⑤ 보이지 않는 쓰레기 문제도 환경 캠페인을 통해 그 인식을 바꿀 수 있다.

FLOWCHART

다음 빈칸에 들어갈 적절한 말을 쓰시오.

많은 사람들이 **1** ______________________ 문제에 대해 생각하지 않음
직접적으로 영향을 미치는 것들에 대해서만 생각하려 함

↓

매년, 인간은 수십억 톤의 쓰레기를 만들고,
우리의 땅과 물을 **2** __________________
그러나 대부분의 사람들은 매일 이 쓰레기를 보지 못하고
큰 문제로 여기지 않음

→

많은 사람들은
같은 양의 쓰레기를 계속
3 __________________

↓

환경 캠페인은 인식을 높이는 데 많은 도움이 됨
사람들은 더 이상 그 문제를 **4** __________________

1 이 글에 쓰인 **affect**와 뜻이 비슷한 단어는?

① swear   ② accept

③ suggest   ④ warn

⑤ influence

2 다음 빈칸에 들어갈 말로 가장 적절한 것은?

> In fact, many people ________________ the same amount of trash.

① pay for   ② take away

③ keep producing   ④ continue to avoid

⑤ unconsciously empty

3 이 글의 제목으로 가장 적절한 것은?

① The Invisible Problem: Trash Pollution

② Recycling: A Solution for a Cleaner Planet

③ Technological Innovations to Reduce Waste

④ The History of Environmental Movements

⑤ The Effects of Trash on Marine Life

PARAPHRASING DRILL

다음 문장들이 같은 뜻이 되도록 빈칸에 들어갈 적절한 말을 <보기>에서 찾아 쓰시오.

> 보기
>
> every day   nevertheless   encounter

However, most people do not see this trash on a daily basis.

= ________________, most people do not see this trash on a daily basis.

= However, most people do not ________________ this trash on a daily basis.

= However, most people do not see this trash ________________.

TRANSLATION DRILL

⭐ 「by + 동명사」 구문은 '~함으로써'로 해석한다.

다음 문장의 밑줄 친 부분에 유의하여 해석을 완성하시오.

1 These work by exposing people to facts and images.
이것들은 사람들을 사실과 이미지에 ________________ 작동한다.

2 She improved her skills by practicing every day.
그녀는 매일 ________________ 그녀의 기술을 향상시켰다.

다음 글의 요지로 가장 적절한 것은?

정답 및 해설 p. 7

Whether it is ancient Greece or merely 100 years ago, most people feel disconnected from history. It's hard to imagine the events of those times happening now. It's even harder to imagine that the people living those events were just like people today. However, author William Faulkner said, "History is not was, it is." To him, history
5 is not just a record of events. Rather, these events have shaped the world we live in today. In many ways, they have set off a chain reaction of events that we are still living. So, they are continuing to shape our world. To understand present-day society, it is important to understand history. The mistakes of the past can be repeated and it is up to us to <u>prevent</u> them from happening again.

① 역사적으로 과거와 현재가 단절된 경우가 있다.
② 과거의 잘못보다 현재에 집중하는 것이 중요하다.
③ 역사를 기록할 때는 비판적인 시각으로 접근해야 한다.
④ 현재의 사회를 이해하기 위해 역사를 이해하는 것은 중요하다.
⑤ 시대적, 공간적 배경에 따라 역사는 종종 다르게 해석될 수 있다.

다음 빈칸에 들어갈 적절한 말을 <보기>에서 찾아 쓰시오.

보기

mistakes	imagine	past	shape

Most people	Feel disconnected from the **1** ____________ Reason: it is not easy to **2** ____________ past events now
Author William Faulkner	Past events have shaped the world we live in today
Facts	The events are continuing to **3** ____________ our world due to a chain reaction of events
Conclusion	By understanding history, we can avoid **4** ____________ we made in the past

1 이 글에 쓰인 **prevent**와 뜻이 비슷한 단어는?

① agree   ② stop

③ ignore   ④ post

⑤ repeat

2 다음 문장이 설명하는 것을 이 글에서 찾아 **두 단어**로 쓰시오.

> The events of the past have shaped the world we live now.

→ ____

3 이 글의 내용과 일치하는 것은?

① Most people feel a sense of connection from historical events.

② History has little impact on shaping the world we live in today.

③ Understanding history helps us avoid repeating previous mistakes.

④ William Faulkner believed that history is simply a list of past events.

⑤ People today find it easy to relate to those who lived in ancient times.

PARAPHRASING DRILL

다음 두 문장이 같은 뜻이 되도록 빈칸에 괄호 안의 단어들을 쓰시오.

1 It's hard to imagine the events of those times happening now.
It's ________________ to picture those events ________________ in the ________________ day. (occurring / present / difficult)

2 In many ways, they have set off a chain reaction of events that we are still living.
= In ________________ ways, they have set off a ________________ ________________ of events that we are still living. (effect / various / domino)

TRANSLATION DRILL

⭐ 「prevent A from + 동명사」는 'A가 ~하는 것을 막다'라는 뜻으로 해석한다. from은 전치사이므로 목적어로 동사가 올 때는 동명사로 바꿔서 써야 한다.

다음 문장의 밑줄 친 부분에 유의하여 해석을 완성하시오.

1 It is up to us to prevent them from happening again.
그것들이 다시 ________________________ 수 있는 것은 바로 우리들이다.

2 We can prevent diseases from spreading.
우리는 질병이 ________________________ 수 있다.

WORDS & PHRASES

practice 통 실행하다 중등필수
given 형 주어진
field 명 밭
plant 통 ~을 심다
multiple 형 다수의, 여러 개의
protect 통 ~을 보호하다 중등필수
soil 명 토양
nutrient 명 영양소
over and over 계속해서
strip out 완전히 제거하다
spoil 통 ~을 상하게 하다
necessity 명 필요성
preserve 통 보호하다, 지키다
impact 명 영향, 영향력

환경

다음 글의 주제로 가장 적절한 것은?   정답 및 해설 p. 8

Many farmers practice crop rotation. This is the process of changing which crops are grown in a given field. For example, a farmer may plant corn in one of his fields. The next year, he will plant a different type of crop. The year after that, he will plant yet another crop. If a farmer has multiple fields, he may simply move his corn crop to a different field each year. He must also do the same with other types of crops. This process is important because it protects the health of the soil. Different crops add different nutrients to the soil. However, planting the same crops over and over can strip out other important nutrients. Over time, this spoils the quality of the soil. After many years, it may be difficult to grow anything at all in that soil.

* crop rotation 윤작(두 가지 이상의 작물을 돌려가면서 농사를 짓는 농법)

① the dangers of not planting crops at the right time
② the best way to choose which crops to plant
③ the necessity of crop rotation in preserving soil
④ the negative impacts of growing corn year after year
⑤ the influence of the government on crop production

👁 지문 한눈에 보기

빈칸에 들어갈 적절한 말을 쓰시오.

도입부 (주제문)	농부들은 **1** ＿＿＿＿＿＿ 순환을 실시한다.
중/후반부 (뒷받침/예시)	첫해에는 옥수수를 심고, 다음 해에는 **2** ＿＿＿＿＿ 종류의 농작물을 심을 것이다. 밭을 **3** ＿＿＿＿＿ 가지고 있다면, 매년 어떤 농작물을 다른 밭으로 옮길지도 모른다. 이 과정은 토양의 건강을 보호하고 영양소를 추가한다. 하지만 계속하여 같은 농작물을 심으면 **4** ＿＿＿＿＿를 없애거나 토양의 품질을 상하게 한다.

🎯 정답 적중하기

글의 핵심 문장을 찾아 빈칸을 완성하시오.

1 Many farmers practice crop ＿＿＿＿＿＿＿＿.

2 This process is important because it ＿＿＿＿＿＿＿ the health of the soil.

3 However, planting the ＿＿＿＿＿＿＿ crops over and over can strip out other important nutrients.

다음 글의 제목으로 가장 적절한 것은?   정답 및 해설 p. 8

When decorating your home, it can be difficult to determine how much is too much. These days, many homeowners prefer to play it safe. Instead of the bold colors and busy patterns of the past, they opt for more neutral colors. Beige, white, and gray are common in a minimalist home. However, some would argue that a lack of color can
5   leave a home feeling boring. A lack of patterns can make a home feel impersonal. Many designers now say, "Decorating your home should be a fun adventure. Don't be afraid to add color." Still, many homeowners are cautious about adding too much color. Designers recommend starting small. Try painting a door. Add wallpaper to just a few walls. Bring in potted plants and small pieces of artwork. Before you know
10 it, your home will reflect your personality.

* opt for ~을 선택하다

① Home Décor: Let Your Personality Shine
② Five Ways to Find Design Inspiration
③ Avoid Overdecorating and Choose Minimalism
④ Paint It All: The More Color, the Better
⑤ Becoming a Homeowner: Dos and Don'ts

WORDS & PHRASES

decorate 통 ~을 장식하다 중등필수
determine 통 결정하다 고등필수
homeowner 명 집주인
instead of ~ 대신에 중등필수
bold 형 대담한
busy 형 복잡한
neutral 형 중간색의, 중립적인
common 형 흔한 중등필수
argue 통 주장하다
lack 명 부족
leave A B A를 B의 상태로 남겨두다
impersonal 형 인간미 없는
cautious 형 신중한
recommend 통 ~을 추천하다 고등필수
wallpaper 명 벽지
bring in ~을 가져오다
potted 형 화분에 심은
artwork 명 작품
before you know it 어느새
reflect 통 ~을 반영하다 고등필수
personality 명 개성, 성격 중등필수

지문 한눈에 보기

빈칸에 들어갈 적절한 말을 쓰시오.

도입부 (일반적인 경향과 그에 대한 반론)	요즘에는 집을 장식할 때 **1** ____________ 색상을 선택한다. 어떤 사람들은 색상이 **2** ____________하면 집이 지루하게 느껴질 수 있다고 주장한다. "집을 꾸미는 것은 재미있는 **3** ____________이 되어야 합니다. 색상을 추가하는 것을 두려워하지 마세요."라고 말하는 디자이너들이 많다.
후반부 (주제문)	당신의 집은 당신의 **4** ____________을 반영할 것이다.

정답 적중하기

글의 핵심 문장을 찾아 빈칸을 완성하시오.

1   A lack of color can leave a home feeling ____________.
2   A lack of patterns can make a home feel ____________.
3   Before you know it, your home will ____________ your personality.

다음 글의 주제로 가장 적절한 것은?   정답 및 해설 p. 8

WORDS & PHRASES

replicate 통 복제하다
search for ~을 찾다
host 명 숙주(기생 생물에게 영양을
        공급하는 생물)
cell 명 세포
attach 통 ~에 달라붙다
genetic 형 유전의
material 명 물질, 재료 고등필수
take over 물려받다, 대신하다
operation 명 작동
instruction 명 지시
protein 명 단백질
come together 모이다
viral 형 바이러스의
severely 부 심각하게
damage 통 ~을 손상시키다 중등필수
destroy 통 ~을 파괴하다 중등필수
otherwise 부 그렇지 않으면
cause 통 ~을 야기[유발]하다 중등필수
deadliest 형 (가장) 치명적인
symptom 명 징후, 증상 고등필수

Viruses are not able to <u>replicate</u> on their own. So, they search for host cells to do so. When a virus enters the body, it attaches itself to a host cell. Then, some of the virus' genetic material enters the cell. This genetic material takes over the cell's operation. It gives the cell instructions to make certain proteins. These proteins are used to
5 create new viruses. Once these proteins come together, the viral cells leave the host cell. This severely damages or even kills the host cell. Then these viruses attach to other nearby host cells. The process repeats, and more host cells are destroyed each time. A host's immune system works hard to find viral cells because it must kill these cells. Otherwise, the virus may cause too much damage to the host.

* immune system 면역 체계(신체를 감염과 질병으로부터 보호하는 방어 시스템)

① the deadliest viruses throughout history
② the symptoms of a weak immune system
③ the importance of being a good host
④ the difficulty of healing after illnesses
⑤ how and why viruses create copies of themselves

FLOWCHART

다음 빈칸에 들어갈 적절한 말을 쓰시오.

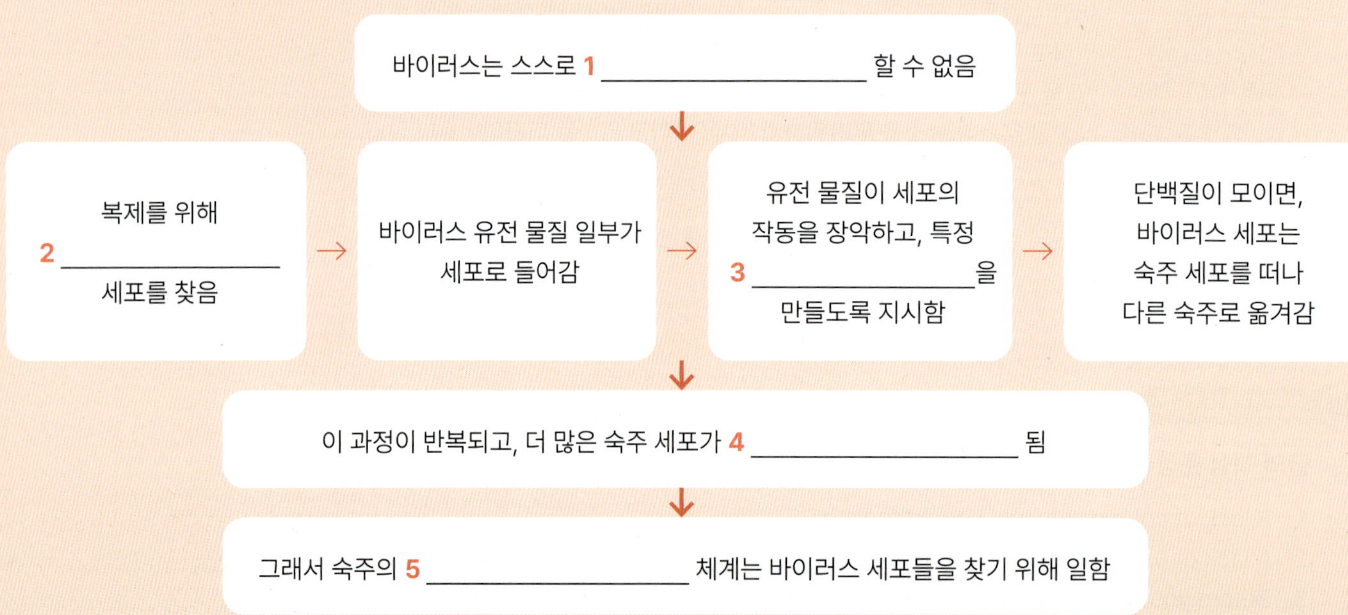

1 이 글에 쓰인 **replicate**와 뜻이 비슷한 표현은?

① make a copy of ② cover for
③ fill in ④ spread out
⑤ relate to

2 밑줄 친 **It**이 가리키는 것을 이 글에서 찾아 <u>두 단어</u>로 쓰시오.

____

3 이 글의 내용과 일치하지 <u>않는</u> 것은?

① Viruses search for host cells to replicate.
② Genetic material controls the cell's operation.
③ New viruses are created by the proteins.
④ Host cells can be damaged when viral cells leave.
⑤ The host's immune system does not need to search for the virus cells.

PARAPHRASING DRILL

다음 두 문장이 같은 뜻이 되도록 빈칸에 괄호 안의 단어들을 쓰시오.

1 This severely damages or even kills the host cell.
= This ________________ ________________ or even ________________ the
host cell. (gets rid of / harms / seriously)
2 Otherwise, the virus may cause too much damage to the host.
= ________________, the virus may ________________ ________________
damage to a host. (severe / if not / result in)

TRANSLATION DRILL

⭐ 수여동사는 간접 목적어와 직접 목적어를 갖는 4형식 동사로 give, send, show, offer 등이 있고, '~에게 …을 (무엇)하다'로 해석한다.

다음 문장의 밑줄 친 부분에 유의하여 해석을 완성하시오.

1 It gives the cell instructions to make certain proteins.
그것은 ________________ 특정 단백질을 만들도록 ________________ 내린다.
2 I will send you a fun story to read before bedtime.
나는 ________________ 자기 전에 읽을 재미있는 ________________ 보낼 것이다.

다음 글의 제목으로 가장 적절한 것은?

정답 및 해설 p. 9

WORDS & PHRASES

loneliness 몡 외로움
emotion 몡 감정 중등필수
survival 몡 생존
theory 몡 이론
suggest 통 ~을 암시[시사]하다 중등필수
form 통 ~을 형성하다
relationship 몡 관계
ensure 통 ~을 보장하다, 반드시 ~하게 하다
receive 통 ~을 받다 중등필수
means 몡 수단
encourage 통 ~을 격려하다 중등필수
raise 통 ~을 기르다 중등필수
individual 몡 개인, 사람 고등필수
face 통 ~에 직면하다
evolve 통 진화하다 고등필수
adapt 통 적응하다
disadvantage 몡 불리한 점

Most people think of loneliness as a negative emotion. However, this emotion had an important role in human survival. Theories suggest that loneliness pushes people to form close relationships with others. Through these relationships, people ensure that they receive help from others in times of need. In the past, loneliness may have been a means of survival in the wild. It encouraged humans to form groups. The members of each group protected each other from wild animals. They also protected each other from rival groups and the elements. Likewise, they worked together to hunt, grow food, and raise children. Thus, individuals had a much better chance of surviving in a group. Humans today may not face the same dangers. But forming groups still helps them stay safe and happy.

* the elements (날씨에 나타나는) 자연의 힘, 악천후

① Why Humans Prefer to Raise Children in Groups
② Loneliness: Another Role in Human Survival
③ How the Human Brain Evolved Over Time
④ Survival: How the Environment Adapts
⑤ The Disadvantages of Being Alone

BREAKDOWN

다음 빈칸에 들어갈 적절한 말을 <보기>에서 찾아 쓰시오.

보기

| protecting | forming | chances | survival | helping |

	Loneliness
Term and Role	Negative emotion, but important role in human **1** ____________
Effects	**2** ____________ close relationships with others due to loneliness
	3 ____________ each other when needed and encouraging humans to form groups
	4 ____________ each other from wild animals, rivals and the elements
	Having more **5** ____________ to survive in a group

1 이 글에 쓰인 **ensure**와 뜻이 비슷한 단어는?

① rely ② guarantee

③ deny ④ realize

⑤ accept

2 밑줄 친 **the same dangers**에 해당하는 것을 이 글에서 찾아 쓰시오.(3개)

_______________ . _______________ . _______________

3 이 글의 내용과 일치하는 것은?

① Most people regard loneliness as a positive emotion.

② Loneliness weakened the chances of surviving in the wild.

③ Loneliness discouraged humans from forming groups.

④ Individuals in the present have the same dangers as in the past.

⑤ Gathering helps keep humans safe and happy.

PARAPHRASING DRILL

다음 문장들이 같은 뜻이 되도록 빈칸에 들어갈 적절한 말을 <보기>에서 찾아 쓰시오.

┌ 보기 ┐

refers to　　almost　　see

Most people think of loneliness as a negative emotion.

= _______________ all people think of loneliness as a negative emotion.

= Most people _______________ loneliness as a negative emotion.

= Most people think that loneliness _______________ a negative emotion.

TRANSLATION DRILL

⭐ encourage는 5형식 동사로 목적격 보어 자리에 to부정사가 오며, '~하도록 격려하다'로 해석한다.

다음 문장의 밑줄 친 부분에 유의하여 해석을 완성하시오.

1 It encouraged humans to form groups.

　그것은 사람들이 무리를 _______________ .

2 Reading books encourages children to explore new ideas.

　책을 읽는 것은 아이들이 새로운 아이디어를 _______________ .

CHAPTER 3
20번대 문제 공략하기 Part 2

UNIT 05 • 함축 의미 파악하기

UNIT 05 **함축 의미 파악하기** [최근 10회 평균 정답률: 60% 난이도 중]

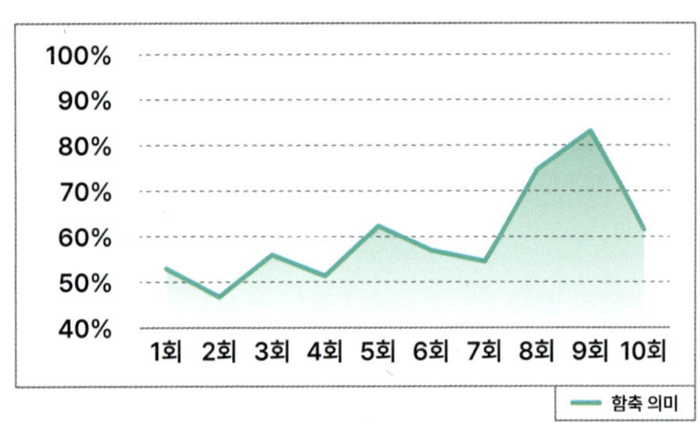

[함축 의미 파악하기 유형]은 고1 모의평가 기준 **평균 정답률이 60%**로 **난이도 중**으로 분류되지만 난이도 중상과의 경계에 있는 **오답률이 높은 유형**이다. 20번대에서는 오답률이 가장 높은 유형으로 **1문제**가 출제되며 **3점 문제로 출제**되는 경우도 있으므로, 충분한 연습이 필요한 유형이라 할 수 있다. 최근 들어 지문의 수준이 높게 출제되는 경향이 있는 점도 주목해야 한다.

학습 전략

밑줄 친 부분은 주로 **표현** 또는 **문장**으로 제시되며, **전체적인 글의 흐름과 요지**가 밑줄 친 부분의 의미를 결정한다. 밑줄 친 부분만 읽고 답을 찾으면 안 되는 이유가 바로 이점이다. 지문의 주제와 핵심 내용을 먼저 파악한 후 **문맥** 속에서 밑줄 친 부분이 갖는 의미를 파악해야 하며, 밑줄 친 부분이 **비유적인 표현**인 경우가 많아 난이도가 높다고 느낄 수 있다. 글의 **도입부**에서 **핵심 문장**을 통해 요지를 파악한 후, 부연 설명한 문장을 통해 글의 전체 흐름을 파악하고 글의 요지와 관련하여 밑줄 친 부분의 **함축적인 의미**를 추론하는 연습이 필요하다.

유형 공략 Q&A

Q1. 주로 어떤 종류의
글이 나오나요?

A1. 최근 경향을 보면 생소하거나 과감한 소재보다는 전반적으로 현대 사회의 변화를 설명하거나 일상적이고 친숙한 소재의 지문들이 자주 나오고 있습니다. 특히 사례나 일화를 통해 주장을 전달하는 지문이 자주 등장합니다.

Q2. 이 유형을 푸는
꿀팁을 알려주세요.

A2. 선택지에서 정답을 고를 때 주제와 무관한 선택지는 버리세요. 일부러 불필요한 내용을 선택지로 넣는 경우가 있답니다. 관련 없는 선택지는 과감히 제외하고 정답을 정했다면, 해당 표현을 밑줄 부분에 넣어서 다시 읽어 보는 것도 좋습니다. 자연스럽다면, 정답일 가능성이 높죠.

Q3. 이 유형을 풀 때
주의할 점이 있나요?

A3. 이 유형의 제목이 '함축' 의미 파악하기인 점을 잊으면 안 됩니다. 함축 의미란 직접적으로 표현되지 않은, 숨겨진 의미랍니다. 단어의 표면적 의미에만 집중해서 오답을 선택하지 않아야 합니다. 평소 독서를 통해 비유적 표현을 이해하는 능력을 키우는 것도 필요합니다.

유형 공략 어휘 ⭐ 알고 있는 어휘에 체크하고 모르는 어휘는 암기하세요.

주제와 요지를 나타내는 어휘	☐ should, must, have to ~ 해야 한다 ☐ I believe ~ ~라고 믿는다 ☐ in my point of view, in my opinion 내 의견으로는	☐ need to ~할 필요가 있다 ☐ I suggest ~ ~라고 제안한다	☐ I think ~ ~라고 생각한다
내용을 강조할 때 쓰는 어휘	☐ especially 특히 ☐ actually 사실 ☐ most of all 무엇보다도	☐ indeed 정말, 확실히 ☐ no doubt 틀림없이 ☐ to sum up 요약하면	☐ truly 진실로 ☐ not at all 전혀
대조를 통해 내용을 반전할 때 쓰는 어휘	☐ but, however, yet 하지만 ☐ otherwise 그렇지 않으면	☐ whereas, on the other hand 반면에 ☐ despite, in spite of ~에도 불구하고	

함축 의미 파악하기

정답률 60% 난이도 ★★☆☆☆

WORDS & PHRASES

psychology 명 심리학 [고등필수]
effect 명 효과 [중등필수]
affect 동 ~에 영향을 주다 [중등필수]
behavior 명 행동 [고등필수]
Egyptian 명 이집트인
treat 동 ~을 치료하다
illness 명 병
shine 동 비추다 [중등필수]
poet 명 시인
notion 명 생각, 개념
further 부 (한 걸음/단계) 더, 조금 더
claim 동 ~을 주장하다
mother tongue 명 모국어
examine 동 조사하다 [중등필수]
identity 명 정체성
translation 명 해석, 번역
be linked to ~와 연관되다

심리

정답 및 해설 p. 10

밑줄 친 Colors are the mother tongue of the subconscious.가 다음 글에서 의미하는 바로 가장 적절한 것은?

Have you ever felt sad after being in a blue room? Perhaps you felt angry when surrounded by red. Color psychology studies this interesting effect. Many believe colors can change a person's mood. Colors can also affect their behavior. Long ago, ancient people believed colors had an emotional effect. The ancient Egyptians used different colors to treat illnesses. They did this by painting a room a certain color. They also shined light through crystals. Much later, the German poet Goethe wrote about colors. He believed colors could reflect human emotions. Famous psychologist Carl Jung took that notion one step further. He claimed, "<u>Colors are the mother tongue of the subconscious.</u>" He believed colors could help people recover from bad experiences.

* subconscious 잠재의식(의식적으로 생각하지 않고도 마음속에서 일어나는 생각이나 감정)

① Illnesses cannot be treated by examining our thoughts.
② A person's first language shapes his or her identity.
③ Colors can help us understand hidden things in our minds.
④ Color psychology has changed due to translation errors.
⑤ Human behavior is always linked to one or more bright colors.

👁 지문 한눈에 보기

빈칸에 들어갈 적절한 말을 쓰시오.

도입부 (글의 요지)	색 심리학에서 많은 사람들이 색이 사람의 **1** ___________ 을 바꿀 수 있고, 행동에 영향을 줄 수 있다고 믿는다.
중반부 (부연 설명)	고대 사람들은 색에는 **2** ___________ 효과가 있다고 믿었다. 독일 시인 Goethe는 색이 사람의 감정을 **3** ___________ 할 수 있다고 믿었다.
후반부 (함축 의미 추론)	Carl Jung은 "색은 **4** ___________ 의 모국어다."라고 주장했다. 그는 색이 사람들이 나쁜 경험에서 회복하도록 도울 수 있다고 믿었다.

🎯 정답 적중하기

글의 핵심 문장을 찾아 빈칸을 완성하시오.

1 Many believe colors can ___________ a person's mood.

2 Colors can also ___________ their behavior.

3 Long ago, ancient people believed colors had an emotional ___________.

정답 및 해설 p. 10

밑줄 친 they are no less equipped for their surroundings가 다음 글에서 의미하는 바로 가장 적절한 것은?

Humans have five main senses: sight, sound, touch, taste, and smell. These senses help us navigate the world safely. For example, the sense of smell helps us avoid dangerous chemicals. Sight helps us move from place to place without injury. However, some animals do not have the best eyesight. They must rely on other special senses to see. The platypus, for example, has many sensors in its bill. These sensors detect electrical impulses. This helps the platypus find prey in deep water. Bats also have an interesting way of seeing. They bounce sounds off nearby objects. This helps them find food and avoid dangers. While some animals may not have traditional human senses, <u>they are no less equipped for their surroundings</u>.

* platypus 오리너구리

① a creature's surroundings determine its lifespan
② most animals have unique ways of seeing and hunting
③ special equipment may be necessary to study bats
④ both the bat and the platypus hunt the same way
⑤ animals have their own ways of surviving in the wild

WORDS & PHRASES

sense 명 감각
navigate 통 ~을 항해하다
avoid 통 ~을 피하다 중등필수
chemical 명 화학물질 고등필수
injury 명 부상
eyesight 명 시력
rely on ~에 의존하다 고등필수
sensor 명 센서, 감지장치
bill 명 부리
detect 통 ~을 감지하다
electrical 형 전기의
impulse 명 자극
prey 명 먹이
bounce 통 반사하다, 튕겨내다
nearby 형 가까이 있는
object 명 물체
traditional 형 전통적인 중등필수
equipped 형 ~에 대해 장비[준비]를 갖춘
surroundings 명 [주변]환경
lifespan 명 수명
equipment 명 장비

 **지문 한눈에 보기**

빈칸에 들어갈 적절한 말을 쓰시오.

도입부 (글의 요지)	인간은 다섯 개의 주요 감각인 시각, 청각, 촉각, 미각, 후각을 가지고 있고, 이것들이 우리가 세상을 **1** ______________ 항해할 수 있도록 도와준다.
중반부 (부연 설명)	어떤 동물들은 시력이 좋지 않아 다른 특별한 감각에 **2** ______________ 해야 한다. 오리너구리는 부리에 많은 센서가 있어 **3** ______________ 을 감지한다. 박쥐는 근처의 물체로 소리를 반사한다.
후반부 (함축 의미 추론)	동물들은 **4** ______________ 에 적응하는 데 있어 덜 갖춰져 있지 않다.

정답 적중하기

글의 핵심 문장을 찾아 빈칸을 완성하시오.

1 However, some animals do not have the best ______________.
2 They must rely on other special senses to ______________.
3 This helps them find food and ______________ dangers.

밑줄 친 place humanity in the position of those ants가 다음 글에서 의미하는 바로 가장 적절한 것은?

WORDS & PHRASES

science fiction 명 공상 과학 소설
fear 통 ~을 두려워하다 중등필수
age 명 시대
depict 통 ~을 묘사하다
futuristic 형 초현대적인
run on ~을 연료로 삼다, ~로 운영되다
advanced 형 발전된
not necessarily 반드시 ~은 아닌
positive 형 긍정적인
indeed 부 실제로
conflict 명 갈등 고등필수
completely 부 완전히
competence 명 능숙함
warn 통 경고하다 중등필수
humanity 명 인류
pest 명 해충
place 통 ~을 두다
atop 전 맨 위에
colony 명 (동·식물의) 군집
cautionary 형 충고[경고]성의
status 명 신분, 지위

Many science fiction writers feared the age of AI. In their stories, they depicted futuristic worlds. These worlds ran on advanced technology. But that was not necessarily a positive thing. Indeed, many writers depicted conflicts between humans and AI. As AI advances, many scientists claim that there is no danger. Instead, AI
5 is just a tool to help humans. However, Stephen Hawking did not completely agree. He said, "The real risk with AI is not malice but competence." He warned of a future in which AI would be very good at achieving its goals. This AI wouldn't necessarily dislike humans. Rather, it would treat humanity like pests. Humans would be viewed the way we view ants. "Let's not place humanity in the position of those ants,"
10 Hawking advised.

* malice 악의(좋지 않은 뜻, 나쁜 마음)

① build our homes atop the colonies of ants
② develop AI to communicate with ants
③ believe the cautionary tales of writers
④ reduce humankind to the status of a pest
⑤ listen to scientists when they develop AI

다음 빈칸에 들어갈 적절한 말을 쓰시오.

공상 과학 소설 작가	- 발전된 기술을 바탕으로 운영되는 **1** ___________ 세계를 묘사 - 인공지능의 시대가 반드시 긍정적이지는 않다고 묘사 - 인간과 인공지능 사이의 **2** ___________을 묘사
3 ___________	- 인공지능은 위험하지 않고, 오히려 인간을 돕는 도구일 뿐이라고 주장
Stephen Hawking	- 인공지능이 목표를 달성하는 데 매우 능숙한 점에 대해 **4** ___________ - 마치 인간이 개미를 바라보는 것처럼 인공지능은 인간을 **5** ___________처럼 취급할 것임을 언급

1 이 글에 쓰인 **depict**와 뜻이 비슷한 단어는?

① imply   ② argue

③ advance   ④ describe

⑤ complete

2 밑줄 친 **it**이 가리키는 것을 이 글에서 찾아 한 단어로 쓰시오.

____

3 이 글의 내용과 일치하지 않는 것은?

① Many writers worried about conflicts between AI and human beings.

② With AI advancing, many scientists believe AI is not harmful.

③ Stephen Hawking totally agreed with scientists.

④ Stephen Hawking argued AI's real risk is competence.

⑤ Stephen Hawking didn't want humans to be considered pests.

PARAPHRASING DRILL

다음 두 문장이 같은 뜻이 되도록 빈칸에 괄호 안의 단어들을 쓰시오.

1 As AI advances, many scientists claim that there is no danger.

= As AI ______________, ______________ scientists claim that there is no ______________. (threat / evolves / a lot of)

2 He warned of a future in which AI would be very good at achieving its goals.

= He warned ______________ a future in which AI would be highly ______________ in reaching its ______________. (aims / skilled / about)

TRANSLATION DRILL

⭐ not necessarily는 '반드시 ~은 아니다'로 해석하며, 전체가 아닌 부분을 부정하는 표현이다.

다음 문장의 밑줄 친 부분에 유의하여 해석을 완성하시오.

1 But that was not necessarily a positive thing.

그러나 그것이 ______________ ______________ 것은 아니었다.

2 Learned men are not necessarily wise.

학식 있는 사람이 ______________ ______________ 것은 아니다.

정답 및 해설 p. 11

밑줄 친 Choose a job you love, and you will never have to work a day in your life.
가 다음 글에서 의미하는 바로 가장 적절한 것은?

WORDS & PHRASES

career path 명 진로
daunting 형 벅찬
task 명 일, 과업 고등필수
pressured 형 부담감을 받는
proud 형 자랑스러워하는
financial 형 재정적인
stability 명 안정성
root 명 근원, 뿌리 중등필수
miserable 형 비참한
devastating 형 충격적인,
　　　　엄청난 손상을 가하는
turn A into B A를 B로 바꾸다
stable 형 안정적인
allow 통 가능하게 하다, 허락하다 중등필수
factor 명 요소, 요인
security 명 보장, 안정성

Choosing the right career path can be a daunting task. Many young people feel pressured to make their parents proud. Their parents also want them to choose a job that will give their son or daughter financial stability. However, money is not the root of all happiness. Sometimes, even the best-paying jobs can make a person miserable.

5 It takes a long time to get a good education for a job. So, it can be devastating to find out that you've chosen a path you don't enjoy. Confucius said, "Choose a job you love, and you will never have to work a day in your life." When it's time to choose a career path, don't think only about money. Think about the things you truly enjoy. Then, think about ways to turn that into a stable career.

* Confucius 공자

① Some careers allow you to avoid working.
② A career you enjoy does not feel like work.
③ Choosing a career is a difficult task to complete.
④ Money should not be a factor when choosing a job.
⑤ The right career path will bring you financial security.

다음 빈칸에 들어갈 적절한 말을 <보기>에서 찾아 쓰시오.

보기

| miserable | enjoy | stability | pressured |

Young People
Feel 1 ___________

Choosing the Right Career Path

Parents
Want their kids to have a financial 2 ___________

Reality
• A good education period takes time
• Even making big money can be 3 ___________

Suggestion
• Don't only think about money
• Consider what you truly 4 ___________ for a stable career

1 이 글에 쓰인 **stable**과 뜻이 비슷한 단어는?

① right ② frequent

③ secure ④ genuine

⑤ successful

2 이 글을 읽고 아래와 같이 제목을 붙일 때, 빈칸에 들어갈 말로 가장 적절한 것은?

From _____________ to Profession: Creating a Stable Career

① Passion ② Money ③ Education ④ Chance ⑤ Ability

3 이 글의 내용과 일치하는 것은?

① Choosing a career path is easy for young people.

② Young people only care about financial stability.

③ Money is essential for all happiness.

④ It takes a short time to obtain a good education for a job.

⑤ Realizing you don't enjoy a chosen job can be devastating.

PARAPHRASING DRILL

다음 문장들이 같은 뜻이 되도록 빈칸에 들어갈 적절한 말을 <보기>에서 찾아 쓰시오.

보기

satisfied   ensure   under

Many young people feel pressured to make their parents proud.

= Many young people feel pressured to _______________ their parents are proud.

= Many young people are _______________ pressure to make their parents proud.

= Many young people feel pressured to make their parents _______________.

TRANSLATION DRILL

⭐ 동사에 ~ing를 붙인 동명사는 '~하는 것'으로 해석하고, 명사 역할을 할 수 있다.

다음 문장의 밑줄 친 부분에 유의하여 해석을 완성하시오.

1 Choosing the right career path can be a daunting task.

올바른 진로를 _______________은 벅찬 일일 수 있다.

2 Cooking delicious meals brings me joy.

맛있는 음식을 _______________은 나에게 기쁨을 가져다준다.

CHAPTER 4
20번대 문제 공략하기 Part 3

UNIT 06 ● 도표 내용 파악하기
UNIT 07 ● 내용 일치/불일치 파악하기

UNIT 06 **도표 내용 파악하기** [최근 10회 평균 정답률: 82% 난이도 중하]

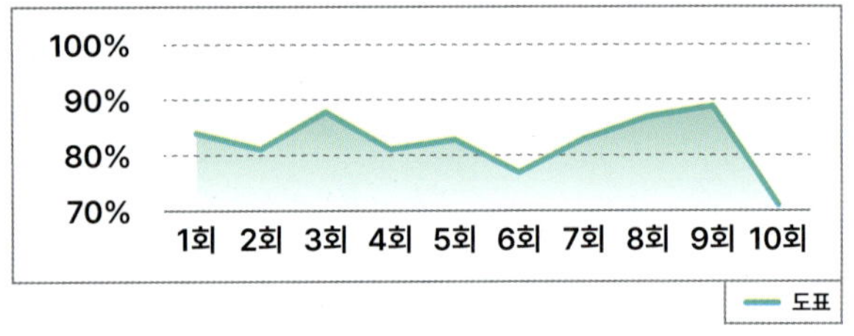

[도표 내용 파악하기 유형]은 **평균 정답률 82%**의 **난이도 중하 유형**으로 기출에서 **1문제**가 출제된다. 지문의 문장 구조 자체는 다소 단순하나 지문에 쓰인 **증가와 감소 표현, 비교와 최상 표현, 배수를 나타내는 표현**에 익숙하지 않을 경우 오답을 도출할 수 있으므로, 해당 표현들을 익히는 것이 필요하다.

학습 전략

지문의 **도입부**를 통해 **도표가 무엇에 관한 것인지 먼저 파악**한다. 지문과 도표에서 비교해야 할 수치가 **순서대로** 출제되는 경향이 있으므로, 도표와 선택지 내용의 **일치 여부를 하나씩 대조**한다. 또한 제시된 **대명사**와 **숫자** 등에 집중해서 정답을 찾아야 하는 유형이다.

유형 공략 어휘 ⭐ 알고 있는 어휘에 체크하고 모르는 어휘는 암기하세요.

증가와 감소를 나타내는 표현	☐ increase-decrease 증가하다-감소하다		☐ grow, go up 늘어나다
	☐ decline, reduce 감소하다	☐ multiply 곱하다, 크게 증가하다	☐ soar-drop 급등하다-급감하다
비교를 나타내는 표현	☐ as ~ as … …만큼 ~한	☐ (the) most/least ~ 가장 많은/적은 ~	
	☐ more/less than ~보다 많은/적은	☐ twice 2배	☐ three times 3배
분수를 나타내는 표현	☐ half 1/2, 절반	☐ a third(= one third) 1/3 ☐ a quarter 1/4	☐ four-fifths 4/5

 내용 일치/불일치 파악하기 *[최근 10회 평균 정답률: 일대기 88% 난이도 중하 / 안내문 92% 난이도 하]*

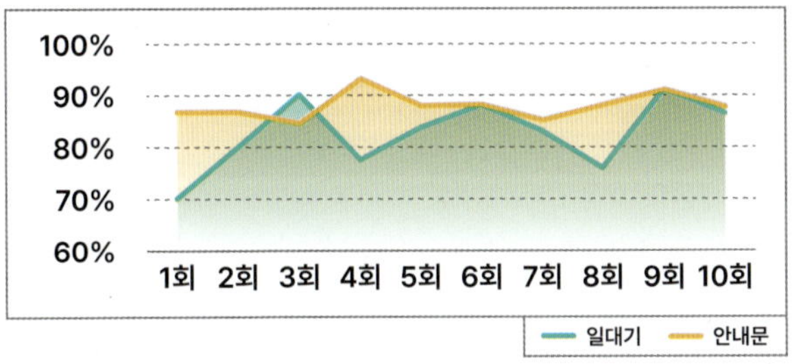

[내용 일치/불일치 파악하기 유형]은 **총 3문제**가 출제되며 **1개**는 **인물의 일대기**를 읽고 일치하지 않는 것을 찾는 문제로, **나머지 2개**는 **안내문**을 보고 일치 또는 불일치하는 내용을 찾는 것으로 출제된다. **일대기 유형**은 **평균 정답률 88%의 중하 난이도**를 보이며, **안내문 유형은 정답률 92%의 난이도 하 유형**이다. 지문에 나오는 정보와 지시문의 순서가 일치하므로 하나씩 일치 또는 불일치 여부를 확인하면서 풀면 된다.

학습 전략

선택지가 한글로 출제되어 전반적으로 난이도가 낮은 유형으로 평가된다. 그렇기 때문에, **지문과 선택지를 함께 읽으면서 시간을 절약**하면, 킬러 문항을 풀 시간을 확보할 수 있다. 글에 담겨 있는 정보 중에서 선택지의 서술 내용에 해당하는 부분을 찾아 비교하면서 일치하거나 일치하지 않는 설명을 찾아 정답을 찾는다.

유형 공략 Q&A

Q1. 이 유형에서 가장 주의할 점은 무엇인가요?

A1. 글의 내용을 대충 보고 '추론'하면 안 됩니다. "~라는 이야긴가 보다"라고 생각하며 문제를 풀지 말고 주어진 정보를 정확하게 확인해야 합니다. 지문 속에서 구체적인 정보를 정확히 찾는지 확인하는 문제이지 추론하는 문제가 아니기 때문이죠.

Q2. 이 유형을 푸는 꿀팁도 한번 알려주세요.

A2. 선택지를 먼저 읽고 지문을 읽는 것도 좋은 방법입니다. 선택지에 나온 내용을 확인한 후 지문에 그 내용이 나오는지 확인해 보는 것이죠. 지문을 다 읽고 선택지로 내려가도 결국 기억이 나지 않아서 다시 지문을 보게 되기도 하거든요. 문제 푸는 순서를 바꿔보는 것도 이 유형을 공략하는 데 좋은 방법이랍니다. 이 방법으로 1분 이내로 해당 유형을 풀어보려고 연습해 보세요. 속도와 정확도를 모두 높일 수 있답니다.

도표 내용 파악하기

정답률 82% 난이도 ★½☆☆☆

WORDS & PHRASES

population 명 인구 [고등필수]
percentage 명 비율
populated 형 인구가 많은
rest 명 나머지
account for 차지하다
make up ~을 만들다, 구성하다
spread across ~에 분포된
highlight 동 강조하다
growth rates 명 성장률
steadily 부 꾸준히 [중등필수]
indicate 동 나타내다
significant 형 상당한 [고등필수]

세계

다음 도표의 내용과 일치하지 <u>않는</u> 것은?

정답 및 해설 p. 12

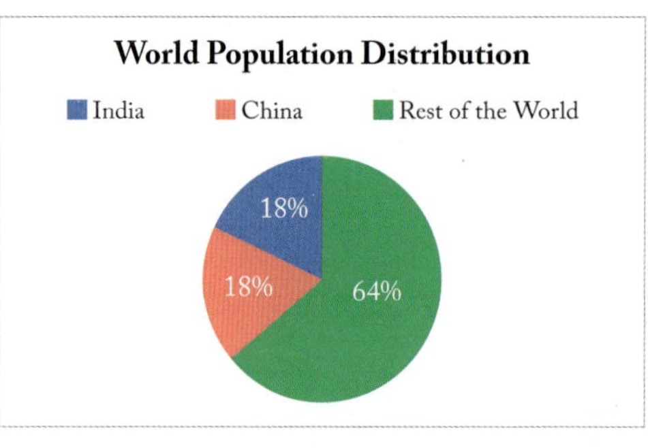

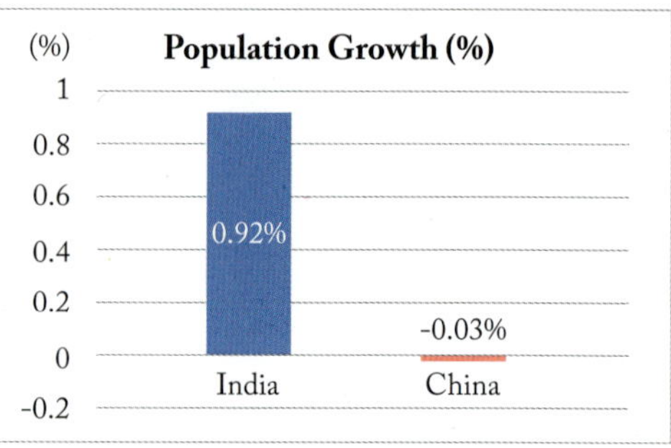

The above charts show three population percentages, focusing on the world's two most populated nations, India and China, and the rest of the world. ① Both India and China each account for 18 percent of the world's population. ② It means that they make up 36 percent together. ③ This leaves 64 percent of the global population spread across other nations. ④ The chart on the right highlights the population growth rates of India and China. ⑤ While India's population is growing steadily at a rate of 0.92 percent, China's growth rate is just 0.03 percent, indicating that significant changes in China's population are likely in the future.

👁 지문 한눈에 보기

빈칸에 들어갈 적절한 말을 쓰시오.

도표 설명	차트들은 각각 세계의 인구 비율과 인도, 중국의 인구 **1** ____________ 을 보여준다.
세계 인구 분포	세계 인구의 각 18%는 **2** ____________ 과 인도에 살고 있다. 나머지 64%는 다른 나라에 살고 있다.
인도와 중국의 인구 성장률	인도의 인구 성장률은 0.92%이다. 중국의 성장률은 **3** ____________ %이다. 이는 **4** ____________ 에 큰 변화가 있을 가능성을 의미한다.

🎯 정답 적중하기

글의 핵심 문장을 찾아 빈칸을 완성하시오.

1 The above charts show three ________________ percentage, focusing on the world's two most populated nations, India and China, and the rest of the world.

2 Both India and China each ________________ 18 percent of the world's population.

3 China's ________________ is just 0.03 percent, indicating that significant changes in China's population are likely in the future.

다음 도표의 내용과 일치하지 <u>않는</u> 것은?

정답 및 해설 p. 12

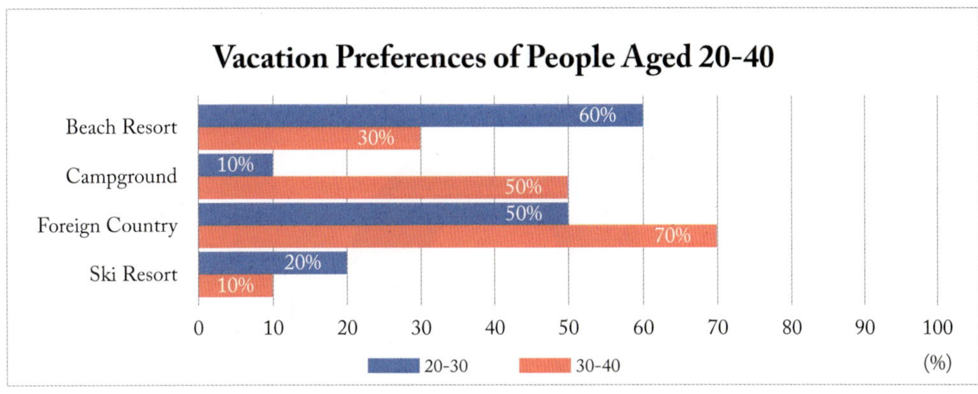

The above graph shows the vacation preferences of people between the ages of 20 and 40. ① 60 percent of people aged 20 to 30 prefer going to beach resorts, but only 30 percent of the older age group do. ② Only 10 percent of the younger age group prefers going to campgrounds, while 50 percent of people aged 30-40 prefer camping. ③ 50 percent of people in their 20s and 30s prefer visiting a foreign country. ④ For people aged 30 to 40, the most popular choice is traveling abroad, with 70 percent preferring it. ⑤ Visiting a ski resort is the least popular option for all age groups.

WORDS & PHRASES

vacation 몡 휴가
preference 몡 선호(도)
prefer 통 ~을 선호하다 중등필수
campground 몡 캠핑장
while 젭 반면에
foreign 혱 외국의 중등필수
popular 혱 인기 있는 중등필수
option 몡 선택

 **지문 한눈에 보기**

빈칸에 들어갈 적절한 말을 쓰시오.

도표 설명	그래프는 20-40세의 사람들이 **1** _____________ 하는 휴가지를 보여준다.
가장 선호하는 휴가지 (나이별)	20-30세의 60%가 **2** _____________ 에 가는 것을 선호하지만 30-40세의 30%만 이곳을 선호한다. 20-30세의 10%가 **3** _____________ 방문을 선호하지만 30-40세는 50%가 선호한다. 20-30세의 50%와 30-40세의 70%가 해외여행을 선호한다. **4** _____________ 리조트는 각각 20%와 10%의 비율을 보인다.

 **정답 적중하기**

글의 핵심 문장을 찾아 빈칸을 완성하시오.

1 The above graph shows the _____________ preferences of people between the ages of 20 and 40.

2 _____________ 10 percent of the younger age group prefers going to campgrounds, _____________ 50 percent of people aged 30-40 prefer camping.

3 For people aged 30 to 40, the most _____________ choice is traveling abroad, with 70 percent preferring it.

다음 도표의 내용과 일치하지 <u>않는</u> 것은?

정답 및 해설 p. 13

WORDS & PHRASES

undergraduate degree 몡 학사 학위
(=university degree)
graduate degree 몡 석사 학위
resident 몡 주민 [고등필수]
diploma 몡 졸업장
go on to ~로 나아가다
complete 통 ~을 마치다 [중등필수]
proportion 몡 비율
specifically 분 명확히, 구체적으로
enter 통 ~에 입학하다

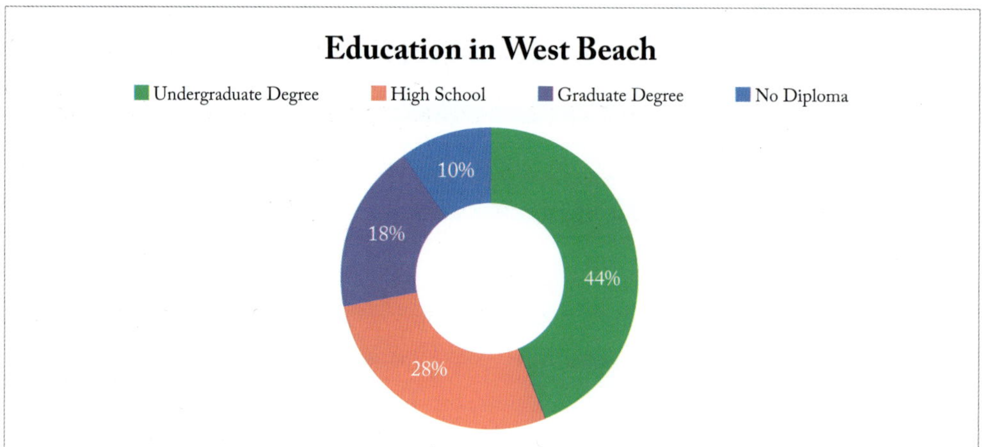

The above graph shows the education levels of people living in West Beach. ① 98 percent of residents have received a diploma of some kind and 28 percent of people finished high school. ② Many of the people who graduated from high school went on to <u>complete</u> a university degree and the proportion of them is 16 percent higher than the proportion of those who only graduated from high school. ③ Specifically, 44 percent of residents received an undergraduate degree and some of them also entered graduate school. ④ 18 percent of residents completed a graduate program and received another degree. ⑤ 10 percent of people in West Beach did not graduate from high school and <u>they</u> do not have any diplomas.

다음 빈칸에 들어갈 적절한 말을 <보기>에서 찾아 쓰시오.

보기

graduate   education   high school   a graduate degree

1 ________________ **Levels of People in West Beach**

	Percentage of people with an undergraduate degree: 44%
Percentage of people who have received some kind of diploma: 90%	Percentage of **2** ________________ graduates only: 28%
	Percentage of people with **3** ________________ : 18%

Percentage of people who did not **4** ________________ from high school: 10%

1 이 글에 쓰인 **complete**와 뜻이 비슷한 단어는?

① attempt   ② attend
③ remain   ④ achieve
⑤ alter

2 밑줄 친 **they**가 가리키는 것을 이 글에서 찾아 일곱 단어로 쓰시오.

____

3 이 글의 내용과 일치하지 <u>않는</u> 것은?

① West Beach 주민의 90%가 어떤 종류든 졸업장을 받았다.
② 고등학교 졸업장을 받은 사람들은 모두 대학 과정을 마쳤다.
③ 44%의 주민이 대학에서 공부를 이어갔다.
④ 대학 학위를 마친 일부 사람들은 대학원에 진학했다.
⑤ 석사 학위를 가진 사람은 West Beach 인구의 18%이다.

PARAPHRASING DRILL

다음 두 문장이 같은 뜻이 되도록 빈칸에 괄호 안의 단어들을 쓰시오.

1 28 percent of people finished high school.

= 28 percent of _______________ _______________ _______________
high school. (from / graduated / residents)

2 10 percent of people in West Beach did not graduate from high school and they do not have any diplomas.

= 10 percent of _______________ in West Beach did not _______________ high
school and they have _______________ diplomas. (complete / individuals / no)

TRANSLATION DRILL

⭐ the proportion of ~는 '~의 비율'이라는 의미로 다음에 비율의 대상이 온다.

다음 문장의 밑줄 친 부분에 유의하여 해석을 완성하시오.

1 <u>The proportion of</u> them is 16 percent higher than <u>the proportion of</u> those who only graduated from high school.
이들_______________은 고등학교만 졸업한 사람들_______________보다 16% 더 높다.

2 <u>The proportion of users</u> has recently increased.
_______________이 최근 증가했다.

다음 도표의 내용과 일치하지 <u>않는</u> 것은?

정답 및 해설 p. 13

WORDS & PHRASES

clean energy 명 청정에너지
investment 명 투자
listed 형 표[명단]에 실린, 나열된
take place 발생하다
invest 통 ~을 투자하다
government 명 정부 고등필수
commit 통 (돈을) 쓰다
billion 명 십억
come in (몇 위를) 차지하다
amount 명 양 중등필수
come out 나오다
slightly 부 약간
ahead of ~보다 앞선
nearly 부 거의
compared to ~와 비교하여

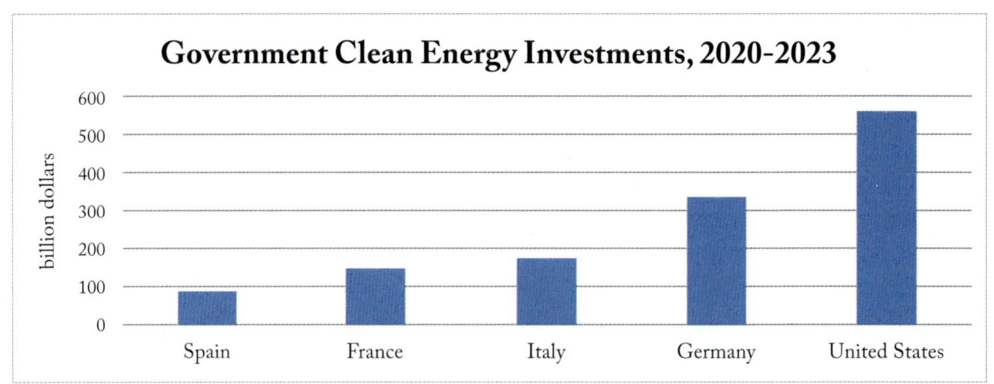

The above chart shows the clean energy investments of five countries. The countries listed are Spain, France, Italy, Germany, and the United States. These investments took place from 2020 to 2023. The United States invested the most money in clean energy. ① The government committed more than 500 billion dollars to clean energy. ② Germany came in second place for the largest investment, and their investment amount was more than 300 billion dollars. ③ Italy and France both invested more than 100 billion dollars. ④ However, France came out <u>slightly</u> ahead of Italy and invested more. ⑤ The Spanish government invested nearly $100 billion in clean energy, the smallest amount compared to other countries.

BREAKDOWN

다음 빈칸에 들어갈 적절한 말을 <보기>에서 찾아 쓰시오.

보기

| less | largest | least | investments |

Clean Energy 1 ____________ 2020 to 2023	
United States	the most money invested, more than 500 billion dollars
Germany	the second 2 ____________, more than 300 billion dollars
Italy	about 200 billion dollars, just ahead of France
France	invested 3 ____________ than Italy
Spain	the 4 ____________ money invested, nearly 100 billion dollars

1 이 글에 쓰인 **slightly**와 바꿔 쓸 수 없는 단어는?

① a bit   ② barely

③ nearly   ④ clearly

⑤ somewhat

2 이 글의 내용을 참고할 때, 빈칸에 들어갈 말로 가장 적절한 것은?

> Germany ranked second ＿＿＿＿＿＿ the largest investment.

① into   ② in terms of   ③ out of   ④ around   ⑤ up to

3 이 글의 내용과 일치하는 것은?

① Only four countries have invested in clean energy.

② Germany invested the largest amount of money.

③ Italy and France invested the same amount.

④ France invested more than 200 billion dollars.

⑤ Spain committed under 100 billion dollars.

PARAPHRASING DRILL

다음 문장들이 같은 뜻이 되도록 빈칸에 들어갈 적절한 말을 <보기>에서 찾아 쓰시오.

> 보기
>
> until   made   occurred

These investments took place from 2020 to 2023.

= These investments ＿＿＿＿＿＿＿ from 2020 to 2023.

= These investments took place from 2020 ＿＿＿＿＿＿＿ 2023.

= These investments were ＿＿＿＿＿＿＿ between 2020 and 2023.

TRANSLATION DRILL

⭐ 「come in + 서수 + place」는 경주나 대회에서 특정 순위를 차지하다는 의미를 나타낼 때 쓴다.

다음 문장의 밑줄 친 부분에 유의하여 해석을 완성하시오.

1 Germany came in second place for the largest investment.

독일은 가장 많은 투자를 한 국가 중 ＿＿＿＿＿＿＿＿＿＿.

2 She came in third place in her first marathon.

그녀는 그녀의 첫 마라톤에서 ＿＿＿＿＿＿＿＿＿＿.

내용 일치/불일치 파악하기

예제 ①

WORDS & PHRASES

throughout 전 ~ 동안
fascinated 형 매료된
due to ~ 때문에
physics 명 물리학
local 형 지역의 중등필수
move to ~로 이주하다
discover 동 ~을 발견하다 중등필수
element 명 원소
win a prize 상을 받다
work 명 업적
chemistry 명 화학
thanks to ~ 덕분에
improve 동 ~을 개선하다 고등필수
accurate 형 정확한

인물

Marie Curie에 관한 다음 글의 내용과 일치하지 <u>않는</u> 것은? 정답 및 해설 p. 14

Marie Curie was born in Poland in 1867. Throughout her life, Marie was fascinated by science. This is likely due to the fact that her father taught her math and physics. However, the local university did not let women study there. So, Marie moved to France to study physics. In 1895, she married Pierre Curie. They worked together
5 and discovered two new elements. Later, they won a Nobel Prize. This made Marie the first woman to win a Nobel Prize. In 1911, Marie won a second Nobel Prize for her work in chemistry. She is the first person to win two Nobel Prizes. Thanks to her work, x-ray machines were improved. They are now able to take more accurate images.

① 1867년에 폴란드에서 태어났다.
② 아버지에게 수학과 물리학을 배웠다.
③ 1895년, Pierre Curie와 결혼했다.
④ 노벨상을 수상한 두 번째 여성이다.
⑤ 노벨상을 두 번 수상한 첫 번째 사람이다.

👁 지문 한눈에 보기

빈칸에 들어갈 적절한 말을 쓰시오.

전반부 (Marie Curie의 일대기)	폴란드에서 태어나 평생 동안 **1** _______에 매료됨 아버지가 수학과 물리학을 가르침 물리학 공부를 위해 **2** _______로 이주함 Pierre Curie와 결혼하고 함께 일함
후반부 (Marie Curie의 업적)	두 가지 새로운 **3** _______를 발견해 노벨상을 수상함 노벨상을 수상한 첫 번째 **4** _______임 화학 분야의 업적으로 두 번째 노벨상을 수상함 **5** _______ 촬영의 개선에 이바지함

🎯 정답 적중하기

글의 핵심 문장을 찾아 빈칸을 완성하시오.

1 So, Marie _______ to France to study physics.
2 They worked together and _______ two new elements.
3 She is the first person to _______ two Nobel Prizes.

여가

Blue Lake Youth Summer Camp에 관한 다음 안내문의 내용과 일치하는 것은?

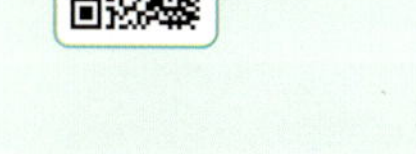

Blue Lake Youth Summer Camp

Do you love the outdoors? Want to learn basic survival skills in a fun and safe environment? Then sign up for our annual youth summer camp. Spend three weeks at the gorgeous Blue Lake. Enjoy boating, fishing, campfires, and many more!

Date: Monday, July 8 to Monday, July 29
Age: For youths aged 11-16
Program Cost: $375 per person
Program Includes: Shared cabin, meals, boat rentals, swimming lessons, fishing rod rentals, nature tours, two camp uniforms, bug spray, and more!

To register, please visit our website at www.bluelakeyouthsummercamp.com/signup.

---

① Blue Lake에서 2주간 진행된다.
② 16세 이상 청소년만 참여가 가능하다.
③ 비용은 2인에 375달러이다.
④ 프로그램 중 낚싯대를 대여받을 수 있다.
⑤ 캠프 신청은 전화로만 가능하다.

WORDS & PHRASES

youth 명 청소년
outdoors 명 야외(활동)
survival 명 생존
environment 명 환경 [고등필수]
sign up for ~에 등록하다
annual 형 연례의, 매년의
spend 동 (시간을) 보내다, (돈을) 쓰다
gorgeous 형 아름다운, 멋진
cost 명 비용
per person 인당
include 동 ~을 포함하다 [중등필수]
cabin 명 오두막집, 객실, 선실
rental 명 대여
fishing rod 명 낚싯대
register 동 ~을 등록하다 [중등필수]

 **지문 한눈에 보기**

빈칸에 들어갈 적절한 말을 쓰시오.

전반부 (Blue Lake 청소년 여름 캠프 소개)	1 ___________을 좋아하거나, 생존 기술을 배우고 싶다면 매년 열리는 청소년 여름 캠프에 2 ___________ 할 것
후반부 (캠프 세부 사항)	일시: 7/8(월)~7/29(월) / 연령: 11~16세 청소년 / 비용: 1인당 375달러 3 ___________ 사항: 공용 오두막집, 식사, 보트 대여, 수영 강습, 낚싯대 대여, 자연 투어, 캠프 유니폼 2벌, 벌레 스프레이 등 등록 방법: 웹사이트 4 ___________ 하기

정답 적중하기

글의 핵심 문장을 찾아 빈칸을 완성하시오.

1 Want to learn basic ___________ skills in a fun and safe environment?
2 Then ___________ for our annual youth summer camp.
3 To register, please ___________ our website.

1 인물

연습문제

C.S. Lewis에 관한 다음 글의 내용과 일치하지 <u>않는</u> 것은?

정답 및 해설 p. 15

WORDS & PHRASES

despite 전 ~임에도 불구하고
celebrated 형 유명한
fight-fought-fought 동 싸우다
novel 명 소설 중등필수
publish 동 ~을 출판하다 고등필수
detail 동 ~을 자세히 묘사하다
adventure 명 모험 중등필수
sibling 명 형제자매
magical 형 마법의
retire 동 은퇴하다 고등필수
pass away 세상을 떠나다
film 명 영화

Born in Ireland in 1898, C.S. Lewis was often ill as a child. Despite this, he became one of the most <u>celebrated</u> writers in the world. Before becoming a writer, Lewis went to England to study. He fought as a soldier in World War I. Later, he became a teacher and began to write novels. Lewis published many stories. But none were as famous as his children's book, *The Lion, the Witch, and the Wardrobe*. It was the first in *The Chronicles of Narnia* series. Lewis wrote seven books detailing the adventures of four siblings in the magical world of Narnia. C.S. Lewis retired from teaching in 1963. He passed away soon after. His stories _______(A)_______ still enjoyed as books and films to this day.

① 1898년 아일랜드에서 태어났으며, 어릴 때 자주 아팠다.
② 작가가 되기 전에 공부하기 위해 영국으로 갔다.
③ 1차 세계대전에 군인으로 참전했다.
④ 출판된 모든 이야기책이 유명해졌다.
⑤ 7권의 《The Chronicles of Narnia》 시리즈를 썼다.

FLOWCHART

다음 빈칸에 들어갈 적절한 말을 쓰시오.

작가가 되기까지	→	유명 작가가 되기까지

작가가 되기까지

1898년 아일랜드에서 태어났고, 어린 시절 자주 아픔

작가가 되기 전에, 공부하기 위해 1 _____________ 으로 감

1차 세계대전에서 군인으로 참전함

선생님이 되었고 2 _____________ 을 쓰기 시작함

유명 작가가 되기까지

많은 이야기를 3 _____________했지만, 《The Lion, the Witch, and the Wardrobe(사자와 마녀와 옷장)》 만큼 유명하지 않음

이 책은 《The Chronicles of Narnia(나니아 연대기)》 시리즈의 첫 번째 이야기였음

마법의 세계인 Narnia에서 네 형제자매의 4 _____________ 을 자세히 묘사한 7권의 책을 씀

1963년에 교직에서 은퇴, 오늘날까지 책과 영화로 사랑받음

1 이 글에 쓰인 **celebrated**와 뜻이 비슷한 단어는?

① criticized ② skillful

③ retired ④ brilliant

⑤ admired

2 이 글의 주어진 빈칸 (A)에 들어갈 말을 한 단어로 쓰시오.

> His stories __________ (A) __________ still enjoyed as books and films to this day.

→ _______________________________________

3 이 글의 제목으로 가장 적절한 것은?

① C.S. Lewis's Childhood and Education
② The World War I Soldier Author, C.S. Lewis
③ A Sickly Child Boy Becomes a World-Renowned Writer
④ *The Chronicles of Narnia*: C.S. Lewis's Masterpiece
⑤ The Adventures and Magic of *The Chronicles of Narnia*

PARAPHRASING DRILL

다음 두 문장이 같은 뜻이 되도록 빈칸에 괄호 안의 단어들을 쓰시오.

1 Despite this, he became one of the most celebrated writers in the world.
= In _______________ of this, he became one of the most _______________ writers all _______________ the world. (over / well-known / spite)

2 Lewis wrote seven books detailing the adventures of four siblings in the magical world of Narnia.
= Lewis _______________ seven books _______________ the adventures of four brothers and _______________ in the magical world of Narnia.
(sisters / describing / published)

TRANSLATION DRILL

⭐ to부정사가 부사적 용법 중 하나인 '목적'을 나타내는 경우에는 '~하기 위해'라고 해석한다.

다음 문장의 밑줄 친 부분에 유의하여 해석을 완성하시오.

1 Before becoming a writer, Lewis went to England to study.
작가가 되기 전에, Lewis는 _______________ 영국으로 갔다.

2 He took a cooking class to learn how to make Italian food.
그는 이탈리아 음식을 만드는 법을 _______________ 요리 수업을 들었다.

2 예술 · 연습문제

New Poets Magazine Novice Contest에 관한 다음 안내문의 내용과 일치하지 <u>않는</u> 것은?

WORDS & PHRASES

poet 명 시인
novice 명 초보자, 신인
poetry 명 (문학의 종류로서의) 시
enter 동 ~에 출전하다
biannual 형 연 2회의
feature 동 (글, 작품 등을) 특집으로 싣다
issue 명 (잡지·신문 등의) 호
submission window 명 제출 기간
sonnet 명 소네트(시의 한 종류)
announce 동 ~을 발표하다 중등필수
spot 명 부분
subscription 명 구독 고등필수

New Poets Magazine Novice Contest

Do you love poetry? Why not enter *New Poets Magazine*'s biannual contest? You could win a <u>chance</u> to be featured in the <u>next</u> issue of *New Poets Magazine*!

Submission Window: Monday, May 13 to Friday, May 17

Type: Any poem or sonnet less than 500 words

Winners Announced: Friday, May 31

You Could Win:

- 1st Prize - a spot in the July issue of *New Poets Magazine*
- 2nd Prize - a year subscription to *New Poets Magazine*
- 3rd Prize - a $50 Abbot's Bookstore gift card

① 콘테스트는 1년에 2회 열린다.
② 제출 기간은 5월 13일부터 4일간이다.
③ 500단어 미만의 시 또는 소네트 형식으로 써야 한다.
④ 수상자 발표는 5월 31일 금요일이다.
⑤ 2등상으로 1년 구독권을 수여한다.

MAPPING 

다음 빈칸에 들어갈 적절한 말을 <보기>에서 찾아 쓰시오.

보기

| period | purpose | contest | requirements |

2 ______________:
Providing an opportunity to be featured in the upcoming issue of *New Poets Magazine*

Winners Announcement: Friday, May 31

Prizes:
1st - feature in magazine
2nd - one-year subscription
3rd - gift card

Contest Name:
New Poets Magazine Novice **1 ______________**

Submission 3 ______________:
Monday, May 13 to Friday, May 17

4 ______________:
Any poem or sonnet less than 500 words

1 이 글에 쓰인 **chance**와 뜻이 비슷한 단어는?

① option ② opportunity

③ selection ④ fairness

⑤ effort

2 밑줄 친 **next**가 의미하는 시기를 이 글에서 찾아 한 단어로 쓰시오.

____

3 이 글의 내용과 일치하는 것은?

① *The New Poets Magazine* Novice Contest isn't held every year.

② The submission should be made from May 13 to June 17.

③ Only poems of more than 500 words are accepted for the contest.

④ The winners of the contest will be announced on May 30.

⑤ Third prize winners will receive a $50 gift card for Abbot's Bookstore.

PARAPHRASING DRILL

다음 문장들이 같은 뜻이 되도록 빈칸에 들어갈 적절한 말을 <보기>에서 찾아 쓰시오.

보기

included	possibility	obtain

You could win a chance to be featured in the next issue of *New Poets Magazine*!

= You could ________________ a chance to be featured in the next issue of *New Poets Magazine*!

= You could win a chance to be ________________ in the next issue of *New Poets Magazine*!

= There is a(n) ________________ to be featured in the next issue of *New Poets Magazine*!

TRANSLATION DRILL

⭐ Why not ~ ?은 권유하는 표현으로 바로 뒤에 동사원형이 와서 '~하는 건 어때(요)?'라는 뜻으로 쓰인다.

다음 문장의 밑줄 친 부분에 유의하여 해석을 완성하시오.

1 Why not enter *New Poets Magazine*'s biannual contest?
   연 2회 열리는 《New Poets Magazine》의 콘테스트에 ________________?

2 Why not explore a new hobby in your free time?
   여가 시간에 새로운 취미를 ________________?

CHAPTER 5
20번대 문제 공략하기 Part 4

UNIT 08 • 어법 적합성 판단하기

UNIT 08 **어법 적합성 판단하기** [최근 10회 평균 정답률: 60% 난이도 중]

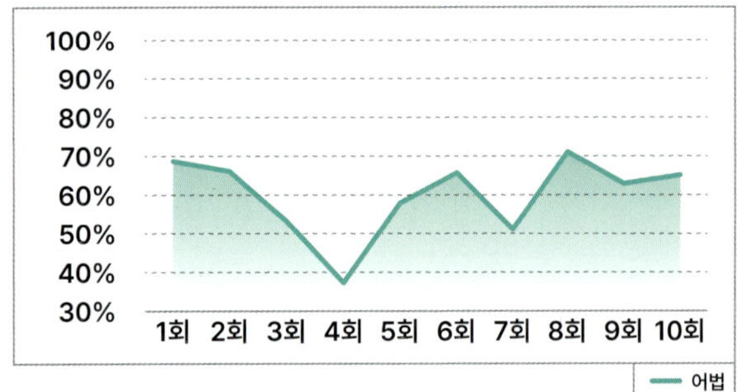

[어법 적합성 판단하기 유형]은 최근 10회분 **평균 정답률이 60%로 난이도 중 유형**으로 분류되나 실제 체감 난이도는 훨씬 어려운 유형이다. **1문제**가 출제되기 때문에 해당 유형을 포기하는 학생들도 많은데, **배점이 3점**이기 때문에 **상위 등급을 목표**로 하는 경우, 포기해서는 안 되는 유형이라고 할 수 있다. 두 가지 형태로 출제되며, 하나는 주어진 두 개의 단어 중 어법상 맞는 것을 찾는 유형, 다른 하나는 밑줄 친 부분 중 어법상 틀린 부분을 찾는 유형이다.

학습 전략

어법은 출제자의 의도가 분명히 있기 때문에, 표시된 부분에서 확인하고자 하는 어법 사항이 무엇인지부터 알아내야 한다. 우선 전체적인 글의 내용을 파악하며 읽고, 해당 부분이 포함된 문장의 구조를 확인하며 문법성을 파악한다. 단순히 문법을 아느냐보다는 문맥 파악이 우선되어야 하며, 문맥 이해를 바탕으로 문장 구조를 이해하여 해당 부분이 어법상 맞는지 판단할 수 있어야 한다.

유형 공략 어법

■ 동사의 수, 시제 일치

관계대명사나 수식어구가 붙어 길어지는 주어가 어디까지인지 실제 주어를 파악하고, 그에 맞는 동사가 오는지 확인하는 문제가 자주 출제된다. 그 이외에도 대명사와 명사의 수 일치 또한 중요하게 출제되므로 항상 단수인지 복수인지 확인하는 습관을 들이도록 한다.

The **team** of researchers that has studied climate change for over five years publish**es** its findings in top journals.

5년 넘게 기후 변화에 대해 연구해 온 연구자들 팀은	출간한다	그것의 결과를	최고의 학술지에
(주어)	(동사)	(목적어)	(부사구)

■ 능동태와 수동태

주어가 동사의 행위를 직접 할 수도 있지만, 그 행위의 영향을 받을 수도 있다. 이때는 수동태를 써야 한다. 동사가 누구에 의해 행해지고 있는지 문맥상 파악하여, 올바른 형태로 썼는지 확인한다.

능동태	The company **launched** a new product.
	그 회사는 (주어)　　출시했다 (동사)　　새로운 제품을 (목적어)

* 주어가 launch 함

수동태	A new product **was launched** by the company.
	새로운 제품이 (주어)　　출시되었다 (동사)　　그 회사에 의해 (부사구)

* 주어가 launch 됨

■ 문장의 성분과 품사

문장의 형식에 맞게 필수 성분이 모두 있는지, 그 성분에 맞는 품사로 쓰였는지 확인하는 문제가 출제될 수 있다. 주어, 동사, 보어, 목적어의 쓰임과 주격 보어, 목적격 보어의 쓰임도 이해해야 한다.

1형식	주어 + 동사	The baby laughed.	4형식	주어 + 동사 + 간접목적어 + 직접목적어	She gave him a gift.
2형식	주어 + 동사 + 주격 보어	She became a doctor.	5형식	주어 + 동사 + 목적어 + 목적격 보어	They elected him president. He made her cry. I saw him leave the house.
3형식	주어 + 동사 + 목적어	He reads a book.			

■ 관계대명사와 관계부사, 접속사

관계대명사의 경우 앞에 오는 선행사가 무엇인지와 주어, 목적어, 소유격 중 무엇을 대신한 것인지에 따라 종류가 다르므로, 관계대명사에 밑줄이 있을 경우 문장 앞뒤를 반드시 살펴봐야 한다. 관계부사는 시간, 장소, 방법, 이유 등을 나타내므로 의미상 적절하게 쓰였는지, 접속사에 밑줄이 있을 경우 의미상 적절한 접속사가 온 것인지, 등위접속사(and, but, or, so 등)의 앞뒤에 같은 구조와 성분이 왔는지 확인해야 한다.

The teacher **who** teaches us math is very kind.　　우리에게 수학을 가르치는 선생님은 매우 친절하다.
The car **which** he bought last week is already broken.　　그가 지난주에 산 차는 벌써 고장 났다.
She is the artist **whose** paintings are displayed in the gallery.　　그녀는 그녀의 그림들이 갤러리에 전시된 예술가이다.

어법 적합성 판단하기

정답률 60% 난이도 ★★½☆☆

WORDS & PHRASES

industrialized 형 산업화된 고등필수
work ethic 명 직업 윤리
prized 형 중요한, 소중한
employer 명 고용주
count A as B A를 B로 간주하다
productivity 명 생산성
period 명 시기, 기간 고등필수
creativity 명 창의성 중등필수
benefit 명 이점
examine 동 조사하다 중등필수
highly 부 매우
intensely 부 극도로, 심하게
productive 형 생산적인
downtime 명 한가한 시간, 여가
engage in ~에 참여하다
stimulate 동 ~을 자극하다
allow 동 가능하게 하다, 허락하다 중등필수
approach 동 다가가다, 접근하다 중등필수
refreshed 형 상쾌한

사회

다음 글의 밑줄 친 부분 중, 어법상 틀린 것은?

정답 및 해설 p. 16

In most industrialized countries, having a good work ethic is prized above all else. Many employers ① to count long hours of work as a sign of productivity. However, studies have shown ② that periods of rest can actually improve a person's productivity and creativity. In his book *Why You Get More Done When You Work Less*, Alex

5 Soojung-Kim Pang showed that ③ resting has many benefits. During his research, Pang examined the lives of highly creative and successful people. He found although they ④ were intensely productive, they often only worked for short periods of time. In their downtime, they engaged in other activities. These activities included hobbies, exercise, and vacations. This type of rest stimulated their brains. It allowed them

10 ⑤ to approach their work again with clear, refreshed minds.

🔍 지문 한눈에 보기

빈칸에 들어갈 적절한 말을 쓰시오.

도입부 (일반적인 경향)	산업화된 국가에서는 좋은 직업윤리(열심히 일하는 것)가 중요하다. 고용주들은 장시간의 근무를 **1** ＿＿＿＿＿＿의 표시로 간주한다.
중반부 (반론/주제문)	**2** ＿＿＿＿＿＿이 한 사람의 생산성과 창의성을 향상시킬 수 있다.
후반부 (근거)	이것은 많은 **3** ＿＿＿＿＿＿이 있다. 창의적인 사람들은 매우 생산적이고 종종 **4** ＿＿＿＿＿＿ 시간 동안만 일한다. 그들은 한가한 시간에 취미, 운동, 휴가 등 다른 활동에 참여했고, 이 휴식은 그들의 뇌를 자극하여, 맑고 상쾌한 정신으로 다시 일하게 했다.

🎯 정답 적중하기

글의 핵심 문장을 찾아 빈칸을 완성하시오.

1 However, studies have shown that periods of rest can actually ＿＿＿＿＿＿ a person's productivity and creativity.

2 He found although they were intensely ＿＿＿＿＿＿, they often only worked for short periods of time.

3 This type of rest ＿＿＿＿＿＿ their brains.

어법상 (A)~(C)에 들어갈 적절한 표현이 바르게 짝지어진 것은?

정답 및 해설 p. 16

When it comes to marketing products to children, Disney is one of the most successful companies. Films, toys, and even theme parks have been (A) created / creating to celebrate and promote Disney's many iconic cartoon characters. However, many of these characters did not originate in the minds of Disney writers.
5 In fact, some fairy tale characters are hundreds of years old. In the 1700s, two German brothers began collecting fairy tale stories. At the time, these stories were told (B) verbal / verbally . The brothers compiled the stories and published them. The tales written by the Brothers Grimm (C) is / are often dark and brutal with frightening endings. Generally, Disney's strategy is to give these characters a happier,
10 more playful treatment. This strategy has been successful in making these old characters beloved among today's children.

	(A)	(B)	(C)
①	created	verbal	is
②	creating	verbal	are
③	created	verbally	is
④	created	verbally	are
⑤	creating	verbally	is

WORDS & PHRASES

when it comes to ~에 관한 한
theme park 몡 테마파크
promote 통 ~을 홍보하다 [중등필수]
iconic 혱 상징적인
character 몡 캐릭터, 등장인물
originate 통 비롯되다
fairy tale 몡 동화
verbally 분 구두로, 말로
compile 통 ~을 엮다
brutal 혱 잔인한
frightening 혱 무서운 [중등필수]
generally 분 일반적으로
strategy 몡 전략 [고등필수]
playful 혱 장난기 많은
treatment 몡 대우, 처리
beloved 혱 사랑받는

지문 한눈에 보기

빈칸에 들어갈 적절한 말을 쓰시오.

도입부 (일반적인 사실)	디즈니는 어린이 상품 판매에 있어 가장 **1**＿＿＿＿＿＿ 회사 중 하나로 디즈니의 상품들은 상징적인 만화 캐릭터들을 **2**＿＿＿＿＿＿하고 홍보하기 위해 만들어졌다.
중반부 (반론)	모든 디즈니 캐릭터들이 디즈니 작가들의 생각에서 처음 시작된 것은 아니다. 독일의 Grimm 형제는 동화 이야기들을 모아서 출판했으며 그 이야기들은 종종 어둡고 잔인하고 **3**＿＿＿＿＿＿이 무섭다.
후반부 (핵심 내용)	디즈니의 **4**＿＿＿＿＿＿은 캐릭터들에게 행복과 장난기를 불어넣는 것이다. 이것 덕분에 옛날 캐릭터들은 오늘날 어린이들 사이에서 사랑받는다.

정답 적중하기

글의 핵심 문장을 찾아 빈칸을 완성하시오.

1 When it comes to marketing products to children, Disney is one of the most ＿＿＿＿＿ companies.
2 Generally, Disney's strategy is to give these characters a happier, more playful ＿＿＿＿＿.
3 This strategy has been successful in making these old characters beloved among today's ＿＿＿＿＿.

다음 글의 밑줄 친 부분 중, 어법상 틀린 것은?

정답 및 해설 p. 17

WORDS & PHRASES

suffer from ~로 고통받다
on the rise 증가하고 있는
edited 형 편집된
conventionally 부 판에 박힌 듯이
attractive 형 매력적인 중등필수
engage 통 관심을 갖다
sort of 종류의
plummet 통 급락하다
psychologist 명 심리학자
negative 형 부정적인
outcome 명 결과 고등필수
impressionable 형 쉽게 영향받는
develop 통 ~을 일으키다 고등필수
eating disorder 섭식 장애
self-esteem 명 자존감
affect 통 ~에 영향을 주다 중등필수
confidence 명 자신감
performance 명 수행 능력, 성과
expert 명 전문가 중등필수
expose 통 노출시키다
genuine 형 진짜인

Many people suffer from poor body image. With the rise in social media, body image issues are steadily on the rise. This is likely ① <u>due to</u> the selected style of social media. Most influencers post highly edited photos and videos that make ② <u>their</u> appear more conventionally <u>attractive</u>. The more users engage with this sort of content, the more their own body image plummets. Psychologists say ③ <u>that</u> poor body image could cause many negative outcomes. Impressionable young people may develop eating disorders. Others may develop poor self-esteem. This may affect their confidence in life and even that can ④ <u>decrease</u> their performance in school and at work. To reduce this, experts suggest ⑤ <u>teaching</u> young people media literacy. This may help <u>them</u> determine if the content they're exposed to is truly genuine.

* media literacy 미디어 리터러시(미디어 정보 해독력)

다음 빈칸에 들어갈 적절한 말을 쓰시오.

문제점	소셜 미디어 증가로 신체 이미지 문제가 꾸준히 **1**____________
문제의 원인	인플루언서들은 더 **2**____________ 보이도록 고도로 편집된 사진과 영상을 게시
부정적 결과	과도하게 편집한 콘텐츠를 더 많이 소비할수록 자신의 신체 이미지를 더 부정적으로 인식하게 됨 좋지 못한 신체 이미지가 많은 **3**____________ 결과를 초래 젊은이들은 자존감이 낮아지고 이것은 성과의 **4**____________로 이어짐
해결 방안	이것을 억제하기 위해, 미디어 리터러시(미디어 정보 해독력)를 가르치는 것을 제안함

1 이 글에 쓰인 **attractive**와 뜻이 비슷한 단어는?

① aggressive   ② passive

③ good-looking   ④ normal

⑤ active

2 밑줄 친 **them**이 가리키는 것을 이 글에서 찾아 두 단어로 쓰시오.

____

3 이 글의 내용과 일치하지 <u>않는</u> 것은?

① 신체 이미지로 인한 문제는 꾸준히 감소 중이다.

② 인플루언서는 더 매력적으로 보이려고 사진을 과하게 보정한다.

③ 쉽게 영향받는 젊은이들은 섭식 장애를 일으킬 수 있다.

④ 자존감이 낮으면 직장에서 성과가 떨어질 수 있다.

⑤ 전문가들은 미디어 리터러시를 가르치는 것을 제안한다.

PARAPHRASING DRILL

다음 두 문장이 같은 뜻이 되도록 빈칸에 괄호 안의 단어들을 쓰시오.

1 Most influencers post highly edited photos and videos that make them appear more conventionally attractive.

= Most influencers ________________ ________________ ________________ photos and videos that make them appear more conventionally attractive.

(modified / upload / significantly)

2 This may help them determine if the content they're exposed to is truly genuine.

= This may help them ________________ ________________ ________________ the content they're exposed to is truly genuine. (whether / out / figure)

TRANSLATION DRILL

⭐ 「with + 명사」는 '~와 함께'로 해석한다.

다음 문장의 밑줄 친 부분에 유의하여 해석을 완성하시오.

1 With the rise in social media, body image issues are steadily on the rise.

소셜 미디어의 ________________, 신체 이미지 문제가 꾸준히 증가하고 있다.

2 With the increase in remote work, flexible schedules are becoming more common.

________________________________, 유연한 일정이 더 일반화되고 있다.

어법상 (A)~(C)에 들어갈 적절한 표현이 바르게 짝지어진 것은?

정답 및 해설 p. 17

WORDS & PHRASES

greenhouse gas 명 온실가스
release 동 ~을 방출하다
individual 명 개인, 사람 고등필수
unsure 형 확신하지 못하는
revolve around ~을 중심으로 돌다
dependent 형 의존하는 고등필수
pollute 동 ~을 오염시키다 중등필수
nevertheless 부 그럼에도 불구하고
recommend 동 ~을 추천하다 고등필수
opt for ~을 선택하다
public transportation 명 대중교통
option 명 선택
purchase 동 ~을 구입하다 중등필수
fuel-efficient 형 연료 효율이 좋은
vehicle 명 자동차
emission 명 (빛·열·가스 등의) 배출(물)
lighting 명 조명
appliance 명 가전제품
install 동 ~을 설치하다
solar panel 명 태양 전지판

A carbon footprint is the amount of greenhouse gases that an activity or product releases into the air. Most experts agree (A) if / that reducing one's carbon footprint is important. However, many individuals are unsure about where to start. Much of their lives revolve around being (B) dependent / dependently on technology that pollutes the environment. Nevertheless, there are a few things scientists now recommend. Firstly, individuals can opt for cleaner transportation. If they live in cities, public transportation is a good option. Those (C) who / whose drive can purchase a fuel-efficient vehicle. Experts also recommend reducing travel by airplane if possible. Individuals can reduce emissions at home as well. This can be done by upgrading lighting and appliances to more efficient models. Installing solar panels on a home could also reduce one's carbon footprint.

* carbon footprint 탄소 발자국(온실 효과를 유발하는 이산화탄소의 배출량)

	(A)	(B)	(C)
①	if	dependently	who
②	that	dependent	who
③	if	dependently	whose
④	that	dependent	whose
⑤	if	dependent	whose

MAPPING

다음 빈칸에 들어갈 적절한 말을 <보기>에서 찾아 쓰시오.

보기

reducing   fuel-efficient   transportation   installing

Not travelling by airplane

Choosing cleaner 1 ＿＿＿＿＿＿＿＿

3 ＿＿＿＿＿＿＿＿ emissions at home

Ways to Reduce Carbon Footprint

Purchasing a 2 ＿＿＿＿＿＿＿＿ vehicle

4 ＿＿＿＿＿＿＿＿ solar panels

Using more efficient lighting and appliances

1 이 글에 쓰인 **opt for**와 뜻이 비슷한 단어는?

① refuse
② ignore
③ explain
④ investigate
⑤ choose

2 이 글의 제목으로 가장 적절한 것은?

① Embracing a Technology-Dependent Lifestyle
② Why Reducing Your Carbon Footprint Is Unimportant
③ Starting Point: Ways to Increase Your Carbon Footprint
④ The Benefits of Increased Air Travel on the Environment
⑤ Small Changes, Big Impact: Reducing Your Carbon Footprint

3 이 글의 내용과 일치하는 것은?

① Reducing one's carbon footprint is not always important.
② Many people know how to reduce carbon emissions.
③ Choosing public transportation can reduce carbon footprint.
④ Experts strongly suggest traveling by airplane if possible.
⑤ Installing solar panels cannot help reduce carbon footprint.

PARAPHRASING DRILL

다음 문장들이 같은 뜻이 되도록 빈칸에 들어갈 적절한 말을 <보기>에서 찾아 쓰시오.

> 보기
>
> begin　　　yet　　　plenty of

However, many individuals are unsure about where to start.

= However, ________________ individuals are unsure about where to start.

= However, many individuals are unsure about where to ________________.

= ________________, many individuals are unsure about where to start.

TRANSLATION DRILL

⭐ 「by + 동명사」는 '~함으로써'로 해석한다.

다음 문장의 밑줄 친 부분에 유의하여 해석을 완성하시오.

1 This can be done by upgrading lighting and appliances to more efficient models.
이것은 조명과 가전제품을 더 효율적인 모델로 ________________ 할 수 있다.

2 By using eco-friendly vehicles, we can help protect the environment.
친환경 차량을 ________________, 우리는 환경을 보호하는 것을 도울 수 있다.

CHAPTER 6
30번대 문제 공략하기 Part 1

UNIT 09 • 어휘 적합성 판단하기

UNIT 09 어휘 적합성 판단하기 [최근 10회 평균 정답률: 53% 난이도 중상]

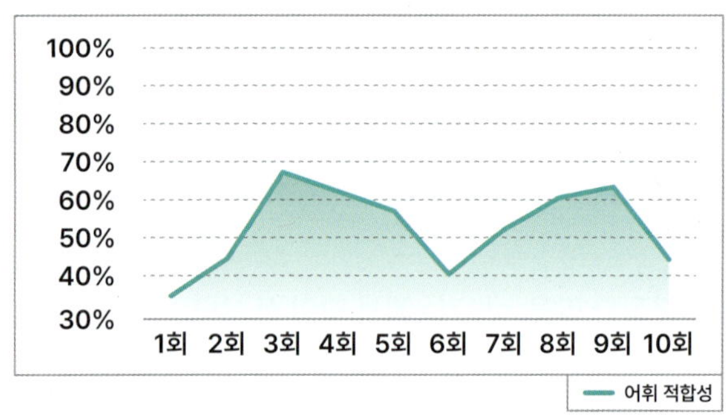

[어휘 적합성 판단하기 유형]은 고1 모의평가 기준 **평균 정답률 53%**, 난이도 **중상의 유형**으로 킬러 유형이라고 볼 수 있다. **문맥상 쓰임이 적절하지 않은 어휘**를 찾는 유형으로 매년 **오답률이 높아지는 유형**이다. **1문제**가 출제되지만 **3점 문제**로 출제되므로 1등급을 위해서는 반드시 정답을 찾아야 하는 유형이라 할 수 있다.

학습 전략

글의 도입부에서 중심 소재를 나타내는 단어를 반복적으로 제시하여 바로 파악할 수 있는 구조로 출제된다. 그렇기 때문에, 앞부분을 잘 읽고 중심 소재를 먼저 파악해야 한다. 중심 소재가 파악되었으면, 밑줄 친 단어가 포함된 문장과 그 전후에서 각 단어의 적절성을 판단할 단서를 찾는다. 갑자기 다른 의미로 흘러가는 단어가 등장하면 답일 가능성이 높다. 원래 들어가야 할 단어 대신에 반의어가 들어가 있는 경우가 많기 때문에 해당 단어를 반의어로 바꿔 보고 문맥상 자연스럽다면 그 부분을 정답으로 선택한다.

유형 공략 Q&A

Q. 사전에 보면 한 단어의 뜻이 너무 많아요.

A. 어떤 언어이든 하나의 단어가 여러 가지 의미를 가지는 것이 당연합니다. 단순히 높은 점수를 받겠다가 아니라 '영어'라는 언어를 익히겠다고 생각하더라도 한 단어를 여러 의미로 활용하는 능력은 필수적입니다. 예를 들어, 'bank'라는 단어는 대부분 '은행'이라는 뜻으로 알고 있지만 강이나 바다의 '둑'이나 '제방'이라는 전혀 다른 뜻을 가지고 있습니다. 완전히 다른 뜻으로 활용될 때 이 뜻을 모른다면 정답을 고를 수 없게 되니 다양한 뜻을 모두 익혀두어야 합니다.

반의어 - 명사

- advantage (이점) - disadvantage (불리)
- courage (용기) - fear (두려움)
- success (성공) - failure (실패)
- increase (증가) - decrease (감소)
- doubt (의심) - certainty (확실)
- pleasure (즐거움) - pain (고통)
- ancestor (조상) - descendant (후손)
- patience (인내) - impatience (조급함)
- strength (힘) - weakness (약함)
- bravery (용기) - cowardice (비겁)
- calm (고요함) - chaos (혼돈)
- fiction (허구) - reality (현실)
- joy (기쁨) - sorrow (슬픔)
- majority (대다수) - minority (소수)
- profit (이익) - loss (손실)
- knowledge (지식) - ignorance (무지)
- wealth (부) - poverty (가난)
- advance (전진) - retreat (후퇴)

반의어 - 동사

- accept (받아들이다) - reject (거절하다)
- grow (자라다) - shrink (줄어들다)
- permit (허락하다) - prohibit (금지하다)
- increase (증가하다) - decrease (감소하다)
- tighten (조이다) - loosen (풀다)
- produce (생산하다) - consume (소비하다)
- arrive (도착하다) - depart (떠나다)
- encourage (격려하다) - discourage (낙담시키다)
- allow (가능하게 하다, 허락하다) - forbid (금지하다)
- include (포함하다) - exclude (제외하다)
- praise (칭찬하다) - criticize (비판하다)
- strengthen (강화하다) - weaken (약화시키다)
- unite (통합하다) - divide (분열하다)
- support (지지하다) - oppose (반대하다)
- admit (인정하다) - deny (부인하다)
- improve (개선하다) - worsen (악화시키다)

반의어 - 형용사

- bold (대담한) - timid (소심한)
- artificial (인공의) - natural (자연의)
- broad (넓은) - narrow (좁은)
- close (가까운) - distant (먼)
- deep (깊은) - shallow (얕은)
- complicated (복잡한) - simple (단순한)
- clear (명확한) - vague (모호한)
- beneficial (유용한) - harmful (해로운)
- calm (차분한) - excited (흥분한)
- common (흔한) - rare (드문)
- essential (필수적인) - optional (선택적인)
- generous (관대한) - selfish (이기적인)

사회

다음 글의 밑줄 친 부분 중, 문맥상 낱말의 쓰임이 적절하지 <u>않은</u> 것은? 정답 및 해설 p. 18

Different parents have different ideas about how to raise their children. Parenting styles can ① <u>differ</u> drastically depending on location and culture. For example, many people would never think of leaving their babies ② <u>outdoors</u> in winter. However, Nordic parents often let their babies nap outside in their strollers. They even believe

5 that the cool air can ③ <u>protect</u> a baby from viruses. Another common point of argument is bedtime. In many Western countries, children are sent to bed rather ④ <u>late</u>. This may be around 7:30 or 8:00 p.m. However, in many Eastern countries, children stay up until 10:00, 11:00, or even later. Regardless, there is no ⑤ <u>single</u> right way to approach parenting. Children in all parts of the world grow up to be

10 stable, healthy adults.

WORDS & PHRASES

different 형 다른
raise 통 ~을 기르다 중등필수
parenting 명 육아
differ 통 다르다
drastically 부 완전히
depending on ~에 따라 고등필수
leave 통 놓아두다 중등필수
outdoors 부 야외에
Nordic 형 북유럽의
nap 통 낮잠을 자다
stroller 명 유모차
protect 통 ~을 보호하다 중등필수
common 형 흔한 중등필수
point 명 요점
argument 명 논쟁
bedtime 명 취침 시간
Western 형 서양의
Eastern 형 동양의
regardless 부 그럼에도 불구하고
single 형 유일한
stable 형 안정적인

👁 지문 한눈에 보기

빈칸에 들어갈 적절한 말을 쓰시오.

도입부 (일반적인 사실)	아이들을 어떻게 키워야 하는지에 대한 생각이 부모마다 다르고, **1** ____________ 방식은 지역과 문화에 따라 완전히 다를 수 있다.
중반부 (근거/예시)	북유럽에서는 종종 아기를 유모차에 태워 **2** ____________ 낮잠을 재운다. 시원한 공기가 아기를 바이러스로부터 보호해 준다고 믿는다. 서양에서는 아이들이 **3** ____________ 잠들고, 동양에서는 늦게 잔다.
후반부 (주제문)	육아에는 **4** ____________ 올바른 방법은 없다. 모든 아이들은 안정적이고 건강한 어른으로 자란다.

🎯 정답 적중하기

글의 핵심 문장을 찾아 빈칸을 완성하시오.

1 Different parents have ____________ ideas about how to raise their children.
2 Regardless, there is no single right way to ____________ parenting.
3 Children in all parts of the world ____________ to be stable, healthy adults.

문맥상 (A)~(C)에 들어갈 적절한 표현이 바르게 짝지어진 것은? 정답 및 해설 p. 19

Clutter can build up in a home quickly, causing an unsightly mess. If your home seems too cluttered, it may be time to (A) ⏐gather around / get rid of⏐ unused items. Decluttering will certainly improve the look of your home, but that's not all. Decluttering can benefit you in numerous other ways. For example, clutter often

5 makes people feel stressed out or (B) ⏐relieved / anxious⏐. On the other hand, a decluttered home can help boost your mood and help you feel better about yourself. It can (C) ⏐increase / decrease⏐ your productivity, so you're able to work or study faster and more efficiently. Finally, a decluttered home will increase feelings of relaxation. This creates a calming effect throughout the day, and you may find that

10 you sleep better at night.

	(A)	(B)	(C)
①	get rid of	relieved	increase
②	get rid of	anxious	decrease
③	gather around	anxious	increase
④	get rid of	anxious	increase
⑤	gather around	anxious	decrease

WORDS & PHRASES

clutter 명 잡동사니
　　　 통 (장소를) 어지르다
build up 쌓이다
unsightly 형 보기 흉한
mess 명 난장판, 엉망인 상태
cluttered 형 어수선한
get rid of ~을 제거하다 [고등필수]
unused 형 사용하지 않는
decluttering 명 잡동사니 정리
certainly 부 확실히
benefit 통 ~에게 혜택을 주다
numerous 형 수많은 [고등필수]
stressed out 스트레스 받는
anxious 형 불안한 [중등필수]
decluttered 형 잡동사니를 정리한
boost 통 ~을 증진시키다
efficiently 부 효율적으로
relaxation 명 휴식
create 통 ~을 만들다 [중등필수]
calming 형 진정하는

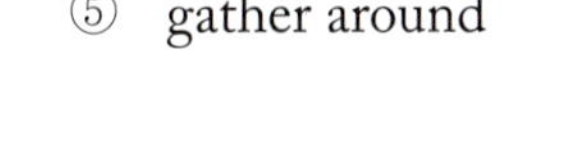 **지문 한눈에 보기**

빈칸에 들어갈 적절한 말을 쓰시오.

도입부 (일반적인 사실)	잡동사니는 집에 보기 흉한 난장판을 유발하며 빠르게 쌓인다. 만일 집이 너무 어수선해 보인다면, 사용하지 않는 물건들을 버릴 때일지도 모른다.
전반부 (주제문)	잡동사니 정리는 집의 모습을 개선시켜 주고, 다른 많은 방법으로 1 ＿＿＿＿＿＿＿＿을 줄 수 있다.
중/후반부 (근거)	기분을 2 ＿＿＿＿＿＿＿＿시키고 자신에 대해 더 좋게 느끼도록 도와줄 수 있다. 3 ＿＿＿＿＿＿＿＿을 증가시킬 수 있어서, 더 빠르고 효율적으로 일할 수 있다. 휴식의 감정을 증가시켜 하루 종일 4 ＿＿＿＿＿＿＿＿ 효과를 만들고, 밤에 더 잘 잠들 수 있다.

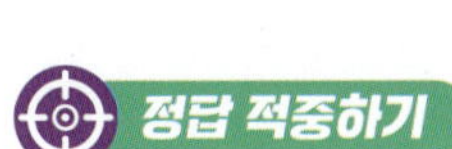 **정답 적중하기**

글의 핵심 문장을 찾아 빈칸을 완성하시오.

1 Decluttering will certainly ＿＿＿＿＿＿＿ the look of your home, but that's not all.

2 Decluttering can benefit you in ＿＿＿＿＿＿＿ other ways.

3 It can increase your productivity, so you're able to work or study faster and more ＿＿＿＿＿＿＿.

과학

다음 글의 밑줄 친 부분 중, 문맥상 낱말의 쓰임이 적절하지 <u>않은</u> 것은? 정답 및 해설 p. 19

WORDS & PHRASES

impossible 혱 불가능한 중등필수
determine 통 ~을 결정하다 고등필수
sense 명 감각
sight 명 시각
block 통 ~을 막다
fully 부 완전히
engage with ~와 관계를 맺다
surroundings 명 [주변]환경
alert 통 ~을 경고하다 고등필수
touch 명 촉각
beneficial 형 유용한
injured 형 다친
navigate 통 ~을 항해하다
work together 함께 작용하다
responsible for ~에 책임이 있는
flavor 명 맛, 풍미 고등필수

It is ① <u>impossible</u> to determine which of the five senses is most important to the human experience. Some might say sight is the most important of all the senses. Sight ② <u>blocks</u> people to experience the world around them fully. It helps them engage with their ③ <u>surroundings</u> and art while also alerting them to dangers.

5 Others, however, might say that a sense of touch is far more beneficial. Without it, people could get injured very easily, and it would be ④ <u>hard</u> to navigate the world. Regardless, many of the senses work together as we experience the world around us. For example, we may think the sense of taste is the only sense <u>engaged</u> when it comes to eating. However, the sense of smell is also ⑤ <u>responsible</u> for the flavors we

10 experience.

BREAKDOWN

다음 빈칸에 들어갈 적절한 말을 쓰시오.

다섯 개의 감각	어떤 감각이 가장 중요한지 결정하는 것은 1 ______________
시각	주변 세계를 완전히 경험하는 것을 돕고, 위험에 대해 2 ______________함 주변 환경과 예술에 참여할 수 있도록 도움
촉각	촉각이 없으면 쉽게 3 ______________, 세계를 항해하는 것이 어려움
미각/후각	4 ______________을 느낄 때 미각뿐만 아니라 후각도 관여함

1 이 글에 쓰인 **engaged**와 뜻이 비슷한 단어는?

① passed　　　　　　② thrown
③ harmful　　　　　　④ strengthen
⑤ participated

2 밑줄 친 **It**이 가리키는 것을 이 글에서 찾아 한 단어로 쓰시오.

____

3 이 글의 제목으로 가장 적절한 것은?

① The Impact of Multiple Senses on Art Appreciation
② The Role of Touch in Exploring the New World
③ The Connection between Taste and Smell
④ The Role of Senses in Human Experience
⑤ How Senses Help People to Engage

PARAPHRASING DRILL

다음 두 문장이 같은 뜻이 되도록 빈칸에 괄호 안의 단어들을 쓰시오.

1 It helps them engage with their surroundings and art while also alerting them to dangers.
= It helps them _______________ with their _______________ and art while also _______________ them to dangers.
(environment / interact / warning)

2 However, the sense of smell is also responsible for the flavors we experience.
= _______________, the sense of smell also _______________ to the flavors we _______________. (perceive / nonetheless / contributes)

TRANSLATION DRILL

⭐ far은 비교급을 강조하는 부사로 '훨씬'으로 해석한다.

다음 문장의 밑줄 친 부분에 유의하여 해석을 완성하시오.

1 Others, however, might say that a sense of touch is far more beneficial.
그러나 다른 사람들은 촉각이 _______________ 하다고 말할지도 모른다.

2 The new restaurant is far better than the old one.
이 새로운 식당은 그 전 식당보다 _______________.

문맥상 (A)~(C)에 들어갈 적절한 표현이 바르게 짝지어진 것은?

정답 및 해설 p. 20

WORDS & PHRASES

represent 동 나타내다
turning point 명 전환점
prior to ~ 이전에
period 명 시기, 기간 [고등필수]
goods 명 상품
produce 동 생산하다, 만들다 [중등필수]
thus 부 따라서, 그리하여
expensive 형 비싼
mechanized 형 기계화된
economy 명 경제 [중등필수]
rapid 형 빠른
pace 명 속도
opportunity 명 기회 [고등필수]
develop 동 발전하다 [고등필수]
carbon dioxide 명 이산화탄소
likewise 부 마찬가지로
pollutant 명 오염 물질
contribute to ~에 일조하다
crisis 명 위기
fare 동 지내다, 살아가다
indeed 부 실제로
force 동 강요하다
wage 명 임금
working environment 명 노동 환경
lead to ~로 이어지다
sickness 명 질병

The Industrial Revolution represented a turning point for human societies. Prior to this period, goods took a long time to (A) [be produced / be progressed]. Thus, they were expensive to buy. The Industrial Revolution saw the beginning of mechanized factories. Economies grew at a rapid pace and job opportunities increased. As a result, cities quickly developed. However, not all of the effects of the Industrial Revolution were (B) [negative / positive]. At the time, factories released a huge amount of carbon dioxide into the air. Likewise, pollutants entered the water and soil, contributing to a rising environmental crisis. Workers did not <u>fare</u> much better during this time. Indeed, they were forced to work long hours for low wages. The factory working environment was often (C) [safe / dangerous], leading to sickness and sometimes death.

* Industrial Revolution 산업혁명(18세기 영국에서 시작된 기술 혁신과 사회경제적 변화)

	(A)	(B)	(C)
①	be progressed	negative	safe
②	be produced	positive	safe
③	be produced	positive	dangerous
④	be progressed	negative	dangerous
⑤	be produced	negative	dangerous

MAPPING

다음 빈칸에 들어갈 적절한 말을 <보기>에서 찾아 쓰시오.

보기

| long | growth | pollution | development |

Industrial Revolution

Advantages

A turning point for human societies, the beginning of mechanized factories / Rapid economic **1** ______________ / More job opportunities / Cities' quick **2** ______________

Disadvantages

A huge amount of carbon dioxide into the air / Water and soil **3** ______________ / Working **4** ______________ hours at a low wage and in a dangerous environment / Falling ill and even death

1 이 글에 쓰인 **fare**와 뜻이 비슷한 단어는?

① succeed　　　　　② expect
③ manage　　　　　④ achieve
⑤ compete

2 이 글의 제목으로 가장 적절한 것은?

① Why Slow Growth Is Right
② Environmental Impact of the Industrial Revolution
③ The Agricultural Revolution: A Defining Turning Point
④ Double-Edged Blade: The Industrial Revolution's Impact
⑤ Solutions to Environmental Problems in Industrialized Countries

3 산업혁명 이후의 변화에 대한 내용으로 알맞은 것은?

① Economies experienced very slow growth.
② Job opportunities decreased and workers faced no health risks.
③ Environmental stability was a positive outcome.
④ Pollutants did not enter the water and soil.
⑤ The workers received lower wages and their working conditions also worsened.

PARAPHRASING DRILL

다음 문장들이 같은 뜻이 되도록 빈칸에 들어갈 적절한 말을 <보기>에서 찾아 쓰시오.

보기

issue　　　leading　　　similarly

Likewise, pollutants entered the water and soil, contributing to a rising environmental crisis.
= _________________, pollutants entered the water and soil, contributing to a rising environmental crisis.
= Likewise, pollutants entered the water and soil, _________________ to a rising environmental crisis.
= Likewise, pollutants entered the water and soil, contributing to a rising environmental _________________.

TRANSLATION DRILL

⭐ 「take + 시간 + to부정사」는 '~하는 데 (시간)이 걸리다'로 해석한다.

다음 문장의 밑줄 친 부분에 유의하여 해석을 완성하시오.

1 Prior to this period, goods took a long time to be produced.
이 시기 이전에는, 상품들은 _________________ 오랜 시간이 걸렸다.
2 We need to take some time to plan our trip.
우리는 _________________ 시간이 좀 필요하다.

CHAPTER 7
30번대 문제 공략하기 Part 2

UNIT 10 ● 빈칸 추론하기

UNIT 10 **빈칸 추론하기** [최근 10회 평균 정답률: 53% 난이도 중상]

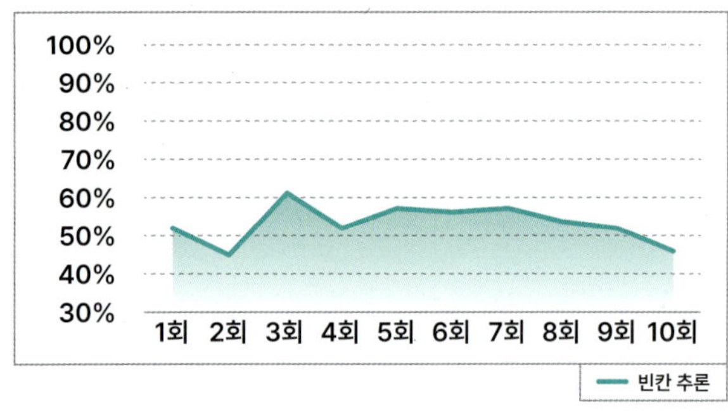

[빈칸 추론하기 유형]은 총 **4문제**가 나오는 **출제 비중이 가장 높은 유형**이다. 특히 **2문제**가 **3점으로 출제**되어 상위권과 중위권을 가르는 유형이라고 할 수 있다. 고1 모의평가 기준 **평균 정답률 53%**로 UNIT 09 어휘 적합성 판단하기와 함께 **난이도 중상의 유형**으로 분류되나 일부 시험에서는 20%대의 정답률을 보인 경우도 있어서 최고 난이도의 킬러 문제로도 출제되고 있음을 알 수 있다. 빈칸에 **짧은 어구**가 들어가는 유형과 **긴 어구**나 **문장**이 들어가는 유형이 있다.

학습 전략

도입 부분부터 정확히 읽어 나가면서 지문의 논리 전개를 먼저 파악한 후 핵심 내용을 파악해야 한다. 지문의 핵심 내용과 관련 있는 문장에 빈칸이 주어지므로 핵심 내용을 파악하는 것이 중요한 전략이라 할 수 있다. 지문을 이해하는 논리력과 사고력, 추론 능력이 함께 요구되는 고난도 유형이며, 특히 빈칸은 핵심 내용을 포함하면서도 다른 단어나 표현으로 다시 쓰여진(paraphrasing) 경우가 많으므로, 문장 구조나 어휘를 바꾸어 다시 쓴 문장을 찾는 능력을 기르는 것도 도움이 된다.

유형 공략 Q&A

Q1. 빈칸이 오는 위치가 항상 똑같은가요?

A1. 빈칸이 있는 문장의 위치는 주로 지문의 마지막 부분인 경우가 많지만, 지문의 중반부인 경우도 있습니다. 이렇게 빈칸의 위치가 다르다는 것은 주제문의 위치가 지문마다 다르다는 의미이기도 합니다. 주제를 중간에 제시하고 후반부에 뒷받침 문장을 두어 논지를 강조할 경우에는 빈칸이 중반부에 위치할 수 있으며, 후반부에서 주제를 강조할 경우에는 마지막에 빈칸이 오게 되는 것이죠. 위치와 관계없이, 빈칸은 핵심 내용을 다른 말로 쓴(paraphrasing) 부분이 된다는 점을 잊지 말아야 합니다.

Q2. 해당 유형을 푸는 꿀팁을 알려주세요.

A2. 도입부부터 차근차근 읽어볼 수도 있지만, 빈칸이 포함된 문장부터 먼저 읽어 보는 것도 요령이 될 수 있습니다. 빈칸 문장을 먼저 읽어 보면서, 필요한 내용을 파악한 후 처음부터 다시 빠르게 읽으면 핵심 내용을 빠르게 파악하는 데 도움이 될 수 있습니다. 난이도가 높아 시간이 많이 필요한 유형이므로 시간 관리도 중요하다는 점을 잊지 말아야 합니다!

Q3. 지문은 이해했는데 선택지를 보면 몇 번이 답인지 모르겠어요.

A3. 일단 지문에 나온 단어가 그대로 다시 나오는 번호는 매력적인 오답일 수 있습니다. 지문의 소재와는 연관성이 있으나, 주제를 정확히 담지 않은 선택지도 오답을 유도하기 위한 함정입니다. 선택지의 내용이 너무 단순하거나, 핵심 내용과 관련이 없지만 일반적인 상식을 담고 있는 경우에도 조심해야 합니다. 익숙한 것에 끌리게 하기 위해서 만들어 놓은 함정이라고 할 수 있습니다. 핵심 문장을 유의어로 다시 쓴 문장이나 표현이 답이 된다는 것을 잊지 마세요.

유형 공략 어휘 🟠 알고 있는 어휘에 체크하고 모르는 어휘는 암기하세요.

고등 빈출 동사와 유의어	☐ accomplish: finish, achieve (완수하다, 성취하다) ☐ assemble: gather, build (모으다, 조립하다)

고등 빈출 동사와 유의어

- ☐ accomplish: finish, achieve (완수하다, 성취하다)
- ☐ assemble: gather, build (모으다, 조립하다)
- ☐ ban: prohibit, forbid (금지하다)
- ☐ cease: stop (멈추다)
- ☐ compose: create, make (작곡하다, 구성하다)
- ☐ decay: rot, break down (부패하다, 썩다)
- ☐ diminish: reduce (줄이다)
- ☐ exaggerate: overstate (과장하다)
- ☐ gaze: look (응시하다)
- ☐ immigrate: move to a new country (이민가다)
- ☐ interpret: explain (해석하다)
- ☐ merge: combine (합병하다)
- ☐ obtain: get (얻다)
- ☐ permit: allow (허가하다)
- ☐ sneak: creep (살금살금 움직이다)
- ☐ translate: change language (번역하다)

경제

다음 빈칸에 들어갈 말로 가장 적절한 것을 고르시오.   정답 및 해설 p. 20

Imagine a beehive as a city. Each section of the honeycomb is a house or a business. Each bee is a citizen going about his or her day. Where then might you find the economy? In truth, an economy is not located in one place. It cannot be witnessed all at once. Rather, an economy is a network. It is made up of businesses, customers, and the connections between them. In the case of a beehive, the worker bees bring in pollen. In a city, merchants may bring in materials. They then use these materials to create goods. The goods are sold in stores to customers. Money then flows through the stores, back to the factories, and back to the merchants. Just like a beehive, this is ______________________________. Any mistake or flaw can upset the entire system.

① operating in silence   ② losing power
③ resembling a queen bee   ④ systematically running
⑤ only serving customers

WORDS & PHRASES

imagine A as B A가 B라고 상상하다
beehive 몡 벌집
section 몡 구역
honeycomb 몡 (벌집 내부의) 육각형 모양의 구조
business 몡 사업체
citizen 몡 시민 중등필수
go about one's day 하루 일과를 보내다
economy 몡 경제 중등필수
in truth 사실은
locate 통 ~을 위치시키다
witness 통 ~을 목격하다 고등필수
all at once 한 번에
rather 뷔 차라리, 오히려
be made up of ~로 구성되다
customer 몡 고객
pollen 몡 꽃가루
merchant 몡 상인 고등필수
material 몡 물질, 재료 고등필수
flaw 몡 결함
upset 통 뒤엎다
entire 혱 전체의 중등필수

👁 지문 한눈에 보기

빈칸에 들어갈 적절한 말을 쓰시오.

도입부 (전제)	벌집이 하나의 도시라면, **1** ____________의 각 구역은 집이나 사업체이며, 각각의 벌들은 바쁘게 하루를 보내는 시민이다.
중반부 (전개/예시)	경제는 하나의 **2** ____________로 사업체, 고객, 그들 사이의 연결로 구성되어 있다. 일벌이 꽃가루를 가져오듯, 상인들은 재료를 가져오고, 그 재료들로 **3** ____________을 만든다. 만들어진 것은 상점에서 고객들에게 판매되고, 돈은 상점을 통해 공장과 상인들에게 다시 흘러간다.
마무리 (주제문)	마치 벌집처럼, 이것은 **4** ____________으로 가동된다. 어떤 실수나 결함도 전체 시스템을 뒤엎을 수 있다.

🎯 정답 적중하기

글의 핵심 문장을 찾아 빈칸을 완성하시오.

1 Each section of the ____________________ is a house or a business.
2 Rather, an economy is a ____________________.
3 It is made up of businesses, customers, and the ____________________ between them.

다음 빈칸에 들어갈 말로 가장 적절한 것을 고르시오. 정답 및 해설 p. 21

Have you ever had a difficult time teaching someone something? Perhaps, the person you were teaching became confused and frustrated. This may be an example of the curse of knowledge. The curse of knowledge occurs when you think others have the same knowledge that you have. It happens when you do not consider
5 the perspective of the person you are teaching, which can cause you to skip over important information. This can lead to a communication breakdown. However, ____. For example, slow down when you are teaching someone something. Try to take their perspective into account. Get a sense of how much knowledge they have. Then aim to explain things in a calm and detailed
10 way.

① there are a few ways to avoid it
② you can find ways to learn better
③ living a slow life has many benefits
④ the curse of knowledge isn't common
⑤ expressing yourself boosts mental health

WORDS & PHRASES

perhaps 〔부〕 아마도
confused 〔형〕 혼란스러운 〔중등필수〕
frustrated 〔형〕 좌절하는
curse 〔명〕 저주
knowledge 〔명〕 지식 〔중등필수〕
occur 〔동〕 발생하다 〔고등필수〕
consider 〔동〕 고려하다, 여기다 〔중등필수〕
perspective 〔명〕 관점 〔고등필수〕
cause 〔동〕 ~을 야기[유발]하다 〔중등필수〕
skip 〔동〕 건너뛰다
breakdown 〔명〕 붕괴
take A into account A를 고려하다
get a sense 이해하다
aim 〔동〕 ~을 목표로 하다
calm 〔형〕 차분한
detailed 〔형〕 상세한
avoid 〔동〕 ~을 피하다 〔중등필수〕
mental health 〔명〕 정신 건강

지문 한눈에 보기

빈칸에 들어갈 적절한 말을 쓰시오.

전반부 (문제 제기)	지식의 **1** ____________는 다른 사람이 나와 **2** ____________ 지식을 가지고 있다고 가정하거나 배우는 사람의 관점을 고려하지 않을 때 발생한다. 이는 중요한 정보를 건너뛰게 만들 수 있고, **3** ____________의 붕괴를 야기할 수 있다.
후반부 (해결책 제시)	그것을 피할 수 있는 몇 가지 방법이 있다. 첫째, 누군가에게 무엇을 가르칠 때 속도를 줄여 보아라. 둘째, 배우는 사람의 관점을 **4** ____________하고, 어느 정도의 지식을 가지고 있는지 이해하라. 셋째, 차분하고 상세한 방법으로 설명하는 것을 목표로 하라.

정답 적중하기

글의 핵심 문장을 찾아 빈칸을 완성하시오.

1 This may be an example of the ________________ of knowledge.
2 This can lead to a communication ________________.
3 Try to take their ________________ into account.

다음 빈칸에 들어갈 말로 가장 적절한 것을 고르시오.

정답 및 해설 p. 21

WORDS & PHRASES

ingest 통 먹다, 삼키다
magical 형 마법의
instance 명 예시
potion 명 물약
shrink 통 줄어들다
fiction 명 소설, 허구
named after ~의 이름을 따서 (이름) 지은
syndrome 명 증후군
rare 형 드문
condition 명 질환, 장애
sufferer 명 고통받는 사람
perceive 통 ~을 인식하다 [고등필수]
view A as B A를 B로 간주하다
object 명 물체
actually 부 실제로, 사실
appear 통 보이다 [중등필수]
symptom 명 증상
permanent 형 영구적인 [고등필수]
over time 시간이 지나면서

In Lewis Caroll's famous novel *Alice's Adventures in Wonderland*, Alice ingests some magical foods. Because of these foods, Alice's body changes in size. In one instance, a potion causes her to <u>shrink</u> to a tiny size. In another, a cake causes her to grow larger again. While magical foods are a thing of fiction, there is a neurological

5 disorder named after this part of Alice's story. Alice in Wonderland Syndrome is a rare condition. <u>It</u> brings errors when the sufferers perceive their bodies and the world around them. They may view the objects around them as smaller than they actually are. In other cases, these same objects may appear ______________. Some objects appear to change their shapes as well. These symptoms are not permanent but rather

10 come and go over time.

* neurological disorder 신경 질환

① healthy
② to be tiny
③ in good shape
④ to be in control
⑤ to be too large

다음 빈칸에 들어갈 적절한 말을 쓰시오.

소재	Lewis Caroll의 유명 소설, 《이상한 나라의 앨리스》
앨리스에게 일어난 일	앨리스가 마법의 음식을 먹자 몸의 1 ____________가 바뀜 물약을 먹으면 아주 작아지고 케이크를 먹으면 다시 커짐
앨리스 증후군	2 ____________ 신경 질환 자신의 몸과 주변 세계에 대해 인식할 때 3 ____________를 일으킴
증상	주변의 물체를 실제보다 4 ____________ 인식하거나 일부 물체는 모양을 바꾸는 것처럼 보임

1 이 글에 쓰인 **shrink**와 뜻이 비슷한 단어는?

① break   ② shorten

③ expand   ④ tighten

⑤ perceive

2 밑줄 친 **It**이 가리키는 것을 이 글에서 찾아 네 단어로 쓰시오.

____

3 이 글의 내용과 일치하지 않는 것은?

① 앨리스는 마법의 음식을 먹고 몸의 크기가 바뀐다.

② 앨리스는 케이크를 먹으면 작은 크기로 줄어든다.

③ 이상한 나라의 앨리스의 이름을 딴 신경 질환이 있다.

④ 앨리스 증후군이 있으면 자신의 몸과 주변 세계 인식 시 오류가 생긴다.

⑤ 앨리스 증후군 환자에게는 물체가 다른 모양으로 바뀌는 것처럼 보이기도 한다.

PARAPHRASING DRILL

다음 두 문장이 같은 뜻이 되도록 빈칸에 괄호 안의 단어들을 쓰시오.

1 Because of these foods, Alice's body changes in size.

= _______________ ______________ these foods, Alice's body _______________ in size. (alters / to / due)

2 In another, a cake causes her to grow larger again.

= In a ______________ situation, a cake ______________ her ______________ larger again. (makes / different / become)

TRANSLATION DRILL

⭐ name after는 '~의 이름을 따서 (이름) 짓다'의 의미를 가진 숙어 표현이다.

다음 문장의 밑줄 친 부분에 유의하여 해석을 완성하시오.

1 There is a neurological disorder <u>named after</u> this part of Alice's story.

앨리스 이야기의 이 부분에서 _______________ 신경 질환이 있다.

2 The restaurant was <u>named after</u> the owner's daughter.

식당 이름은 주인의 _______________________________.

② 교육

연습문제

다음 빈칸에 들어갈 말로 가장 적절한 것을 고르시오.   정답 및 해설 p. 22

WORDS & PHRASES

stubborn 형 고집불통의
creature 명 생명체
let go of ~에서 손을 놓다
goal 명 목표
even if 비록 ~일지라도
practical 형 실용적인 고등필수
give up 포기하다
refuse 동 ~을 거부하다 중등필수
failure 명 실패
bring A down A를 무너뜨리다
instead 부 대신에
treat A as B A를 B로 여기다
lesson 명 교훈
look for ~을 찾다
alternate 형 대안의
reach 동 ~에 이르다, 도달하다 중등필수
resilient 형 탄력적인
so long as ~하는 한
pass on A to B B에게 A를 전달하다
identify 동 ~을 확인하다
inherited 형 유전의
trait 명 특성

Some might say humans are stubborn creatures. In fact, some people have a difficult time letting go of dreams or goals even if it would be easier and more practical to give up. These examples can be found in successful people. The most successful people in the world often <u>refuse</u> to let failure bring them down. Instead, they

5 treat failure as a lesson and so should you. When we fail, we are forced to look for alternate ways to reach success. This helps to boost our creativity. Likewise, failure teaches us to be more resilient. It is not the end of the world if we fail, so long as we pick ourselves back up and try again. Failure can also be a great learning experience because ____. We can also

10 pass on this knowledge to others.

① we see failure as something to fear
② we should value the process more than failure
③ we believe that we cannot forget and overcome failure
④ we can identify what went wrong and how to improve
⑤ there is an opinion that stubbornness is an inherited trait of ours

MAPPING

다음 빈칸에 들어갈 적절한 말을 <보기>에서 찾아 쓰시오.

보기

boost   resilient   lesson   difficult

When Failing
Searching alternatives to help **3** ________________ creativity

Stubborn Creature
Feel **1** ________________ to let go
of dreams or goals

Humans

Failure
Teaching us to be more **4** ________________

Successful People
Refuse to let failure bring them down and treat
failure as a **2** ________________

Trying Again
A great learning experience for us and others

1 이 글에 쓰인 **refuse**와 뜻이 비슷한 단어는?

① accept　　　　　　② restart

③ insert　　　　　　 ④ boost

⑤ reject

2 이 글의 제목으로 가장 적절한 것은?

① How to Avoid Challenges in Life
② The Role of Failure in Growth and Success
③ The Importance of Following the Initial Plan
④ Why You Should Avoid Failure at All Costs
⑤ Ignoring Failures: The Key to Happiness

3 이 글의 내용과 일치하는 것은?

① Some people find it easy to give up on their dreams.
② Successful people never experience failure.
③ Failure can help us become more creative and resilient.
④ Humans are described as creatures who easily let go of their goals.
⑤ The most successful people avoid learning from their failures.

PARAPHRASING DRILL

다음 문장들이 같은 뜻이 되도록 빈칸에 들어갈 적절한 말을 <보기>에서 찾아 쓰시오.

> 보기
>
> frequently　　　individuals　　　accomplished

The most successful people in the world often refuse to let failure bring them down.

= The most ________________ people in the world often refuse to let failure bring them down.

= The most successful ________________ in the world often refuse to let failure bring them down.

= The most successful people ________________ refuse to let failure bring them down.

TRANSLATION DRILL

⭐ so long as는 접속사로 뒤에 완전한 절이 오며 '~하는 한'이라는 의미로 조건을 나타낸다.

다음 문장의 밑줄 친 부분에 유의하여 해석을 완성하시오.

1 It is not the end of the world if we fail, so long as we pick ourselves back up and try again.
　우리가 다시 일어서서 ________________, 실패해도 세상이 끝난 것은 아니다.

2 So long as you study diligently, you will succeed in your exams.
　당신이 성실히 ________________, 시험에서 성공할 것이다.

CHAPTER 8
30번대 문제 공략하기 Part 3

UNIT 11 • 무관한 문장 파악하기
UNIT 12 • 글의 순서 파악하기
UNIT 13 • 주어진 문장 위치 파악하기

UNIT 11 **무관한 문장 파악하기** *[최근 10회 평균 정답률: 61% 난이도 중]*

[무관한 문장 파악하기 유형]은 실제 기출에서 **1문제**가 출제되며, 고1 기출 기준 평균 **정답률 61%, 난이도 중** 유형이다. 글의 논리적 구조를 파악하여 관련이 없는 문장을 선택하는 유형으로 쉽게 출제될 때는 70%대의 정답률을 보이나 어려운 경우 절반 정도의 학생들만 정답을 찾는, 중위권과 하위권을 가르는 유형이라고 할 수 있다.

학습 전략

반복적인 어구 또는 특정 소재와 관련된 어구를 통해 글의 요지를 먼저 파악한다. 특히 대명사, 연결사 등에 초점을 맞추어 글의 요지와의 연결성을 확인하면서 읽어야 한다. 이점에 중점을 두고 통일성과 연결성에 초점을 맞추어야 하며, 문장 하나하나를 해석만 해내는 것은 적절한 공략법이 아니라고 할 수 있다. 주제와 관련되어 있는 단어가 등장하더라도, 글의 요지와 **문맥상 연계성이 떨어질 경우 정답**이라고 할 수 있다.

UNIT 12 **글의 순서 파악하기** *[최근 10회 평균 정답률: 62% 난이도 중]*

[글의 순서 파악하기 유형]은 고1 기출 기준 평균 **정답률 62%**로 [무관한 문장 파악하가 유형]과 함께 **난이도 중**의 유형이다. 총 **2문제**가 출제되며 주로 두 번째 출제되는 문제가 다소 난이도가 높다. 주어진 글 뒤에 이어질 내용을 **문맥상 바르게 배열**하는 유형으로 지문 전체에 대한 문맥 이해가 필요한 유형이다. **지시어**와 **연결어**에 유의하여 올바른 순서를 찾는 연습이 필요하다.

유형 공략 어휘 ⭐ 알고 있는 어휘에 체크하고 모르는 어휘는 암기하세요.

순서	☐ first	☐ next	☐ then	☐ finally	☐ lastly	
시간	☐ at the moment	☐ as soon as	☐ suddenly	☐ soon	☐ while	☐ by the time
인과	☐ because	☐ since	☐ as	☐ now that	☐ due to	☐ therefore	☐ as a result
예시	☐ for example	☐ for instance	☐ especially	☐ specifically		

 주어진 문장 위치 파악하기 [최근 10회 평균 정답률: 48% 난이도 상]

[주어진 문장 위치 파악하기 유형]은 최근 기출에서 고1 기준 **정답률 48%**로 가장 어려운 유형 중에 하나인 난이도 상의 유형이다. 글의 논리성, 통일성, 일관성에 대한 이해가 있어야 풀 수 있는 문제로, 3점으로 출제되지는 않지만 정답률이 낮은 편이다. 총 **2문제**가 출제되며 [글의 순서 파악하기 유형]과 함께 **지시어**와 **연결어**에 주목하여 읽으면서 문장과 문장 사이의 흐름이 부자연스럽거나 단절되는 곳을 찾는 연습이 필요하다.

학습 전략

주어진 문장을 먼저 읽고, 핵심 내용이 무엇인지, 지시어와 연결어와 같은 단서가 되는 표현은 무엇인지 찾아본다. 대명사와 정관사는 앞에 나온 대상을 지칭하는데, 지칭하는 대상이 무엇인지 주의하며 흐름상 누락된 내용이 있는지 파악하는 것이 필요하다. 주어진 문장이 들어가기에 적절한 위치를 찾았다면, **문장을 넣어 다시 읽어 보고** 흐름이 자연스러운지 확인해 본다.

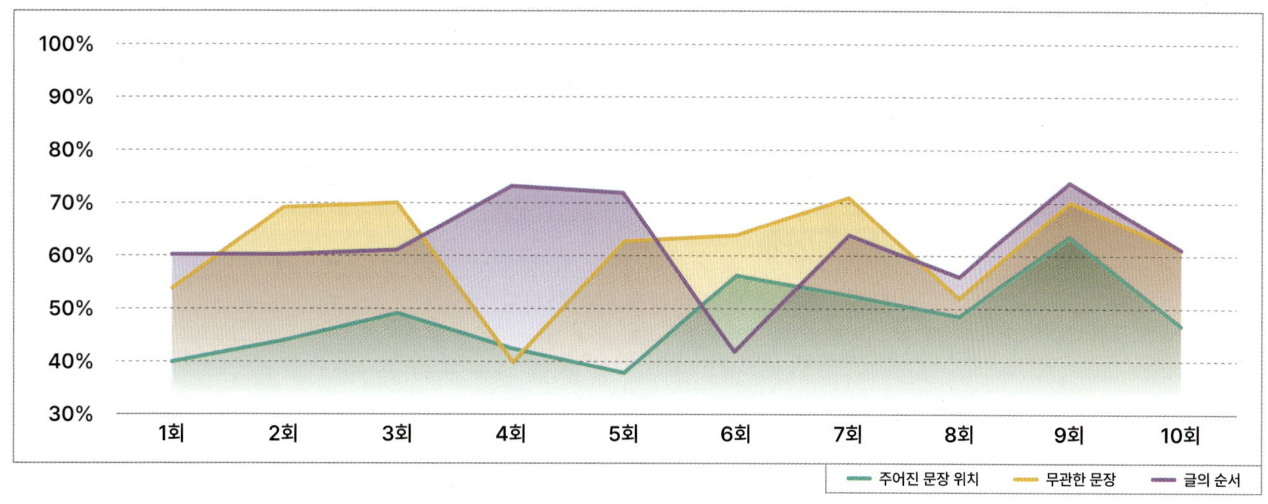

WORDS & PHRASES

predict 통 ~을 예측하다 [고등필수]
certainty 명 확실함
probability 명 확률
likely 형 가능성이 있는
flip 통 튀겨 올리다, 가볍게 던지다
land 통 ~에 떨어지다
heads 명 (동전의) 앞면
tails 명 (동전의) 뒷면
chance 명 기회, 가능성
odds 명 가능성, 확률
win a lottery 복권에 당첨되다
divide 통 ~을 나누다 [중등필수]
outcome 명 결과 [고등필수]
slim 형 희박한
at once 한꺼번에
million 명 백만

통계

다음 글에서 전체 흐름과 관계 없는 문장은? 정답 및 해설 p. 22

It is difficult to predict events with certainty. However, probability can help you determine how likely something is. Flipping a coin is a simple example of probability. It can land on heads or tails. ① You have a 50 percent chance of landing on heads, and you also have a 50 percent chance of landing on tails.
5 ② Probability can also be used to determine the odds of winning the lottery, and the easiest way is to divide the number of winning numbers by the number of possible numbers. ③ There are more than five possible outcomes when winning the lottery. ④ The chances of winning the lottery are slim, and this is because so many people are playing the lottery at once. ⑤ In some cases, you would
10 have around a one-in-15-million chance of winning, and it could be one in 150 million!

👁 지문 한눈에 보기

빈칸에 들어갈 적절한 말을 쓰시오.

도입부 (주제문)	사건을 확실하게 예측하는 것은 어렵지만, 확률은 어느 정도의 1 _____________이 있는지 알아내는 데 도움을 줄 수 있다.
중/후반부 (구체적 예시)	동전을 던졌을 때 앞면이 나올 확률이 50%이고 뒷면이 나올 확률도 2 _____________이다. 확률은 3 _____________에 당첨될 가능성을 알아내는 데 사용된다. 너무 많은 사람들이 한꺼번에 구매하기 때문에 당첨될 가능성은 4 _____________하다. 낭첨 가능성이 1,500만 분의 1이 될 수도 있고, 1억 5천만 분의 1이 될 수도 있다.

🎯 정답 적중하기

글의 핵심 문장을 찾아 빈칸을 완성하시오.

1 However, probability can help you _____________ how likely something is.
2 Flipping a coin is a simple example of _____________.
3 The chances of winning the lottery are _____________, and this is because so many people are playing the lottery at once.

다음 글에서 전체 흐름과 관계 <u>없는</u> 문장은?

정답 및 해설 p. 23

In most stories, the hero is the main character. Through the hero's eyes, we experience the world and events and we naturally sympathize with and root for this character. However, shifting this point of view to a villain's may turn everything we thought we knew about the story upside down. ① In L. Frank Baum's *The Wizard of Oz*, the story is told through the heroine, Dorothy. ② Through her point of view, the reader learns to fear and dislike the story's villain, the Wicked Witch of the West. ③ However, the musical *Wicked* does not tell Dorothy's story; it is the villain who the story centers on. ④ Comic book villains are often the ones fans identify with. ⑤ Through her perspective, readers understand how she became a villain and might even sympathize with her story.

WORDS & PHRASES

main character 명 주인공
naturally 부 자연스럽게
sympathize with ~에 공감하다
root for ~을 응원하다
shift 동 ~을 바꾸다
point of view 명 관점
villain 명 악당
heroine 명 여주인공
fear 동 ~을 두려워하다 [중등필수]
dislike 동 ~을 싫어하다
wicked 형 사악한
center on ~에 중심을 두다
identify with ~와 동질감을 느끼다
perspective 명 관점 [고등필수]

 지문 한눈에 보기

빈칸에 들어갈 적절한 말을 쓰시오.

도입부 (주제문)	대부분의 이야기는 **1** ______________의 관점에서 전개되어 독자들이 자연스럽게 **2** ______________하게 만든다.
중/후반부 (구체적 예시)	예를 들어, 《오즈의 마법사》에서는 도로시의 시점을 통해 독자들이 서쪽 마녀를 싫어하게 된다. 그러나 **3** ______________의 관점으로 시점을 바꾸면 이야기가 새로워진다. 뮤지컬 《위키드》는 서쪽 마녀의 이야기를 **4** ______________으로 전개되며, 관객은 그녀가 어떻게 변하게 되었는지 이해하고 심지어 공감할 수도 있다.

정답 적중하기

글의 핵심 문장을 찾아 빈칸을 완성하시오.

1 In most stories, the hero is the ______________ character.

2 However, ______________ this point of view to a villain's may turn everything we thought we knew about the story upside down.

3 Through her perspective, readers ______________ how she became a villain and might even sympathize with her story.

다음 글에서 전체 흐름과 관계 없는 문장은?

정답 및 해설 p. 23

WORDS & PHRASES

entirely 〔부〕 전적으로, 완전히
constantly 〔부〕 계속해서 〔고등필수〕
adulthood 〔명〕 성인기
billion 〔명〕 십억
neuron 〔명〕 뉴런, 신경 세포
grow 〔동〕 키우다, 확대하다 〔중등필수〕
pathway 〔명〕 경로
connection 〔명〕 연결
adapt to ~에 적응하다
adaptability 〔명〕 적응성
face 〔동〕 ~에 직면하다
challenge 〔명〕 어려움
damage 〔명〕 손상
stroke 〔명〕 뇌졸중
neural 〔형〕 신경의, 신경과 관련된
victim 〔명〕 환자, 피해자 〔고등필수〕

The human brain is thought to be fully developed by age twenty-five, but this is not entirely true. In fact, the brain is <u>constantly</u> changing well into adulthood and this is called neuroplasticity. The brain is made up of billions of neurons and grows pathways or connections between these neurons. ① This happens as we experience things around us, and these connections help us learn, think, and adapt to new situations. ② This adaptability helps us face the challenges and understand our environment. ③ Without neuroplasticity, it would be difficult to learn anything and solve problems. ④ Neuroplasticity can also cause various forms of brain damage like a stroke which can cause neural connection damage. ⑤ Over time, the brain forms new neurons, which help people with brain damage, such as stroke victims, relearn to speak, walk, and solve problems.

* neuroplasticity 신경 가소성(인간의 뇌는 고정되어 있지 않고 변화한다는 뇌신경학적 이론)

다음 빈칸에 들어갈 적절한 말을 쓰시오.

소재	1 ______________ : 뇌의 지속적 성장
뇌의 성장	인간의 뇌는 2 ______________ 에도 계속해서 변화함 뇌는 수십억 개의 3 ______________ 으로 구성되며 이들 사이의 경로 또는 연결을 확대시키고 이것은 상황 적응력을 도움
신경 가소성의 중요성	신경 가소성이 없다면 학습이나 문제 해결에 어려움이 생김 신경 가소성은 4 ______________ 환자와 같은 뇌 손상이 있는 사람이 말하고, 걷고, 문제를 해결하는 데 도움을 줌

1 이 글에 쓰인 **constantly**와 뜻이 비슷한 단어는?

① partly   ② entirely
③ strongly   ④ continuously
⑤ simultaneously

2 이 글의 제목으로 가장 적절한 것은?

① Types of Brain Diseases in Adults
② Neurons: Fixed Connections for Life
③ The Unchanging Structure of the Brain
④ What Keeps the Human Brain Growing
⑤ The Difference Between an Adult's Brain and a Child's Brain

3 이 글의 내용과 일치하지 <u>않는</u> 것은?

① 인간의 뇌가 반드시 25세까지 완전히 발달되는 것은 아니다.
② 뇌는 성인기에도 계속해서 변화한다.
③ 뉴런들 사이의 연결은 우리가 새로운 상황에 적응하도록 돕는다.
④ 적응성은 어려움에 직면하고, 환경을 이해하도록 돕는다.
⑤ 시간이 지남에 따라 뇌는 새로운 뉴런을 형성하지 못할 수도 있다.

PARAPHRASING DRILL

다음 두 문장이 같은 뜻이 되도록 빈칸에 괄호 안의 단어들을 쓰시오.

1 The brain is made up of billions of neurons and grows pathways or connections between these neurons.
= The brain _______________ billions of neurons and _______________ pathways or connections _______________ themselves. (among / develops / consists of)

2 This happens as we experience things around us, and these connections help us learn, think, and adapt to new situations.
= This happens as we _______________ things around us, and these connections _______________ us to learn, think, and adapt to new _______________. (circumstances / engage / enable)

TRANSLATION DRILL

⭐ help는 5형식 준사역동사로 목적격 보어 자리에 동사원형 혹은 to부정사가 올 수 있고, '목적어가 ~하도록 돕다'라고 해석한다.

다음 문장의 밑줄 친 부분에 유의하여 해석을 완성하시오.

1 This adaptability <u>helps us face</u> the challenges and understand our environment.
이러한 적응성은 _______________ 어려움에 직면하고, 우리의 환경을 _______________.

2 The software <u>helps users complete</u> their tasks more efficiently.
그 소프트웨어는 _______________ 더 효율적으로 작업을 _______________.

다음 글에서 전체 흐름과 관계 없는 문장은?

정답 및 해설 p. 24

WORDS & PHRASES

under the weather 몸이 좋지 않은
suddenly 〔부〕 갑자기
mood 〔명〕 기분
lift 〔동〕 (기분이) 좋아지다
symptom 〔명〕 증상 〔고등필수〕
ease 〔동〕 (증상 등이) 덜해지다
profound 〔형〕 엄청난, 심오한
effect 〔명〕 영향 〔중등필수〕
psychologist 〔명〕 심리학자
therapy 〔명〕 치료법
mental illness 〔명〕 정신 질환
patient 〔명〕 환자
compose 〔동〕 ~을 작곡하다
original 〔형〕 독창적인
result 〔명〕 결과
greatly 〔부〕 크게
participant 〔명〕 참가자
emotional 〔형〕 감정적인

Imagine you are feeling under the weather. You put on your favorite song and suddenly, your mood lifts. The same might be true if you are feeling down. You may find your symptoms ease a little. ① This is because music has a profound effect on the human mind, and that is the reason some psychologists have begun experimenting with music therapy. ② They did a study to test the effects of music on mental illnesses. ③ During this study, patients were grouped together and sang songs, and some even composed their own original music. ④ People achieve better results when they work in groups. ⑤ Psychologists found that these activities greatly improved the mental health of the participants, and some participants reported feeling less emotional turmoil.

* turmoil 혼란

FLOWCHART

다음 빈칸에 들어갈 적절한 말을 쓰시오.

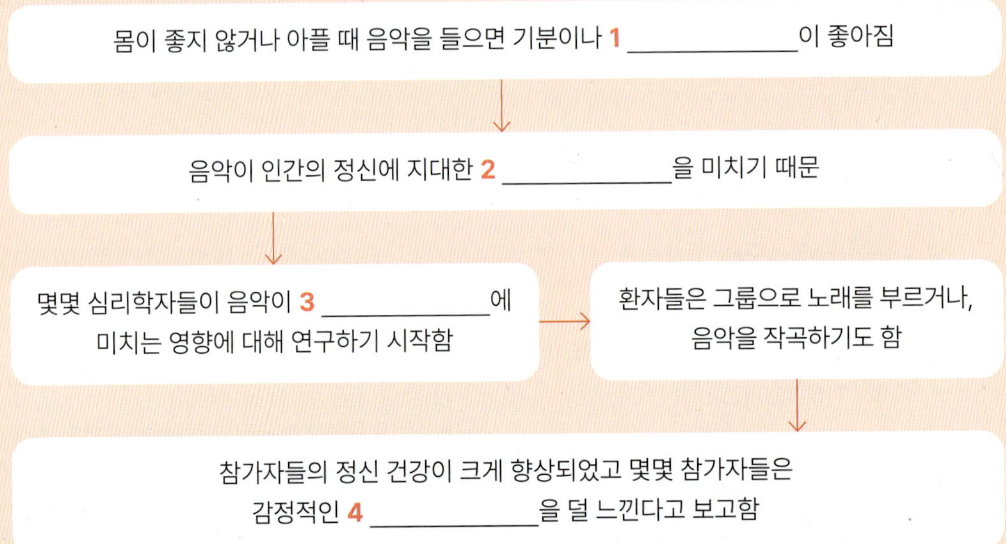

1 이 글에 쓰인 **profound**과 뜻이 비슷한 단어는?

① great
② negative
③ frequent
④ improved
⑤ accomplished

2 밑줄 친 <u>They</u>가 가리키는 것을 이 글에서 찾아 <u>두 단어</u>로 쓰시오.

____

3 이 글의 내용과 일치하지 <u>않는</u> 것은?

① Listening to your favorite song can improve your mood.
② Music has an effect on easing symptoms when you are sick.
③ Psychologists found that music affects the human mind.
④ In the experiment, composition was not performed by the patients.
⑤ Participants felt less emotional turmoil after music therapy.

PARAPHRASING DRILL

다음 문장들이 같은 뜻이 되도록 빈칸에 들어갈 적절한 말을 <보기>에서 찾아 쓰시오.

> • 보기 •
>
> investigate   motivates   influence

This is because music has a profound effect on the human mind, and that is the reason some psychologists have begun experimenting with music therapy.

= This is because music has a profound _________________ on the human mind, and that is the reason some psychologists have begun experimenting with music therapy.

= This is because music has a profound effect on the human mind, which _________________ psychologists to have begun experimenting with music therapy.

= This is because music has a profound effect on the human mind, which leads psychologists to _________________ music therapy.

TRANSLATION DRILL

⭐ during은 특정 기간을 나타내는 전치사로 '~ 동안(에)'로 해석한다. for는 구체적인 숫자로 표현하는 기간을 나타내므로 구분하여 사용해야 한다.

다음 문장의 밑줄 친 부분에 유의하여 해석을 완성하시오.

1 <u>During this study</u>, patients were grouped together and sang songs, and some even composed their own original music.

_________________, 환자들은 그룹으로 나뉘어져 노래를 불렀고, 몇몇은 심지어 그들만의 독창적인 음악을 작곡했다.

2 <u>During the storm</u>, trees fell across the road.

_________________, 나무들이 도로 위에 넘어졌다.

1 예제

WORDS & PHRASES

popular 형 인기 있는
include 통 ~을 포함하다 중등필수
depending on ~에 따라
require 통 ~이 필요하다 중등필수
non-round 형 둥글지 않은
pointed 형 뾰족한
allow 통 가능하게 하다, 허락하다 중등필수
spin 통 회전하다
dimple 명 옴폭 파인 곳
exterior 명 외부, 바깥쪽
reduce 통 ~을 줄이다
resistance 명 저항
fly through ~을 통과해서 날아가다
batter 명 타자
headbutt 통 (머리로) 들이받다
injury 명 부상
bounce 통 반사하다, 튕겨내다
regardless of ~와 상관없이
regarding 전 ~에 관하여
dictate 통 ~을 좌우하다, 지시하다
fair 형 공정한 중등필수

스포츠

주어진 글 다음에 이어질 글의 순서로 가장 적절한 것을 고르시오.　　정답 및 해설 p. 24

> Many of the most popular sports include a ball. Depending on the sport, the ball may look very different.

(A) However, some sports require a non-round ball. American footballs do not have a round shape. Rather, they are pointed on either end. This allows the ball to spin as it is thrown. Golf balls have dimples across their exteriors. These dimples reduce wind resistance. That allows them to fly through the air easily.

(B) Some sports require a small, round ball. Baseballs, for example, must be small and round in order for the batter to hit them. Soccer balls are larger and softer than baseballs. This allows players to kick or headbutt them without injury. Basketballs are round and filled with air. This makes them perfect for continuous bouncing.

(C) Regardless of the shape, all sports have rules regarding balls. These rules dictate the weight and softness of the ball. They also dictate which materials may be used. These rules help to keep the games fair.

① (A) - (C) - (B)　　　　② (B) - (A) - (C)
③ (B) - (C) - (A)　　　　④ (C) - (A) - (B)
⑤ (C) - (B) - (A)

👁 **지문 한눈에 보기**

빈칸에 들어갈 적절한 말을 쓰시오.

도입부 (주제문)	인기 있는 스포츠는 공을 1 ____________ 하며 스포츠에 따라 공 모양이 다르다.
중반부 (구체적 예시)	야구공은 타자가 칠 수 있도록 작고 둥글다. 축구공은 크고 부드러워 선수들이 부상 없이 발로 차거나 머리로 들이받게 해준다. 농구공은 둥글고 공기로 가득 차 있어 계속해서 2 ____________ 에 완벽하다. 미식 축구공은 양쪽 끝이 뾰족해서 회전할 수 있다. 골프공은 옴폭 파인 부분이 있어 바람의 3 ____________ 을 줄여 쉽게 날아갈 수 있게 한다.
후반부 (내용 추가)	공에 관한 규칙들은 공의 무게와 부드러움, 그리고 어떤 4 ____________ 가 쓰일 수 있는지 결정하고, 공정한 경기를 유지하게 한다.

🎯 **정답 적중하기**

글의 핵심 문장을 찾아 빈칸을 완성하시오.

1　Many of the most ____________ sports include a ball.
2　Depending on the sport, the ball may look very ____________.
3　Regardless of the shape, all sports have ____________ regarding balls.

주어진 글 다음에 이어질 글의 순서로 가장 적절한 것을 고르시오.   정답 및 해설 p. 25

> Have you ever slipped on a polished floor? This happened due to a lack of friction, but what is friction?

(A) Likewise, ice has very little friction. This is what makes ice skating possible. Your skate blades are designed to glide across the ice. They can also dig in to help you pick up speed and turn. Figure skaters use low friction to spin at top speeds.

(B) It is everywhere in our daily lives and occurs when two surfaces slide against each other. These surfaces tend to resist each other. Bumpy surfaces will resist a lot. Smoother surfaces will resist less.

(C) Imagine you have fallen on some pavement. Your pants tear at the knee. You get a painful scrape. Now imagine you have fallen on a snowy hill. Your pants do not tear. Instead, you slide down the hill. This is because the snow is less bumpy than pavement. So, there is less friction.

① (A) - (C) - (B)   ② (B) - (A) - (C)
③ (B) - (C) - (A)   ④ (C) - (A) - (B)
⑤ (C) - (B) - (A)

WORDS & PHRASES

polished 혱 (윤이 나도록) 닦인
floor 몡 바닥
due to ~ 때문에
lack 몡 부족
friction 몡 마찰(력)
possible 혱 가능한 [중등필수]
blade 몡 (칼·도구 등의)날
designed 혱 설계된
glide 통 미끄러지다
dig in ~을 파고들다
pick up speed 속도를 올리다
everywhere 떼 모든 곳
occur 통 발생하다 [고등필수]
surface 몡 표면
slide 통 미끄러지다
tend to ~하는 경향이 있다
resist 통 저항하다 [고등필수]
bumpy 혱 울퉁불퉁한
pavement 몡 포장도로
tear 통 찢어지다
scrape 몡 찰과상

 **지문 한눈에 보기**

빈칸에 들어갈 적절한 말을 쓰시오.

도입부 (일반적 사실/질문 제시)	잘 닦인 바닥에서 미끄러지는 것은 **1** ＿＿＿＿＿＿이 부족하기 때문이다.
전반부 (설명과 예시)	마찰력은 일상생활 어디에나 있고, 두 표면이 맞닿아 미끄러질 때 발생한다. 울퉁불퉁한 표면에 비해 부드러운 표면은 덜 **2** ＿＿＿＿＿＿한다. 포장도로에서 넘어지면 바지가 찢어지고 찰과상을 입는다. 눈 덮인 언덕에서 넘어지면 **3** ＿＿＿＿＿＿ 마찰력으로 바지가 찢어지지 않고 언덕을 미끄러져 내려간다.
후반부 (추가 예시)	얼음은 마찰력이 매우 적어 아이스 스케이팅을 가능하게 한다. 스케이트 날은 얼음을 가로질러 미끄러지도록 설계되어 있고, 피겨 스케이트 선수들은 최고 **4** ＿＿＿＿＿＿로 회전하기 위해 낮은 마찰력을 이용한다.

 **정답 적중하기**

글의 핵심 문장을 찾아 빈칸을 완성하시오.

1 Likewise, ice has very ＿＿＿＿＿＿ friction.

2 It is ＿＿＿＿＿＿ in our daily lives and occurs when two surfaces slide against each other.

3 This is because the snow is less ＿＿＿＿＿＿ than pavement.

주어진 글 다음에 이어질 글의 순서로 가장 적절한 것을 고르시오.

정답 및 해설 p. 25

WORDS & PHRASES

numerous 형 수많은 [고등필수]
deliver 통 ~을 전달하다 [중등필수]
ancient 형 고대의
be known for ~로 알려져 있다
efficient 형 효율적인 [고등필수]
delivery 명 전달
on foot 걸어서
hut 명 오두막
located 형 (~에) 위치한
order 명 명령 [중등필수]
region 명 지역
distance 명 거리 [중등필수]
near 통 다가오다
rush 통 서두르다
verbally 부 구두로, 말로
memorize 통 ~을 외우다 [중등필수]

Today, we have <u>numerous</u> ways of delivering messages, but these are very different from how ancient people sent messages.

(A) As an example, the Inca people are known for their efficient message delivery. Unlike some cultures, they did not deliver messages on horseback. Rather, they delivered them on foot. The messengers had to be good runners. They lived in huts located along major roads.

(B) Usually, the messages were from the king. He often sent information and orders to other regions this way. Thanks to the runners, his messages could travel great distances in only a few days.

(C) Each day, the messengers watched the road for runners. When a runner neared, they rushed out of the huts to receive the message. Rather than using paper, the messages were delivered verbally. Each runner memorized the message. Then he passed <u>it</u> on to the next runner. Like a relay, the message traveled for hundreds of miles along the roads.

① (A) - (B) - (C) ② (A) - (C) - (B)
③ (B) - (A) - (C) ④ (C) - (A) - (B)
⑤ (C) - (B) - (A)

다음 빈칸에 들어갈 적절한 말을 쓰시오.

소재	고대 사람들의 메시지 전달 방법
잉카 사람들의 메시지 전달 방법	잘 달리는 사람이 말을 이용하지 않고 **1** ______________ 메시지를 전달 전달자들은 주요 도로를 따라 위치한 **2** ____________에서 생활 메시지를 외워서 **3** ____________로 전달함
메시지 전달의 목적과 효과	메시지들은 다른 지역에 정보와 명령을 보내기 위해 **4** ____________이 보낸 것 주자들 덕분에 며칠 만에 먼 거리까지 메시지를 전달할 수 있었음

1 이 글에 쓰인 **numerous**와 바꿔 쓸 수 없는 단어는?

① various ② plentiful
③ diverse ④ countless
⑤ limited

2 밑줄 친 **it**이 가리키는 것을 이 글에서 찾아 두 단어로 쓰시오.

____

3 이 글의 내용과 일치하지 않는 것은?

① 잉카 사람들은 걸어서 메시지를 전달했다.
② 전달자들은 한곳에 모여 함께 생활했다.
③ 메시지는 문자가 아닌 사람의 말로 전달되었다.
④ 메시지는 전달자들을 통해 수백 마일을 이동했다.
⑤ 여러 주자들 덕분에 메시지는 며칠 만에 먼 거리까지 전달됐다.

PARAPHRASING DRILL

다음 두 문장이 같은 뜻이 되도록 빈칸에 괄호 안의 단어들을 쓰시오.

1 As an example, the Inca people are known for their efficient message delivery.
= As an example, the Inca people are _______________ for their
_______________ message _______________. (passing / effective / famous)

2 Thanks to the runners, his messages could travel great distances in only a few days.
= _______________ to the runners, his messages could _______________
great distances in _______________ a few days. (just / due / cover)

TRANSLATION DRILL

⭐ hundreds of는 '수백의'를 의미하며, 이렇게 숫자 단위 뒤에 's'를 붙이면 '수 배의' 숫자를 의미한다. 예를 들어, thousands of는 '수천의', millions of는 '수백만의'로 해석한다.

다음 문장의 밑줄 친 부분에 유의하여 해석을 완성하시오.

1 Like a relay, the message traveled for hundreds of miles along the roads.
이어달리기처럼, 메시지는 도로를 따라 _______________을 이동했다.

2 Thanks to the system, his messages reached hundreds of people in days.
시스템 덕분에, 그의 메시지는 며칠 만에 _______________에게 도달했다.

주어진 글 다음에 이어질 글의 순서로 가장 적절한 것을 고르시오.

정답 및 해설 p. 26

WORDS & PHRASES

government 몡 정부 [고등필수]
rule 통 ~을 통치하다
    몡 통치
preserve 통 보호하다, 지키다
refuse 통 ~을 거부하다 [중등필수]
marry 통 ~와 결혼하다
crown 몡 왕위, 왕관
    통 왕위에 앉히다
fall to ~에게 돌아가다, ~의 것이 되다
male 몡 남자
relative 몡 친족
cousin 몡 사촌
nephew 몡 (남자) 조카
female 몡 여자
entire 형 전체의 [중등필수]
normally 閉 보통

> In the past, monarchies were a common form of government. These governments were led by one leader for many years.

(A) Elizabeth I was the daughter of King Henry VIII. She ruled England from 1558 to 1603. To <u>preserve</u> her rule, she refused to marry. If she had done so, she would have lost power to her husband. Instead, she ruled as both queen and king.

(B) Sometimes, however, there were no children. Thus, the crown would fall to the next male relative. This could be a cousin or nephew. In some cases, a female was crowned ruler instead. One of the most powerful rulers was Queen Elizabeth I.

(C) In many cases, this leader ruled for his or her entire life. He or she would normally have the title of king or queen. Upon his or her death, the crown would fall to a relative. Usually, this was the eldest son.

* monarchy 군주제(세습 군주가 나라를 다스리는 정치 형태)

① (A) - (C) - (B)   ② (B) - (A) - (C)
③ (B) - (C) - (A)   ④ (C) - (A) - (B)
⑤ (C) - (B) - (A)

MAPPING

다음 빈칸에 들어갈 적절한 말을 <보기>에서 찾아 쓰시오.

> 보기
>
> marry   the eldest son   monarchy   male relative

Led by one leader for many years — **1** _____________ — **Queen Elizabeth I**
Ruled England / Refused to **4** _____________

The crown
Falling to **3** _____________

The 2 _____________
Titled as king when there were no children

1 이 글에 쓰인 **preserve**와 뜻이 비슷한 단어는?

① presume   ② predict

③ produce   ④ protect

⑤ protest

2 이 글의 제목으로 가장 적절한 것은?

① The Unique Succession Rules of Monarchies

② The Life and Times of Queen Elizabeth I

③ The Political Strategies of Elizabeth I

④ The Problems of Monarchy

⑤ The History of Monarchies

3 이 글의 내용과 일치하지 <u>않는</u> 것은?

① Monarchies were a common form of government in the past.

② One leader led his or her monarchy for many years.

③ Upon the king's or queen's death, the crown sometimes fell to a relative.

④ Queen Elizabeth I ruled England from 1558 to 1603.

⑤ Because Elizabeth I never married, she couldn't maintain her power.

PARAPHRASING DRILL

다음 문장들이 같은 뜻이 되도록 빈칸에 들어갈 적절한 말을 <보기>에서 찾아 쓰시오.

보기

> remained   keep   power

To preserve her rule, she refused to marry.

= To ________________ her rule, she refused to marry.

= To preserve her ________________, she refused to marry.

= To preserve her rule, she ________________ unmarried.

TRANSLATION DRILL

⭐ 「from ~ to …」는 일정 범위를 나타내며 '~부터 …까지' 혹은 '~에서 …로'라고 해석한다.

다음 문장의 밑줄 친 부분에 유의하여 해석을 완성하시오.

1 She ruled England <u>from 1558 to 1603</u>.

그녀는 ________________________ 잉글랜드를 통치했다.

2 The population grew rapidly <u>from 10,000 to 50,000</u> over a decade.

인구가 10년 동안 ________________________ 급증했다.

주어진 문장 위치 파악하기

정답률 48%
난이도 ★★★★☆

예제

WORDS & PHRASES

ocean 명 바다
simply 부 단순히
uniform 형 균일한 중등필수
body of water 명 수역(水域), 물줄기
actually 부 실제로, 사실
be made up of ~로 구성되다
separate 동 구분 짓다, 분리하다
chemical 형 화학적인 고등필수
makeup 명 구성
temperature 명 온도 고등필수
vinegar 명 식초
remain 동 ~대로이다, 여전히 ~이다
mixture 명 혼합물
content 명 함유량
determine 동 ~을 결정하다 고등필수

해양

글의 흐름으로 보아, 주어진 문장이 들어가기에 가장 적절한 곳은?　　　정답 및 해설 p. 26

> Now, imagine removing the cups, leaving only the water behind.

You may think Earth's oceans are simply one large, uniform body of water. However, the oceans are actually made up of different bodies of water, and in many places, no land separates these bodies of water. This is due to the chemical
5　makeup and temperatures of the water. ① Imagine you have two cups of water, and you add some vinegar to one of them. ② The amount of water you have remains unchanged at a total of 2 cups, but the vinegar mixture now has a different chemical makeup. ③ The two types of water will mix a little where they're touching, but they will not fully mix and the same is true for the oceans.
10　④ An ocean's salt content determines its chemical makeup. ⑤ So, oceans do not fully mix where they meet, having different salt contents.

👁 지문 한눈에 보기

빈칸에 들어갈 적절한 말을 쓰시오.

도입부 (주제문)	바다는 크고 균일한 하나의 수역이 아니라 **1** ＿＿＿＿＿＿ 수역들로 구성되어 있고 바다를 분리하는 것은 육지 자체라기 보다는 화학적인 구성과 물의 **2** ＿＿＿＿＿＿ 차이이다.
중/후반부 (구체적 예시)	물 두 컵 중 하나에 식초를 넣은 후 물만 남기고 컵을 제거한다고 상상해 볼 때 식초 혼합물은 이제 다른 **3** ＿＿＿＿＿＿ 구성을 가지게 된다. 두 종류의 물은 그들이 닿는 곳에서 약간 섞이지만, 완전히 섞이지 않으며, 바다도 이와 마찬가지다. 바다들이 만나는 곳에서는 서로 다른 소금 **4** ＿＿＿＿＿＿ 을 가지고 있기 때문에 완전히 섞이지 않는다.

🎯 정답 적중하기

글의 핵심 문장을 찾아 빈칸을 완성하시오.

1 However, the oceans are actually made up of different bodies of water, and in many places, no land ＿＿＿＿＿＿ these bodies of water.

2 The two types of water will mix a little where they're touching, but they will not ＿＿＿＿＿＿ mix and the same is true for the oceans.

3 So, oceans do not fully mix where they meet, having different ＿＿＿＿＿＿.

글의 흐름으로 보아, 주어진 문장이 들어가기에 가장 적절한 곳은?　　　정답 및 해설 p. 27

> Repeat this process again and again, and you may discover something amazing.

Have you ever envisioned a beautiful image and tried to draw it? Perhaps, your drawing came out looking all wrong and you just couldn't make it match the image in your head. This is quite a common situation. Even experienced artists may have trouble creating an image from scratch. ① However, you should not throw away your work. ② Instead, try copying your drawing, and you will find that it improves slightly as you clean up errors. ③ Your drawing now looks a lot more like the image in your mind. ④ This technique has been used by artists throughout the ages: Renaissance artists often created multiple versions of a single work. ⑤ Many of them also admired the art of ancient Egypt, Greece, and Rome, and they repeatedly copied these famous pieces in order to improve their own artistic skills.

WORDS & PHRASES

process 명 과정
discover 통 ~을 발견하다 중등필수
envision 통 ~을 상상하다
make it 해내다
match 통 ~을 일치시키다
quite 부 꽤
situation 명 상황 고등필수
experienced 형 경험이 많은, 숙련된
have trouble -ing ~하는 데 어려움을 겪다
from scratch 처음부터
throw away ~을 버리다
work 명 작품
slightly 부 약간
clean up 정리하다
throughout 부 ~에 걸쳐
multiple 형 여러 개의
admire 통 ~에 감탄하다
repeatedly 부 반복적으로
in order to ~하기 위해서

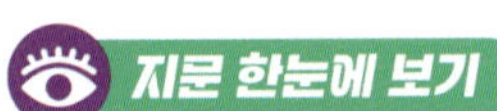 지문 한눈에 보기

빈칸에 들어갈 적절한 말을 쓰시오.

도입부 (소재 소개)	아름다운 이미지를 상상하고 그림으로 그려 보려고 노력해도 머릿속 이미지와 1____________ 하지 않는 상황은 경험 많은 2____________들에게도 일어나며 그들도 어떤 이미지를 처음 만드는 데는 어려움을 겪을 수 있다.
중/후반부 (주장/구체적 예시)	자신이 그린 그림을 따라 그리면서 실수를 정리하다 보면 조금씩 그림을 3____________시킬 수 있고 이 과정을 반복하면 놀라운 것을 발견할 수 있을 것이다. 르네상스 예술가들은 종종 한 작품의 여러 버전을 만들었고 고대 이집트, 그리스, 로마의 예술에 감탄하며 그들의 예술적인 기술을 향상시키기 위해 4____________ 작품들을 반복적으로 모방했다.

정답 적중하기

글의 핵심 문장을 찾아 빈칸을 완성하시오.

1. Even experienced artists may have trouble ____________ an image from scratch.
2. Instead, try ____________ your drawing, and you will find that it improves slightly as you clean up errors.
3. Repeat this process again and again, and you may discover something ____________.

글의 흐름으로 보아, 주어진 문장이 들어가기에 가장 적절한 곳은?

정답 및 해설 p. 27

WORDS & PHRASES

tongue 명 혀
be capable of ~할 수 있다
flavor 명 맛, 풍미 고등필수
certain 형 특정한
region 명 부위, 구역 고등필수
sweetness 명 단맛
tip 명 끝부분
sourness 명 신맛
bitterness 명 쓴맛
notion 명 생각, 개념
completely 부 완전히
false 형 거짓인
translation 명 해석, 번역
study 명 연구
unfortunately 부 불행히도
be separated into ~로 분리되다
register 동 ~을 인식하다
bitter 형 (맛이) 쓴
given 형 주어진

> Actually, every part of the tongue is capable of tasting a variety of flavors.

Long ago, scientists believed that the tongue had certain regions that could taste certain flavors. Sweetness was tasted at the tip of the tongue, sourness on the sides, and bitterness at the back of the mouth. However, in the 1980s and 1990s, researchers
5 realized that the notion of taste regions was completely false. The idea had come from a translation of a German study, but unfortunately, the translation included numerous errors. ① Today, researchers understand a lot more about taste buds. ② In truth, taste buds cannot be separated into regions. ③ However, different parts of your tongue may register a flavor before the rest of the tongue. ④ For example,
10 imagine you are eating something bitter. ⑤ You will likely taste it at the back of your mouth first and this is why it seems like only one part of the tongue can taste a given flavor.

* taste bud 미뢰(미각을 가진 꽃봉오리 모양의 기관)

다음 빈칸에 들어갈 적절한 말을 쓰시오.

소재	과거에는 혀에 특정한 맛을 느끼는 특정한 **1** ____________가 있다고 믿었음
기존 전제	단맛은 혀의 끝, 신맛은 혀의 옆, 쓴맛은 구강 뒤쪽에서 느껴짐 1980년대와 1990년대에, 연구원들은 **2** ____________라는 개념이 완전히 잘못되었음을 깨달음
현재 밝혀진 사실	미뢰들은 부위로 분리될 수 없고, 혀의 모든 부분에서 **3** ____________ 맛을 느낄 수 있음 각각의 부위가 나머지 부위보다 **4** ____________ 맛을 인식할 수도 있음

1 이 글에 쓰인 **separated**와 뜻이 비슷한 단어는?

① completed   ② combined
③ registered   ④ divided
⑤ given

2 이 글의 제목으로 가장 적절한 것은?

① Different Ways to Taste
② Personal Taste Preference
③ The Various Roles of the Tongue
④ Improving the Functioning of the Tongue
⑤ A Truth about the Taste Regions of the Tongue

3 이 글의 내용과 일치하지 <u>않는</u> 것은?

① 과거에는 혀의 특정 부분에서 특정 맛을 느낀다고 믿었다.
② 신맛은 혀의 옆쪽에서 느낄 수 있다고 믿었다.
③ 쓴맛은 혀의 어느 부분에서도 감지되지 않는다.
④ 사실은 혀의 모든 부분에서 다양한 맛을 느낄 수 있다.
⑤ 혀의 일부 부위가 나머지 부위보다 먼저 맛을 느낄 수 있다.

PARAPHRASING DRILL

다음 두 문장이 같은 뜻이 되도록 빈칸에 괄호 안의 단어들을 쓰시오.

1 However, in the 1980s and 1990s, researchers realized that the notion of taste regions was completely false.
= However, in the 1980s and 1990s, researchers _______________ that the _______________ of taste regions was entirely _______________.
(incorrect / discovered / idea)

2 You will likely taste it at the back of your mouth first and this is why it seems like only one part of the tongue can taste a given flavor.
= You will _______________ notice the taste at the back of your mouth first, which _______________ it seem as though only one area of the tongue can detect a _______________ flavor. (makes / particular / probably)

TRANSLATION DRILL

⭐ a lot은 비교급 강조 부사로 '훨씬'으로 해석한다. 이외에도 much, still, far, even 등이 비교급 강조 부사로 쓰인다.

다음 문장의 밑줄 친 부분에 유의하여 해석을 완성하시오.

1 Today, researchers understand a lot more about taste buds.
오늘날, 연구원들은 미뢰에 대해 _______________ 이해한다.

2 The latest model of the laptop is a lot lighter than the previous one.
최신 노트북 모델은 이전 것보다 _______________.

2 연습문제 — 끼리, 문화

글의 흐름으로 보아, 주어진 문장이 들어가기에 가장 적절한 곳은?

정답 및 해설 p. 28

WORDS & PHRASES

symbol 명 상징
share 통 ~을 공유하다 [중등필수]
moreover 부 게다가
view 명 관점 [중등필수]
literature 명 문학 [고등필수]
source 명 공급원
treat 통 ~을 대우하다, 취급하다
cruelly 부 잔인하게
sacred 형 신성한
associated 형 연관된
evil 명 악 [고등필수]
on the other hand 반면에
worship 통 ~을 숭배하다
fertility 명 비옥함
greatly 부 크게
even though 비록 ~일지라도

> Yet, these symbols are not always shared across cultures.

Throughout history, humans have built a place for themselves in the natural world. Moreover, different cultures have developed different views of animals. These views have become symbols in art, song and literature. ① For example, cows are mostly seen as a food source in Western countries, and in many cases, they are treated cruelly. ② However, in Nepal, cows are sacred animals and are treated very well. ③ Likewise, many Western cultures dislike snakes, which are thought to be dangerous or even associated with evil. ④ On the other hand, the ancient Egyptians worshipped snakes and thought them to be symbols of power and fertility. ⑤ Within a given culture, views can also differ greatly, and even though many people in the U.S. dislike snakes, some people keep them as pets in their homes.

MAPPING

다음 빈칸에 들어갈 적절한 말을 <보기>에서 찾아 쓰시오.

> 보기
>
> sacred   views   dangerous   cultures

Symbols
In art, song, and literature but not shared across
2 ____________

Different cultures and different
1 ____________ of animals

Snakes
4 ____________ animal in Western cultures but symbols of power and fertility in ancient Egypt

Cows
Food source in Western countries but 3 ____________ animals in Nepal

People in U.S
Dislike snakes but some keep them as pets

1 이 글에 쓰인 **sacred**와 뜻이 비슷한 단어는?

① holy   ② safe

③ harsh   ④ ancient

⑤ modern

2 밑줄 친 **them**이 가리키는 것을 이 글에서 찾아 한 단어로 쓰시오.

____

3 이 글의 내용과 일치하는 것은?

① Views on animals within a culture are uniform.

② Cows are treated as sacred animals in Western countries.

③ Ancient Egyptians believed snakes were symbols of destruction.

④ Snakes are universally admired as symbols of power and fertility.

⑤ Some people in the U.S. keep snakes as pets despite widespread dislike.

PARAPHRASING DRILL

다음 문장들이 같은 뜻이 되도록 빈칸에 들어갈 적절한 말을 <보기>에서 찾아 쓰시오.

> 보기
>
> regarded   unkind   mainly

For example, cows are mostly seen as a food source in Western countries, and in many cases, they are treated cruelly.

= For example, cows are _________________ seen as a food source in Western countries, and in many cases, they are treated cruelly.

= For example, cows are mostly _________________ as a food source in Western countries, and in many cases, they are treated cruelly.

= For example, cows are mostly seen as a food source in Western countries, and in many cases, they receive _________________ treatment.

TRANSLATION DRILL

⭐ not always는 부분 부정으로 '항상 ~인(하는) 것은 아니다'라고 해석한다.

다음 문장의 밑줄 친 부분에 유의하여 해석을 완성하시오.

1 Yet, these symbols are <u>not always shared</u> across cultures.
   그러나, 이러한 상징들은 문화들 사이에서 _________________________________.

2 People's first impressions of others are <u>not always accurate</u>.
   사람들이 다른 사람들에 대해 가지는 첫인상은 _________________________________.

CHAPTER 9
40번대 문제 공략하기 Part 1

UNIT 14 • 요약문 완성하기

UNIT 14 **요약문 완성하기** [최근 10회 평균 정답률: 56% 난이도 중상]

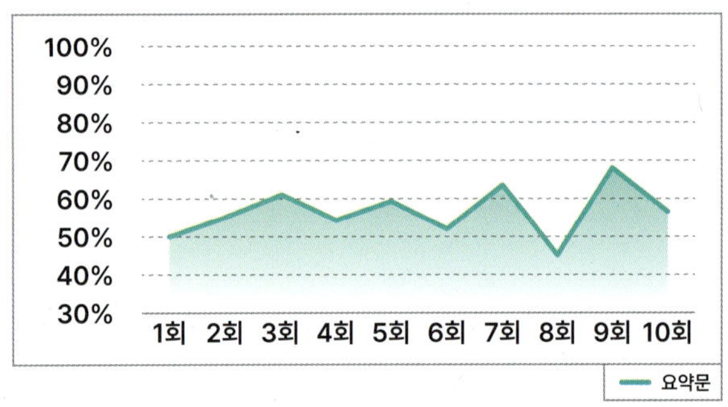

[요약문 완성하기 유형]은 글의 전체 내용을 요약한 한 문장을 완성하는 유형으로 **1문제**가 출제된다. **정답률 56%, 난이도 중상**의 유형으로 40번대 문제 중에서는 정답률이 다소 낮은, 어려운 유형이라고 할 수 있다. 독해력뿐만 아니라, **어휘력**도 중요한 유형이다.

학습 전략

요약문과 선택지를 먼저 훑어보며 글의 주제를 추론해 보고 요약문에서 빈칸의 위치와 앞뒤 문장 구조를 분석하여 글의 주제에 대한 단서를 파악해 본다. 요약문을 통해 얻은 단서들을 바탕으로 글을 다시 읽으면서, 요약문의 빈칸에 들어갈 말로 가장 적절한 단어를 선택지에서 고른다. Unit 10 [빈칸 추론하기 유형]과 마찬가지로 핵심 문장을 유의어로 **다시 쓰는(paraphrasing)** 경우가 많으므로, paraphrasing 연습을 꾸준히 해 보는 것도 도움이 된다.

유형 공략 Q&A

Q1. 주로 어떤 지문이
많이 나오나요?

A1. 기본적으로 정보를 전달하는 non-fiction 지문이 나옵니다. 사회 현상이나 과학적 사실, 정치, 경제 등 다양한 영역에서 출제되며 일반적으로 대학에서 배울만한 수준 높은 지문들이 출제되고 있습니다. 특히, 실험이나 연구에 대해 설명한 후 해당 실험이나 연구를 요약하는 형식도 많이 출제됩니다.

Q2. 해당 유형을 풀 때
어떤 순서로 풀면
좋을까요?

A2. 지문을 건너뛰고 요약문부터 먼저 보는 것이 좋아요. 빈칸이 있긴 하지만 해당 요약문이 지문의 핵심적인 내용을 담고 있기 때문에 이 부분을 먼저 파악하는 것이 도움이 됩니다. 단, 요약문만 보고 유추하려고 하면 안 됩니다. 요약문을 통해 핵심적인 내용을 파악한 후 반드시 지문을 전체적으로 읽어봐야 합니다. 내용의 일부분만 해석하고 답을 찾으려고 할 경우 분명히 출제자가 만들어둔 함정에 빠져 오답을 찾게 될 거예요.

유형 공략 어휘   ⭐ 알고 있는 어휘에 체크하고 모르는 어휘는 암기하세요.

고등 빈출 명사와 유의어	agriculture (농업) - farming (농사)	burden (부담) - load (짐)
	chaos (혼돈) - disorder (무질서)	device (장치) - gadget (도구)
	emphasis (강조) - stress (중점)	evolution (진화) - development (발전)
	heritage (유산) - legacy (유산)	incident (사건) - event (사건)
	myth (신화) - legend (전설)	passion (열정) - enthusiasm (열광)
	status (지위) - position (위치)	sympathy (동정) - compassion (연민)

요약문 완성하기

정답률 56% 난이도 ★★★☆☆

기출

정답 및 해설 p. 29

다음 글의 내용을 한 문장으로 요약하고자 한다. 빈칸 (A), (B)에 들어갈 말로 가장 적절한 것은?

The passage of time has been important to humans throughout history. To measure it, people have come up with a variety of clocks. The pocket watch was the first portable clock. It was originally invented in the 16th century. This small clock was usually attached to a chain. The chain was pinned to a jacket or a vest. The clock face was tucked inside
5   a small pocket. However, these early watches were heavy and expensive. Thus, it was not until a hundred years later that they became a common fashion accessory. In 1810, the first wristwatch was created for the Queen of Naples. Wristwatches soon gained popularity. Over time, they replaced the pocket watch as the preferred fashion accessory. Like all other accessories, they changed greatly in appearance due to emerging trends.
10 Today, there are numerous watch styles and brands. Each one makes a certain statement. In many ways, however, the smartwatch has begun to replace traditional watches.

While modern watches are worn on the wrist as _____(A)_____ items, the first portable watches were attached to strings and kept in pockets, which was not _____(B)_____ in the past.

	(A)		(B)		(A)		(B)
①	simple	–	fashionable	②	stylish	–	widespread
③	favorable	–	notable	④	stylish	–	expensive
⑤	simple	–	popular				

📖 지문 한눈에 보기

빈칸에 들어갈 적절한 말을 쓰시오.

도입부 (주제문)	시간의 흐름은 인간에게 중요하여, 시간을 측정하기 위해 사람들은 **1** ____________ 시계를 생각해 냈다.
중/후반부 (구체적 예시)	회중시계는 16세기 발명된 최초의 **2** ____________ 시계로 보통 체인에 붙어 있고, 체인은 재킷이나 조끼에 고정됐다. 초기 시계들은 **3** ____________ 비쌌기 때문에 백 년 후에야 일반적인 패션 액세서리가 되었고 나폴리 여왕을 위해 만들어진 손목시계는 곧 인기를 얻었다. 오늘날, 수많은 시계는 각각이 가진 특정한 메시지를 전달하고 있으며, **4** ____________ 는 전통적인 시계를 대체하기 시작했다.

🎯 정답 적중하기

글의 핵심 문장을 찾아 빈칸을 완성하시오.

1 The pocket watch was the first ____________ clock.

2 Over time, they replaced the pocket watch as the ____________ fashion accessory.

3 In many ways, however, the smartwatch has begun to ____________ traditional watches.

WORDS & PHRASES

passage 명 흐름
measure 동 ~을 측정하다 고등필수
come up with ~을 생각해 내다
a variety of 다양한
pocket watch 명 회중시계
portable 형 휴대용의
originally 부 본래, 원래
century 명 세기 중등필수
attach to ~에 붙이다
pin 동 ~을 고정시키다
vest 명 조끼
clock face 명 시계 문자판
tuck 동 ~을 집어넣다
wristwatch 명 손목시계
gain 동 ~을 얻다 중등필수
popularity 명 인기
replace 동 ~을 대체하다
preferred 형 선호되는
appearance 명 외관
emerging 형 최근에 생겨난
statement 명 진술, 메시지
traditional 형 전통적인 중등필수

정답 및 해설 p. 29

다음 글의 내용을 한 문장으로 요약하고자 한다. 빈칸 (A), (B)에 들어갈 말로 가장 적절한 것은?

Have you ever studied with your phone in sight? Perhaps you felt this was fine since you did not check your phone. However, researchers think there may be more to this than meets the eye. In one study, students were put into three groups. In one group, they were asked to take a test with their cell phones on their desks. In another, the students kept their phones in their bags. In the third group, the students left their phones in another room. Overwhelmingly, the "desk" group received the worst scores. The students who had left their phones in the other room did the best. This suggested that students perform much better without their phones in sight. After the test, the students were asked to rate their own performance. All of the students felt that they were unaffected by their phones. This was noteworthy because we may not even realize it when our phones are affecting us negatively.

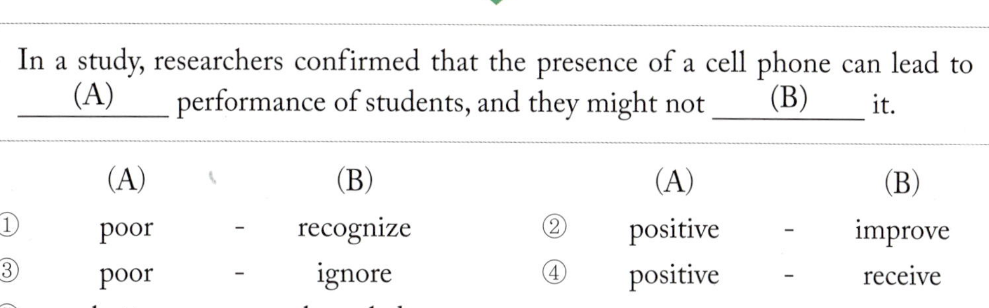

In a study, researchers confirmed that the presence of a cell phone can lead to _________(A)_________ performance of students, and they might not _________(B)_________ it.

	(A)		(B)		(A)		(B)
①	poor	-	recognize	②	positive	-	improve
③	poor	-	ignore	④	positive	-	receive
⑤	better	-	acknowledge				

WORDS & PHRASES

sight 명 시야
researcher 명 연구자
meet the eye 눈에 보이다, 드러나다
put into ~에 넣다, 두다
overwhelmingly 부 압도적으로
receive 동 ~을 받다 중등필수
worst 형 가장 나쁜
suggest 동 ~을 암시[시사]하다 중등필수
perform 동 수행하다 중등필수
performance 명 수행 능력, 성과
unaffected 형 영향을 받지 않는
noteworthy 형 주목할 만한
realize 동 ~을 깨닫다 중등필수
affect 동 ~에 영향을 주다 중등필수
negatively 부 부정적으로
presence 명 존재

👁 지문 한눈에 보기

빈칸에 들어갈 적절한 말을 쓰시오.

도입부 (일반적인 생각/반론)	**1** _____________ 할 때 휴대전화가 옆에 있어도 확인만 하지 않으면 괜찮다고 생각하지만, 연구원들은 눈에 보이는 것 이상의 것이 있을 수도 있다고 생각한다.
중/후반부 (근거/예시)	한 연구에서, 학생들은 **2** _____________ 으로 나누어 시험을 치르도록 요청받았고, 각 그룹은 책상 위에, 가방에, 혹은 다른 방에 휴대전화를 두었다. "책상" 그룹이 가장 **3** _____________ 점수를 받았고, 다른 방에 두고 온 학생들이 가장 잘했다. 모든 학생들이 휴대전화의 영향을 받지 않았다고 느꼈는데, 휴대전화가 우리에게 **4** _____________ 으로 영향을 미칠 때조차도 깨닫지 못할 수도 있다는 점에서 주목할 만하다.

🎯 정답 적중하기

글의 핵심 문장을 찾아 빈칸을 완성하시오.

1 However, researchers think there may be _____________ to this than meets the eye.

2 The students who had left their phones in the other room did the _____________.

3 This was _____________ because we may not even realize it when our phones are affecting us negatively.

정답 및 해설 p. 30

다음 글의 내용을 한 문장으로 요약하고자 한다. 빈칸 (A), (B)에 들어갈 말로 가장 적절한 것은?

WORDS & PHRASES

currently 甼 현재
dependent 톙 의존하는 [고등필수]
fossil fuel 톙 화석 연료
crust 톙 지각
decompose 톙 ~을 분해하다
coal 톙 석탄
natural gas 톙 천연가스
non-renewable 톙 재생 불가능한
limited 톙 제한적인
supply 톙 공급 [중등필수]
run out of ~을 다 써버리다, ~이 고갈되다
lessen 톙 ~을 줄이다
dependence 톙 의존
attempt 톙 시도하다
renewable 톙 재생 가능한
unlimited 톙 무한한
environment 톙 환경 [고등필수]
solar 톙 태양의
abundant 톙 풍부한
experiment 톙 실험하다 [중등필수]
organism 톙 생물체, 유기체
turn into ~으로 변하다
aim 톙 ~을 목표로 하다
reliance 톙 의존, 의지
in favor of ~에 지지[찬성]하여

Currently, much of the world is still dependent on fossil fuels. Fossil fuels are found deep below Earth's crust. They form from <u>decomposing</u> animals and plants. This process takes millions of years. Some examples are oil, coal, and natural gas. These are all non-renewable energy sources. This means that there is a limited supply of
5 them, and we will run out of them someday. Many nations hope to lessen their dependence on fossil fuels. Thus, they are attempting to use more renewable energy. Renewable energy is any unlimited energy source. Gathering <u>this type of energy</u> does not impact the environment in a negative way. Wind and solar energy are two of the most popular examples. As there is an abundant supply of wind and sunlight, we will
10 never run out of these things. Researchers are also experimenting with biomass. This is energy that comes from living organisms, such as plants, trees, crops, seaweed, and animal waste. It can be burned for heat or turned into fuel.

* biomass 바이오매스(특정 지역 내의 생물량)

Many nations aim to lessen their _____(A)_____ on fossil fuels in favor of renewable energy because it is _____(B)_____ and safe for the environment.

	(A)		(B)			(A)		(B)
①	effect	-	controlled		②	independence	-	unchecked
③	independence	-	limited		④	reliance	-	unlimited
⑤	reliance	-	checked					

다음 빈칸에 들어갈 적절한 말을 쓰시오.

소재	1 ___________ : 지구의 지각 깊은 곳에서 발견, 동식물이 분해된 것
화석 연료의 예시와 특징	석유, 석탄, 천연가스 같은 화석 연료에 대한 의존도가 여전히 높음 재생 불가능한 에너지, 공급이 2 ___________ , 언젠가 고갈됨
화석 연료 의존도를 줄이는 방법	3 ___________ 에너지를 사용하려고 시도하는 나라들이 많음 재생 가능 에너지: 4 ___________ 에너지원, 환경에 부정적 영향을 미치지 않음, 바람과 태양 에너지가 예시, 풍부하고 절대 고갈되지 않음 바이오매스 실험: 동식물 등 살아있는 생물체에서 나오는 에너지, 열을 얻기 위해 태우거나 연료화할 수 있음

1 이 글에 쓰인 **decomposing**과 뜻이 비슷한 단어는?

① demanding ② supplying
③ gathering ④ feeding
⑤ decaying

2 밑줄 친 **this type of energy**가 가리키는 것을 이 글에서 찾아 두 단어로 쓰시오.

____

3 이 글의 내용과 일치하지 <u>않는</u> 것은?

① 많은 국가들이 현재 여전히 화석 연료에 의존하고 있다.
② 화석 연료는 모두 재생 불가능한 에너지다.
③ 화석 연료는 무제한으로 공급될 가능성이 있다.
④ 재생 가능한 에너지 사용을 시도하는 국가들이 많아지고 있다.
⑤ 연구자들은 바이오매스 실험을 통해 새로운 에너지를 연구하고 있다.

PARAPHRASING DRILL

다음 두 문장이 같은 뜻이 되도록 빈칸에 괄호 안의 단어들을 쓰시오.

1 Currently, much of the world is still dependent on fossil fuels.
= _______________, many _______________ are still _______________ on fossil fuels. (relying / nowadays / nations)

2 Thus, they are attempting to use more renewable energy.
= _______________, they are _______________ to _______________ more renewable energy. (utilize / therefore / trying)

TRANSLATION DRILL

⭐ 동명사는 '~하는 것'으로 해석하고, 주어로 올 때 단수로 취급하므로 동사도 단수 형태가 와야 한다.

다음 문장의 밑줄 친 부분에 유의하여 해석을 완성하시오.

1 Gathering this type of energy does not impact the environment in a negative way.
이런 종류의 에너지를 _______________은 환경에 부정적인 방식으로 영향을 미치지 않는다.

2 Reading books expands your knowledge.
책을 _______________은 당신의 지식을 확장시킨다.

다음 글의 내용을 한 문장으로 요약하고자 한다. 빈칸 (A), (B)에 들어갈 말로 가장 적절한 것은?

WORDS & PHRASES

toxic 형 독성이 있는
plant 명 식물, 나무
instead of ~ 대신에 [중등필수]
harm 동 해를 입히다 [중등필수]
ability 명 능력
substance 명 물질 [고등필수]
release 동 ~을 방출하다
layer 명 층
absorb 동 ~을 흡수하다
stem 명 줄기
eventually 부 결국
dry out 마르다
surrounding 형 인근의, 주위의
decay 동 썩다
effect 명 영향 [중등필수]
nearby 형 근처의
die out 죽다
ensure 동 ~을 보장하다,
　　　　반드시 ~하게 하다

Manganese is <u>toxic</u> to many plants. But one special plant uses manganese in an interesting way. Instead of being harmed by manganese, the blackberry plant has the ability to use and move this substance. With its roots, the plant gathers manganese from deep within the soil. It then moves the manganese upwards. The roots release
5　it into the upper layers of the soil. This act does not harm the blackberry plant. In fact, the plant even has the ability to absorb some of this manganese. As it grows, it pulls the manganese up its roots and stems. It lets the manganese collect in its leaves. Eventually, these leaves dry out and fall onto the surrounding ground. As the leaves decay, more manganese is added into the soil. All of this manganese has a toxic effect
10　on nearby plants. These plants easily die out, leaving the area clear. This ensures the blackberry plant has enough space to grow.

* manganese 망간(백색의 광택이 나는 중금속 원소)

The blackberry plant ______(A)______ manganese to the surrounding soil to kill off other plants and ensure it ______(B)______ from the result.

	(A)		(B)		(A)		(B)
①	transfers	-	originates	②	removes	-	protects
③	transfers	-	benefits	④	removes	-	damages
⑤	collects	-	disappear				

FLOWCHART

다음 빈칸에 들어갈 적절한 말을 쓰시오.

망간은 많은 식물들에게 **1** ________________이 있음

↓

블랙베리 나무는 망간에 의해 해를 입는 대신, 이 물질을 이용하고 **2** ________________ 능력이 있음

↓

뿌리는 망간을 토양의 상층으로 방출하지만 이것이 블랙베리 나무에게 해를 끼치지는 않음 → 블랙베리의 뿌리는 토양 속 깊은 곳에서 망간을 모아 위로 이동시켜 잎에 모이도록 하고, 잎은 결국 **3** ________________ → 주변 땅에 잎이 떨어지고 그것이 **4** ________________, 더 많은 망간이 토양으로 주입되며 근처의 식물들에게 독성이 있는 영향을 미침

↓

주변 식물들이 죽어서 주변이 깨끗해지면서 블랙베리 나무는 자랄 수 있는 **5** ________________을 보장받음

1 이 글에 쓰인 <u>toxic</u>과 뜻이 비슷한 단어는?

① necessary ② poisonous
③ practical ④ abundant
⑤ critical

2 이 글의 제목으로 가장 적절한 것은?

① How to Grow a Blackberry Tree Productively
② The Effect of Manganese on All Plant Growth
③ How Blackberry Plants Avoid Manganese Toxicity
④ Blackberries and Manganese: the Benefits of Toxicity
⑤ Alternative Toxins Released by Blackberry Plants

3 이 글의 내용과 일치하는 것은?

① The blackberry plant can't use and move manganese.
② Manganese collects in the leaves of the blackberry plant.
③ Blackberry plants are harmed by the manganese they absorb.
④ Nearby plants thrive in the presence of manganese.
⑤ Manganese helps nearby plants grow and flourish.

PARAPHRASING DRILL

다음 문장들이 같은 뜻이 되도록 빈칸에 들어갈 적절한 말을 <보기>에서 찾아 쓰시오.

> 보기
>
> transport   rather   utilize

Instead of being harmed by manganese, the blackberry plant has the ability to use and move this substance.

= ________________ than being damaged by manganese, the blackberry plant has the ability to use and move this substance.

= Instead of being harmed by manganese, the blackberry plant can ________________ and move this substance.

= Instead of being harmed by manganese, the blackberry plant has the ability to use and ________________ this substance.

TRANSLATION DRILL

⭐ 접속사 as는 여러 뜻을 가진다. 그중에 '~함에 따라, ~하면서'라고 해석되는 경우에는 비교적 긴 시간에 걸쳐 동시에 진행되는 두 가지 변화에 대해 말할 때 쓴다.

다음 문장의 밑줄 친 부분에 유의하여 해석을 완성하시오.

1 <u>As it grows</u>, it pulls the manganese up its roots and stems.
________________, 그것은 망간을 뿌리와 줄기 위로 끌어 올린다.

2 <u>As she grow older</u>, she looked more and more like her mother.
________________, 그녀는 점점 더 그녀의 어머니처럼 보였다.

CHAPTER 10
40번대 문제 공략하기 Part 2

UNIT 15 • 장문 독해

UNIT 15 **장문 독해** [최근 10회 평균 정답률: 69% 난이도 중]

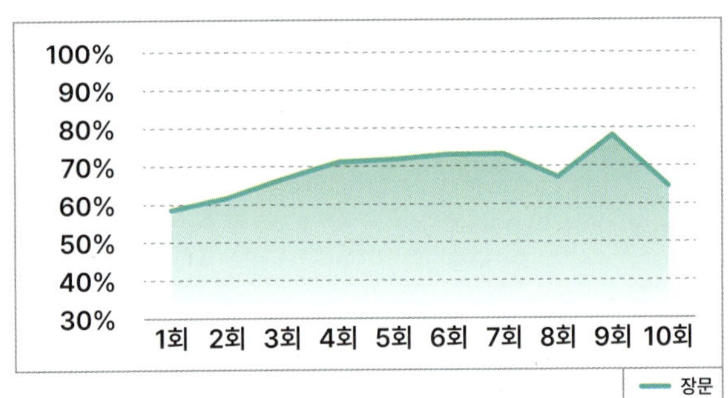

[장문 독해 유형]은 **41번부터 45번**까지 **총 5문제**가 출제된다. 각 문제별로 정답률의 차이를 보이나 평균적으로 **정답률 69%**의 **난이도 중** 유형이다. 41~42번이 두 문제가 출제되는 세트 문제로, 43~45번이 세 문제가 출제되는 세트 문제로 출제된다. 번호별로 출제 유형이 정해져 있고 대부분 앞에서 출제된 유형이므로, 장문이라는 점 이외에 킬러 문항이라고는 볼 수 없다. 다만 길이가 길고, 전체 시험의 마지막 문제들이므로, **시간 관리가 필요한 유형**이라고 할 수 있다.

학습 전략

41~42번 단일 지문 유형의 경우 제목 찾기와 문맥상 어색한 어휘 찾기 문제로 출제된다. 43~45번 지문에 비해 길이는 짧지만 지문의 난이도는 더 높다. 지문의 내용을 핵심적이고 함축적으로 요약한 제목을 찾고, 앞뒤 맥락을 확인하여, 적절하지 않은 어휘를 파악해야 한다. 43~45번 복합 지문 유형의 경우, 지문의 길이는 길지만 내용은 쉬운 편이며, 주로 이야기, 일화 등의 지문이 나온다. 글의 순서를 파악하는 문제와 지칭 대상을 추론하는 문제, 내용 불일치를 확인하는 문제가 나오며, 연결어, 지시어, 대명사 등을 중점으로 지문을 읽으면서 전체 흐름을 파악하고, 지칭 대상을 추론해야 한다. 내용 일치 문제를 공략하기 위해서는 선택지에 나온 내용을 지문에서 정확히 확인하는 연습이 필요하다.

유형 공략 Q&A

Q1. 긴 지문을 읽는 데 시간이 너무 오래 걸려요.

A1. 지문을 읽기 전에 문제부터 먼저 확인해 보세요. 장문 독해를 풀 시간대는 시험이 완료되기 직전인 경우가 많습니다. 정답 표기도 해야 하는 만큼 최대한 시간을 아낄 수 있도록 문제를 먼저 읽고, 핵심 내용을 파악한 후 지문으로 올라가서 전략적으로 접근하는 것이 필요합니다.

Q2. 중하위권도 장문 독해 문제를 맞힐 수 있을까요?

A2. 실전에서 모든 시험을 풀 수 없다면 30번대 킬러 문항을 패스하고 장문 독해를 먼저 푸는 것도 하나의 전략이 될 수 있습니다. 3점 문제들 보다 지문의 길이만 길 뿐 독해가 어렵지는 않기 때문입니다. 한 지문을 해석해서 여러 문제를 풀 수 있기 때문에 시간이 부족하다면 장문 독해 유형을 먼저 푸는 것이 점수 획득에 효율적입니다.

유형 공략 어휘 🌟 알고 있는 어휘에 체크하고 모르는 어휘는 암기하세요.

고등 빈출 형용사와 반의어		
available (이용 가능한) - unavailable (이용 불가능한)		reliable (믿을 수 있는) - unreliable (믿을 수 없는)
valuable (가치 있는) - valueless (가치 없는)		hopeful (희망에 찬) - hopeless (희망이 없는)
careful (신중한) - careless (부주의한)		useful (유용한) - useless (쓸모없는)
possible (가능한) - impossible (불가능한)		mature (성숙한) - immature (미성숙한)
capable (유능한) - incapable (무능한)		accurate (정확한) - inaccurate (부정확한)
efficient (효율적인) - inefficient (비효율적인)		flexible (유연한) - inflexible (경직된)
legal (합법적인) - illegal (불법적인)		rational (합리적인) - irrational (비합리적인)

WORDS & PHRASES

writing system 명 문자 체계
evidence 명 증거 고등필수
Sumerian 명 수메르인
　　　　형 수메르 사람[말]의
Egyptian 명 이집트인
　　　　형 이집트 사람[말]의
Akkadian 명 아카드인(고대 아카드
　　　　제국에 속했던 사람들),
　　　　아카드어
　　　　형 아카드 사람[말]의
prior to ~ 이전에
rely on ~에 의존하다 고등필수
spoken word 명 구어(口語)
civilization 명 문명
expert 명 전문가 중등필수
claim 동 ~을 주장하다
gesture 명 몸짓
produce 동 생산하다, 만들다 중등필수
complex 형 복잡한
gene 명 유전자
allow 동 가능하게 하다, 허락하다 중등필수
a wide range of 다양한 범위의
vocal 형 발성의
grammar system 명 문법 체계
form 동 ~을 형성하다
emerge 동 생겨나다
artificial 형 인공적인

언어

다음 글을 읽고, 물음에 답하시오. 　　　　정답 및 해설 p. 31

The oldest writing systems we have as evidence are the ones used by ancient Sumerians, Egyptians, and Akkadians. Prior to that, humans relied on the (a) <u>spoken</u> word to communicate. Ancient civilizations used complex spoken languages, but how did these languages develop? Some experts claim that languages developed
5　from various sounds and gestures. However, early humans did not have the ability to produce (b) <u>complex</u> sounds. It wasn't until around 70,000 years ago that humans developed a speech gene. This gene (c) <u>allowed</u> the brain to get meaning from sounds. At that time, the vocal organs were not yet fully developed. Thus, it was (d) <u>easy</u> for humans to produce a wide range of sounds. Around 50,000 years ago, the
10　vocal organs finished developing. Humans began to make a wider variety of sounds. Over thousands of years, these sounds (e) <u>changed</u> into more complex sounds. From them, words developed, and grammar systems eventually formed. Experts suggest that complex languages began to emerge as late as 20,000 years ago. Through these languages, societies began to form. Ideas were shared, and technologies developed.

* vocal organ 발성 기관

1 　**윗글의 제목으로 가장 적절한 것은?**

① The Invention of Writing: Key Dates and Facts
② Human Evolution and Changes in Vocal Organs
③ Human Development: Genetic Changes from 70,000 Years Ago
④ Language of the Future: Conversations with Artificial Intelligence
⑤ The Evolution of Language: The History of Human Communication

2 　**밑줄 친 (a)~(e) 중에서 문맥상 낱말의 쓰임이 적절하지 <u>않은</u> 것은?**

① (a)　　　② (b)　　　③ (c)　　　④ (d)　　　⑤ (e)

빈칸에 들어갈 적절한 말을 쓰시오.

도입부 (주제 제시)	문자 체계가 생겨나기 이전에는 인간은 의사소통을 하기 위해 **1** ____________ 에 의존했다. 고대 문명은 복잡한 음성 언어를 사용했는데 어떻게 이러한 언어들이 발달했을까?
중반부 (구체적 진술)	초기 인류는 **2** ____________ 소리를 낼 수 있는 능력이 없었고 발성 기관이 완전히 **3** ____________ 하지 않아 다양한 소리를 내기가 어려웠다. 약 5만 년 전, 발성 기관의 발달이 끝나자 인간은 **4** ____________ 소리를 내기 시작했다. 수천 년 동안, 이러한 소리들은 더 복잡한 소리로 발달했다.
후반부 (마무리)	마침내, **5** ____________ 가 형성되었고, 약 2만 년 전부터 복잡한 언어가 생겨났다. 이러한 언어들을 통해 사회가 형성되기 시작했고, 아이디어의 공유와 기술의 발달이 이루어졌다.

글의 핵심 문장을 찾아 빈칸을 완성하시오.

1 Ancient civilizations used complex spoken languages, but how did these languages ____________?
2 At that time, the ____________ organs were not yet fully developed.
3 Humans began to make a ____________ variety of sounds.

다음 글을 읽고, 물음에 답하시오. 정답 및 해설 p. 32

WORDS & PHRASES

peaceful 형 평화로운 중등필수
in the heart of ~의 한가운데에
kingdom 명 왕국
hideous 형 흉측한
stumble 동 비틀거리다
creature 명 생명체, 생물 중등필수
covered in ~로 덮인
sticky 형 끈적한
mud 명 진흙
matted 형 엉겨 붙은
swamp 명 늪
stand 명 가판대
feature 명 얼굴 생김새, 이목구비
soften 동 부드러워지다
curse 명 저주
reward 명 보람, 보상
vendor 명 상인
join in ~에 합류[동참]하다
call names 욕을 하다
cruel 형 잔인한
anger 동 화나게 하다
deadly 부 치명적인
fang 명 송곳니
crowd 명 군중 중등필수
lone 형 하나뿐인
stride-strode-stridden 동 성큼성큼 걷다
gently 부 부드럽게, 다정하게
offer 동 제공하다

(A)

There once was a peaceful village in the heart of a beautiful kingdom. One morning, a hideous monster stumbled into the village market. The creature was green and covered in sticky mud. His hair was matted, and (a) <u>he</u> smelled like a swamp. He stumbled toward a fruit stand and said, "Please give me something to eat."

(B)

The monster took the shiny fruit from the boy's hand. Suddenly, the monster looked a little smaller. (b) <u>His</u> features softened, and his green skin turned normal. Soon, a prince was standing before the little boy. "Thank you for saving me from my curse," (c) <u>he</u> told the little boy. "Only kindness could do so. As a reward, I will give you ten bags of gold."

(C)

The vendor stepped back and shouted, "Go away, ugly creature! This is no place for a monster!" The other villagers joined in, calling the monster cruel names, and some of them threw rocks at him. This only angered the monster, and he began to grow taller. (d) <u>His</u> teeth grew into sharp, deadly fangs.

(D)

A poor boy was watching from the crowd. The other children were still throwing rocks at the monster. Instead of a rock, the little boy took the lone apple from his bag. It was the only food he had, but he pushed through the crowd and strode toward the angry monster. Gently, (e) <u>he</u> offered his apple to the monster.

3 **주어진 글 (A)에 이어질 내용을 순서에 맞게 배열한 것으로 가장 적절한 것은?**

① (B) - (D) - (C)   ② (C) - (B) - (D)
③ (C) - (D) - (B)   ④ (D) - (B) - (C)
⑤ (D) - (C) - (B)

4 밑줄 친 (a)~(e) 중에서 가리키는 대상이 나머지 넷과 <u>다른</u> 것은?

① (a)　　　　② (b)　　　　③ (c)　　　　④ (d)　　　　⑤ (e)

5 윗글에 관한 내용으로 적절하지 <u>않은</u> 것은?

① 흉측한 괴물이 비틀거리며 시장으로 들어왔다.

② 마을 사람들 중 일부는 괴물에게 돌을 던졌다.

③ 화가 난 괴물은 덩치가 더 커졌고 송곳니도 자랐다.

④ 괴물은 마을에서 아무것도 얻을 수 없었다.

⑤ 왕자는 어린 소년에게 금을 주기로 했다.

👁 지문 한눈에 보기

빈칸에 들어갈 적절한 말을 쓰시오.

도입부 (사건의 발단)	한 아름다운 왕국에 흉측한 괴물이 마을 시장에 나타나 **1** ＿＿＿＿＿＿＿에 가서 먹을 것을 요구했다.
중반부 (사건의 전개)	상인과 마을 사람들이 그 괴물에게 욕을 하고 돌을 던졌고 괴물은 화가 나서 몸이 커지고 **2** ＿＿＿＿＿＿＿가 자랐다. 한 소년이 지켜보다가 **3** ＿＿＿＿＿＿＿ 하나를 꺼내어 괴물에게 건넸다.
후반부 (결말)	소년에게서 과일을 받은 괴물은 몸이 작아지고, 외모가 부드러워졌으며, 피부색도 정상이 되었고 곧, 왕자로 변하여 소년에게 고마워하며 **4** ＿＿＿＿＿＿＿을(를) 보답으로 주었다.

◎ 정답 적중하기

글의 핵심 문장을 찾아 빈칸을 완성하시오.

1 One morning, a hideous monster stumbled into the ＿＿＿＿＿＿ market.

2 It was the only ＿＿＿＿＿＿ he had, but he pushed through the crowd and strode toward the angry monster.

3 "Only kindness could do so. As a ＿＿＿＿＿＿, I will give you ten bags of gold."

다음 글을 읽고, 물음에 답하시오.

정답 및 해설 p. 32

WORDS & PHRASES

journaling 몡 일기 쓰기
adult 몡 성인
keep a journal 일기를 쓰다
participant 몡 참가자
diagnose 통 ~을 진단하다
anxiety 몡 불안
disorder 몡 질환, 장애
significantly 뷔 상당히 [고등필수]
analyze 통 ~을 분석하다 [고등필수]
take over 지배하다, 장악하다
gratitude 몡 감사
form 몡 형태
grateful 혱 감사하는
detail 통 자세히 설명하다
depressed 혱 우울한
worsen 통 ~을 악화시키다
depression 몡 우울증

Over the years, many studies have been done on the (a) <u>benefits</u> of journaling. In 2018, a group of 70 adults was asked to keep a journal. Over the course of 12 weeks, they wrote in their journals every day. Each of the participants had been diagnosed with an anxiety disorder. At the end of the study, the participants' anxiety levels had significantly (b) <u>increased</u>. This was probably because people with anxiety often focus on negative thoughts. Journaling can help them put these thoughts into words. This helps them analyze their feelings, and it (c) <u>stops</u> these feelings from taking over. A study done in 2021 also noted the benefits of keeping a <u>gratitude</u> journal. A gratitude journal can take (d) <u>many</u> forms. It can be a list of things you are grateful for each day. It can also be a letter detailing all of the good things happening in your life. Researchers found that keeping a gratitude journal helped some people feel less (e) <u>depressed</u>. It helped to break the negative thought patterns that worsen depression.

1 윗글의 제목으로 가장 적절한 것은?

① How to Start a Travel Journal
② How to Write a Bestselling Journal
③ Famous Authors Who Kept Journals
④ How Journaling Can Help People with Anxiety
⑤ The History of Journaling throughout the Ages

2 밑줄 친 (a)~(e) 중에서 문맥상 낱말의 쓰임이 적절하지 <u>않은</u> 것은?

① (a)　　② (b)　　③ (c)　　④ (d)　　⑤ (e)

BREAKDOWN

다음 빈칸에 들어갈 적절한 말을 쓰시오.

일기 쓰기 연구	2018년에 70명의 성인들에게 12주 동안 매일 일기를 쓰게 했음
연구 참가자의 특징	1____________ 진단을 받았고 종종 2____________ 생각에 집중하는 경향이 있음
일기 쓰기의 효과	생각을 말로 표현하고 감정을 3____________할 때 도움을 줌
감사 일기의 형태와 효과	감사하는 것들의 목록 또는 좋은 일들을 자세히 설명하는 편지 형식 일부 사람들의 4____________ 증상 완화에 도움을 줌

1 이 글에 쓰인 **gratitude**와 뜻이 비슷한 단어는?

① appreciation
② significance
③ improvement
④ participation
⑤ analyzation

2 밑줄 친 **It**이 가리키는 것을 이 글에서 찾아 두 단어로 쓰시오.

____

3 이 글의 내용과 일치하지 <u>않는</u> 것은?

① 수년에 걸쳐 일기 쓰기의 이점에 대한 연구가 수행되었다.
② 2018년의 연구에 참가한 사람들은 불안 장애 진단을 받았던 이들이다.
③ 불안감을 가진 사람들은 부정적인 생각에 집중하는 경향이 있다.
④ 일기 쓰기는 감정 분석에 도움을 주어 부정적 감정의 지배를 막는다.
⑤ 감사 일기 쓰기는 기본 형식이 정해져 있어 이에 맞춰서 써야 한다.

PARAPHRASING DRILL

다음 두 문장이 같은 뜻이 되도록 빈칸에 괄호 안의 단어들을 쓰시오.

1 Each of the participants had been diagnosed with an anxiety disorder.
= _______________ participant had been _______________ as having a
_______________ of anxiety. (condition / every / identified)

2 This was probably because people with anxiety often focus on negative thoughts.
= This was _______________ because _______________ who have anxiety tend
to _______________ on negative thoughts. (concentrate / individuals / likely)

TRANSLATION DRILL

⭐ 「stop A from + 동명사(-ing)」 구문은 'A가 ~하는 것을 막다'라고 해석하고, 동사 keep, prevent, prohibit 등도 stop 대신에 비슷한 의미로 쓰일 수 있다.

다음 문장의 밑줄 친 부분에 유의하여 해석을 완성하시오.

1 It stops these feelings from taking over.
그것은 이러한 감정들이 ___________________________.

2 Taking deep breaths stops anger from clouding my judgment.
깊게 숨을 마시는 것은 분노가 ___________________________.

다음 글을 읽고, 물음에 답하시오.

정답 및 해설 p. 33

WORDS & PHRASES

recital 명 발표회
burrito 명 (멕시코 요리) 부리토
nacho 명 (멕시코 요리) 나초
rub 동 ~을 문지르다
tummy 명 배
starving 형 몹시 배고픈
lean 동 기울이다
whisper 동 속삭이다 [중등필수]
shake-shook-shaken 동 ~을 흔들다
reply 동 대답하다
turn out ~인 것으로 밝혀지다
car crash 명 자동차 충돌사고
injure 동 다치다 [중등필수]
end up -ing 결국 ~하다
elderly 형 나이가 지긋한, 연세가 드신
sidewalk 명 인도
rusty 형 녹슨
stare 동 응시하다 [중등필수]
organize 동 ~을 조직하다
fundraiser 명 모금 행사
be proud of ~을 자랑스러워하다 [중등필수]
compassion 명 동정심, 연민
kindness 명 친절

(A)

Last week, my daughter Anna had a dance recital. To celebrate, I took Anna to her favorite Mexican restaurant for dinner. Anna would always order the same thing: a chicken burrito with a side of nachos. "I can't wait to eat," Anna said in the car, rubbing (a) her tummy. "I'm starving!"

(B)

Anna leaned in close to me to whisper, "Does that man have a home, Mom?" I shook my head sadly and replied, "I don't think so." (b) She stopped to say hello to the man. It turned out his name was Fred, and he had gotten in a bad car crash. His leg had been injured, which meant he couldn't work anymore, so he ended up losing his home.

(C)

We arrived at the restaurant and parked the car. As we walked to the restaurant, (c) she noticed an elderly man lying on the sidewalk. He looked messy and wasn't wearing shoes. A small cup sat at his feet with a few rusty coins inside.

(D)

After hearing his story, we said goodbye and went into the restaurant. When the food arrived, Anna only stared out the window at Fred. "I'm not that hungry anymore," (d) she said and asked the waitress to put her food into a to-go box. After Anna got the box from (e) her, she took the food out to Fred. The next day, Anna called all her friends. Together, they organized a fundraiser to help Fred. I was so proud of Anna's compassion and kindness!

3 주어진 글 **(A)**에 이어질 내용을 순서에 맞게 배열한 것으로 가장 적절한 것은?

① (B) - (D) - (C)   ② (C) - (B) - (D)
③ (C) - (D) - (B)   ④ (D) - (B) - (C)
⑤ (B) - (C) - (D)

4 밑줄 친 (a)~(e) 중에서 가리키는 대상이 나머지 넷과 <u>다른</u> 것은?

① (a) ② (b) ③ (c) ④ (d) ⑤ (e)

5 윗글에 관한 내용으로 적절하지 <u>않은</u> 것은?

① Anna와 그녀의 어머니는 함께 멕시코 식당에 갔다.
② 한 노인이 인도에 누워 있는 것을 발견했다.
③ 그 노인은 심각한 자동차 사고를 당해서 다리를 다쳤다.
④ Anna는 식당 방침상 음식을 포장할 수 없었다.
⑤ Anna는 그녀의 친구들을 모아 모금 행사를 조직했다.

다음 빈칸에 들어갈 적절한 말을 쓰시오.

지난주, 딸 Anna와 멕시코 식당에 갔을 때 한 노인이 인도에
1 __________________을 발견함
그는 지저분하고 신발도 신고 있지 않았으며, 구걸을 하고 있었음

↓

Anna는 Fred가 심각한 **2** __________________로 다리를 다쳐 일을 할 수 없게 되었고,
결국 집까지 잃게 된 것을 알게 됨

↓

Anna는 자신의 음식을 받았지만 **3** __________________에게 부탁하여 포장한 후
Fred에게 그것을 나눠 줌

↓

다음 날 Anna는 친구들을 불러 Fred를 돕기 위한 **4** __________________를 조직함
Anna의 어머니는 Anna의 동정심과 **5** __________________에 자랑스러움을 느낌

1 이 글에 쓰인 **starving**과 뜻이 비슷한 단어는?

① hurt   ② anxious
③ hungry   ④ diligent
⑤ indifferent

2 이 글의 제목으로 가장 적절한 것은?

① A Sad Experience One Evening
② Homeless People: Problems and Solutions
③ Famous Mexican Restaurants and Their Origins
④ When We Met Homeless People: Dos and Don'ts
⑤ A Kind Heart: A Change That Started with One Shared Meal

3 이 글의 내용과 일치하는 것은?

① Anna had a dance recital last month.
② Anna always ordered a beef burrito with cheese.
③ Anna met a young boy sitting on the street.
④ Anna didn't talk to the man injured in a car accident.
⑤ Anna requested the waitress to pack her food into a box.

PARAPHRASING DRILL

다음 문장들이 같은 뜻이 되도록 빈칸에 들어갈 적절한 말을 <보기>에서 찾아 쓰시오.

> 보기
>
> loss   get   injury

His leg had been injured, which meant he couldn't work anymore, so he ended up losing his home.
= Due to his leg ____________, he couldn't work anymore, ending up losing his home.
= His leg had been injured, which meant he couldn't ________________ any job, so he ended up losing his home.
= His leg had been injured, which meant he couldn't work anymore, resulting in the ________________ of his home.

TRANSLATION DRILL

⭐ 동사 stop은 동명사가 목적어로 올 때 '~하는 것을 멈추다'라고 해석하지만, to부정사가 뒤에 오는 경우에는 to부정사의 부사적 용법이 되어 '~하기 위해 멈추다'로 해석한다.

다음 문장의 밑줄 친 부분에 유의하여 해석을 완성하시오.

1 She stopped to say hello to the man.
그녀는 그 남자에게 ____________________.
2 He stopped to ask for directions to the nearest gas station.
그는 가장 가까운 주유소 방향을 ____________________.

UNIT 01 목적 파악하기

 ⑤  ③

해설

학생들을 위한 직업 박람회에 전문가로 참석이 가능한지 문의하며 연설을 부탁하는 내용이므로, 글의 목적으로 가장 적절한 것은 ⑤이다.

해석

George Knight 씨께,

제 이름은 Rita Sparks입니다. 저는 Grove 고등학교의 선생님입니다. 매년, 학교는 학생들을 위한 직업 박람회를 개최합니다. 시 전역에서 온 전문가들이 이 행사에 참석합니다. 그들은 워크숍에서 가르치고 발표를 하는 데 자원합니다. 많은 우리 학생들이 시의 새로운 박물관을 설계하는 당신의 작업에 친숙합니다. 저는 당신이 우리의 다음 직업 박람회에 참석할 수 있는지 궁금합니다. 그것은 다음 달에 열릴 것입니다. 우리는 당신이 건축가로서의 도전과 보람에 대해 연설을 해주시면 좋겠습니다. 저는 학생들이 당신으로부터 많은 것을 배울 수 있을 것이라 생각합니다.

Rita Sparks 드림

구문 이해

1 They **volunteer to teach and give** presentations in workshops.
→ '자원하다, 자진하다'라는 뜻의 동사 volunteer 뒤에 to부정사(to teach, to give)가 와서 동사의 목적어 역할을 하는 명사적 용법으로 쓰였다. 등위접속사 and와 동사 give 사이에는 to가 생략되어 있다.
2 I **think** the students could learn a lot from you.
→ 동사 think 뒤에 목적절을 이끄는 접속사 that이 생략되어 있다.

지문 한눈에 보기

1 선생님 **2** 직업 박람회 **3** 건축가 **4** 연설

정답 적중하기

1 if you're available to attend our next career fair
2 if you could give a speech

해설

학교 체육관 보수 공사로 인해 학생들에게 변동 사항에 대해 안내를 하는 내용이므로, 글의 목적으로 가장 적절한 것은 ③이다.

해석

학생들을 위한 공지:

학교 체육관 공사는 월요일에 시작할 것입니다. 보수는 6주가 걸릴 것입니다. 그 기간 동안, 학생들에게 체육관은 출입 금지가 될 것입니다. 모든 체육 수업은 길 건너 King Park에서 진행될 것입니다. 그러나, 일부 체육 수업은 좋지 못한 날씨 때문에 연기될 수 있습니다. 또한, 봄 도서 전시회는 올해는 체육관에서 열리지 않을 것입니다. 대신에 중앙 도서관에서 열릴 것입니다. 버스들이 행사 당일 학생들을 태우고 도서관을 오고 갈 것입니다. 여러분의 협조와 인내에 감사드립니다. 모두 우리의 새 체육관을 기대합시다!

Prince 중학교 직원

구문 이해

1 **During** that time, the gym will be off-limits to students.
→ '~ 동안'이라는 의미의 전치사 during 뒤에는 특정 기간을 나타내는 명사(구)가 온다. for는 숫자가 포함된 기간과 함께 쓰이는데 이 차이를 기억해야 한다.
2 All P.E. classes **will be held** at King Park across the street.
→ will be held는 조동사와 수동태(be + 과거분사(p.p))가 결합된 형태이다. be held는 '(행사 등이) 열리다, 개최되다'라는 의미의 수동태 표현이다.

지문 한눈에 보기

1 체육관 공사 **2** 금지(제한) **3** 체육 **4** 도서 전시회

정답 적중하기

1 Notice
2 Construction on the school gym
3 your cooperation and patience

연습문제

① ⑤   ② ②

해설

호텔에 투숙했던 고객이 쓴 편지로 불만족스러웠던 호텔 서비스에 대해 항의하는 내용이므로, 글의 목적으로 가장 적절한 것은 ⑤이다.

해석

관계자분께,

최근에 저희 가족은 Sunside Beach에 있는 귀하의 호텔에 투숙했습니다. 안타깝게도, 저희는 숙박에 만족하지 못했습니다. 첫째, 우리가 도착했을 때 방이 엉망진창인 상태였습니다. 바닥에는 먼지가 가득했고, 침대보도 정리된

것처럼 보이지 않았습니다. 둘째, 우리는 음식에도 역시 감동받지 못했습니다. 조식 뷔페의 계란은 묽고 식어 있었습니다. 팬케이크는 타버렸고, 베이컨은 너무 익혀졌습니다. 추가적으로, 우리는 모닝콜을 예약했지만 전화가 늦게 왔습니다. 결과적으로, 우리는 서핑 수업을 놓쳤습니다. 다시는 귀하의 호텔에 머물지 않을 것입니다.

진심을 담아,

Peter Black으로부터

구문 이해

1 Firstly, our room was a mess **when** we arrived.

→ when이 의문사일 때는 주로 문장의 앞에 와서 '언제'라는 의미로 쓰이지만 접속사로 두 문장을 연결할 때는 '~할 때'의 의미로 쓰인다.

2 The eggs at the breakfast buffet **were** runny and cold.

→ 문장의 주어가 The eggs이므로 동사는 복수형인 were가 쓰였다. The eggs 뒤의 「전치사 + 명사구」 형태의 at the breakfast buffet는 The eggs를 수식하는 형용사 역할을 한다.

FLOWCHART

1 만족하지 못함   **2** 엉망이었음   **3** 음식   **4** 늦게 옴   **5** 호텔

COMPREHENSION CHECK-UP

1 ⑤   **2** the bed sheets   **3** ③

1 satisfied는 '만족한'이라는 의미의 형용사로 ⑤ disappointed(실망한)는 유의어라고 볼 수 없다.
① 기쁜
② 행복한
③ 아주 기뻐하는
④ 만족하는
2 앞에 나온 침대보(the bed sheets)를 가리킨다.
3 ③ The eggs at the breakfast buffet were runny and cold.를 통해 조식 뷔페에서 계란이 제공되었음을 알 수 있다.
① Peter는 Sunside Beach에 있는 호텔에서 혼자 머물렀다.
② 호텔의 객실은 매주 청소된다.
④ 호텔에는 모닝콜 서비스가 없다.
⑤ Peter는 나중에 또 그 호텔에 머무를 것이다.

PARAPHRASING DRILL

1 as soon as
2 Additionally, unsatisfied with

TRANSLATION DRILL

1 팬케이크는 타버렸고, 베이컨은 너무 익혀졌다.
2 자유의 여신상은 1886년에 지어졌다.

②
연습문제

본문 p. 14

해설

Bright Studios에서 제공하는 다음 학기 미술 수업 과정에 대해 안내하는 내용이므로, 글의 목적으로 가장 적절한 것은 ②이다.

해석

미술 애호가 여러분 주목하세요!

당신은 미술 실력을 향상시키는 데 관심이 있나요? Bright Studios는 지금 다양한 과정을 제공하고 있습니다. 저희 강사들은 재능 있으며 지식도 풍부합니다. 그들은 당신의 미술 여정을 따라서 당신을 안내할 준비가 되어 있습니다. 초보자들은 미술 기초 과정에 등록할 수 있습니다. 당신은 스케치와 색칠하는 법을 배울 것입니다. 만약 당신이 조각하는 것에 관심이 있다면, 조각하기 1, 2, 또는 3단계 수업을 들으세요. 저희는 또한 사진 촬영, 도자기, 그리고 뜨개질 수업을 제공합니다. 다음 학기는 1월 초에 시작합니다. 수업은 일주일에 두 번, 7주에 걸쳐 열립니다. 12월 28일까지 등록하고 10% 할인을 받으세요! 더 많은 정보를 원하시면 저희 웹사이트 www.brightstudios.com을 방문하세요.

구문 이해

1 The next semester **begins** in early January.

→ 가까운 미래의 확정된 일정이나 계획은 현재시제로 나타낸다.

2 Classes will be held **twice a week** over seven weeks.

→ '두 번'이라는 의미의 부사 twice는 a week, a month, a year 등과 같이 기간을 나타내는 명사와 함께 쓰여 '일주일에 두 번', '한 달에 두 번', '일 년에 두 번'이라는 뜻을 나타낸다.

MAPPING

1 knowledge   **2** sketch   **3** levels   **4** twice   **5** signing up

COMPREHENSION CHECK-UP

1 ④   **2** ③   **3** Early January.

1 sign up (for)는 '~에 등록하다'라는 의미로 ④ register로 바꿔 쓸 수 있다.
① 해결하다
② 고르다
③ 유발하다
⑤ 버리다
2 조각 수업은 1단계부터 3단계까지 있으므로 ③ Art lovers can take various sculpture classes.(미술 애호가들은 다양한 조각 수업을 받을 수 있다.)가 가장 적절하다.
① 상급 수업에만 등록할 수 있다
② 기초 수업에서는 스케치만 배울 수 있다
④ 주 1회 수업에 참여할 수 있다
⑤ 12월 28일까지 20% 할인을 받을 수 있다
3 The next semester begins in early January.를 통해 1월 초임을 알 수 있다.

PARAPHRASING DRILL

prepared, lead, throughout

TRANSLATION DRILL

1 당신은 스케치하고 색칠하는 방법을 배울 것이다.
2 이 소프트웨어를 사용하는 방법을 보여줄 수 있나요?

예제 ①

본문 p. 16

해설

다양한 농작물을 수확한 후에 맛있는 음식을 준비하며, 모닥불 주위에서 춤을 추는 모습을 묘사하고 있으므로, ① festive(축하하는, 축제의)가 가장 적절하다.

해석

매년 가을, Kabelo의 마을은 수확을 기념했다. Kabelo는 9살의 아이 치고는 작았지만, 여름 내내 그의 마을을 돕기 위해 열심히 일했다. 그들은 함께 감자, 호박 그리고 옥수수와 같은 농작물을 키웠다. 농작물을 수확하는 것은 힘든 일이었지만, 마침내 일은 끝이 났다. 마을 사람들은 큰 모닥불 주위에 모였다. 그들은 자신들이 재배한 음식으로 맛있는 진수성찬을 준비했다. 진수성찬 후에, 마을 원로들은 불 주변에 둘러앉아 그들의 용감한 조상들의 이야기를 들려주었다. 그러고 나서 드럼 연주자들이 드럼을 치기 시작했고, 가수들이 합류했다. Kabelo는 어린 소년들과 소녀들이 불 주변에서 빙글빙글 도는 것을 보았다. 그것은 매우 재미있어 보여서, 그는 그들과 함께했다. 다 함께, 그들은 별 아래에서 춤을 추고 또 추었다. Kabelo는 모든 수확이 그렇게 멋지기를 희망했다.
② 무서운
③ 지루한
④ 느긋한
⑤ 긴급한

구문 이해

1 **Harvesting** the crops **was** hard work, but finally, the job was done.
→ 동명사가 주어로 오는 경우 단수로 취급하므로 동사도 단수 형태(was)가 왔다.
2 Kabelo **watched** young boys and girls **twirl** around the fire.
→ watch는 대표적인 지각동사로 목적어를 보충 설명하는 목적격 보어로 동사원형이나 현재분사가 올 수 있다. 위 문장에서도 twirl 대신에 twirling으로 진행 중임을 강조할 수 있다.

 **지문 한눈에 보기**

1 수확   **2** 옥수수   **3** 진수성찬   **4** 불(모닥불)

정답 적중하기

1 celebrated
2 beat their drums
3 so much fun

예제 ②

본문 p. 17

해설

오디션 결과를 알기 전에는 손이 축축하고 이마에 땀이 날 정도로 nervous(긴장한)한 감정이었다가 합격자 명단에서 자신의 이름을 확인한 후 delighted(아주 기뻐하는)한 감정으로 변한 상황을 담고 있는 글이다. 따라서 가장 적절한 것은 ⑤ nervous → delighted이다.

해석

그가 복도에 있는 한 무리의 학생들에게 다가갈수록 Thomas의 손바닥은 축축했다. 그들은 모두 벽에 테이프로 붙여져 있는 안내문 주위에 옹기종기 모여 있었다. 연극 선생님이 오디션 결과를 붙여 두셨다. 지난주, Thomas는 《가장 어린 사자》의 주연 역할에 지원했었다. 이제, 그는 마침내 자신이 합격했는지를 알 수 있을 것이다. 사람들을 뚫고 나아갈 때 Thomas의 이마에 땀이 났다. 그는 종이 위의 명단을 읽었다. '주연'이라는 말 바로 옆에 그의 이름이 있었다. 학생들은 Thomas의 등을 토닥거리며 그의 이름을 환호했다. Thomas는 이렇게 멋지게 느낀 적이 없었고 마침내 그의 꿈은 이루어졌다!
① 매혹된 → 비극적인
② 걱정스러운 → 느긋한
③ 절망적인 → 감사한
④ 낙담한 → 안도한

구문 이해

1 The drama teacher **had posted** the audition results.
→ 과거보다 한 시제 앞선 시간을 나타낼 때 「had + 과거분사(p.p)」 형태를 쓰며 과거완료 또는 대과거라고 한다.
2 Now, he would finally know **if** he made the cut.
→ if는 명사절에서 '~인지 아닌지'라는 의미로 쓰이고, 어떤 상황이나 사실에 대한 의문이나 불확실성을 나타내며 whether로 바꿔 쓸 수 있다.

 **지문 한눈에 보기**

1 축축   **2** 안내문   **3** 주연(주인공)   **4** 환호

 **정답 적중하기**

1 clammy as he approached
2 Sweat broke out
3 never felt so wonderful

 **연습문제** 

① ③   ② ②

연습문제 ①

본문 p. 18

해설

텐트 근처에서 정체 모를 동물이 땅을 긁는 소리가 나서 Anna가 두려움에 떨고 잠을 못 이루는 모습을 묘사하고 있으므로, ③ strange and frightening(기괴하고 무서운)이 가장 적절하다.

해석

Anna는 깨어나서 텐트의 칠흑같이 어두컴컴한 곳을 응시했다. Glenview 캠핑장에서의 한밤중이었고 숲은 소음으로 가득했다. 부엉이들이 울고 멀리서 늑대들이 울부짖었다. Anna는 각각의 소리에 주의 깊게 귀를 기울였다. 한 소리가 점점 더 가까워지고 있었다. 무엇인가가 Anna의 텐트 문 근처의 땅을 긁고 있었다. 텐트는 마치 거대한 어떤 것이 막 스치고 지나간 것처럼 흔들렸다. 아마도 그것은 코요테나 어쩌면 곰이었을 것이다. Anna는 소리를 질러 그녀의 부모님을 깨우고 싶었지만, 두려움이 그녀를 얼어붙게 했다. 그

녀는 단 한마디의 소리도 낼 수 없었다. 곧, 그 긁는 소리가 희미해졌다가 다시 나타났다. 밤새, Anna는 긁는 소리에 귀를 기울이면서 깬 채로 누워 있었다. 그녀는 그것이 무엇이든 사라지기를 기다렸다.
① 유쾌하고 재미있는
② 축제 같고 흥겨운
④ 차분하고 편안한
⑤ 조용하고 따분한

구문 이해

1 Anna wanted to scream and wake her parents, but fear **kept** her **frozen**.
→ keep은 「주어 + 동사 + 목적어 + 목적격 보어」의 5형식 동사로 쓰였고, 목적격 보어 자리에는 목적어의 상태를 나타내는 frozen(얼어붙은)이 왔다.
2 She waited for **whatever** it was to disappear.
→ whatever은 관계대명사 what에 ever을 붙여 쓴 것으로 '무엇이든'이라는 의미의 복합관계대명사이다.

FLOWCHART

1 소음　　**2** 가까워지고 있었음　　**3** 두려움　　**4** 깨어 있었음

COMPREHENSION CHECK-UP

1 ②　　**2** noise　　**3** ④

1 carefully가 포함된 문장은 'Anna는 각각의 소리를 주의 깊게 들었다'는 의미이므로, '자세히, 면밀히'라는 의미의 ② closely가 적절하다.
① 거의 ~하지 않는
③ 정중히
④ 꾸준히
⑤ 소극적으로
2 forest was alive with noise 부분을 통해 소음(noise) 때문에 잠에서 깨어났음을 알 수 있다.
3 ④ '큰 코요테와 곰이 Anna의 텐트를 찢으려고 했다'는 내용은 나와 있지 않다.
① Anna는 멀리서 동물들이 울부짖는 소리를 들을 수 있었다.
② 그 소리 중 하나가 점점 가까워지고 있었다.
③ 무엇인가가 Anna의 텐트 근처 땅바닥을 긁고 있었다.
⑤ Anna는 두려움 때문에 단 한마디도 하지 못했다.

PARAPHRASING DRILL

1 trembled as though
2 had a desire to shout

TRANSLATION DRILL

1 한 소리는 점점 더 가까워지고 있었다.
2 그 새들은 하늘로 점점 더 높이 올라가고 있었다.

②
연습문제

본문 p. 20

해설

Jenny가 과학 박람회에서 자신이 만든 모형이 상을 받을 것이라 기대했으

나 모형을 땅에 떨어뜨려 금이 가면서 frustrated(좌절한)의 감정이었다가 친구의 도움으로 다시 접착제로 고치면서 hopeful(희망찬)의 감정으로 변화한 과정을 담고 있는 글이다. 따라서 Jenny의 심경 변화로 가장 적절한 것은 ② frustrated → hopeful(좌절한 → 희망찬)이다.

해석

Jenny는 과학 박람회에서 상을 받을 것이라고 확신하고 있었다. 결국, 그녀는 태양계 모형을 만드는 데 3주를 보냈다. 하지만 그 모형은 Jenny가 예상한 것보다 더 무거웠다. 그녀가 그것을 학교로 옮길 때 강한 바람이 불어왔다. 갑자기, 그 모형은 땅에 떨어졌다. 행성들이 인도로 굴러 떨어졌고, 일부는 반으로 갈라졌다. "망쳤어!" Jenny는 무언가를 차고 싶은 충동과 싸우며 말했다. 그때, Jenny의 가장 친한 친구 Mindy가 달려왔다. 그녀는 가방 안을 뒤져서, 접착제 한 병을 꺼내며 "함께 고쳐 보자."라고 말했다. Jenny는 웃으며 금이 간 행성들을 줍기 시작했다. 그녀가 상을 받을 가능성은 여전히 있었다.
① 감사한 → 긴장한
③ 당황한 → 느긋한
④ 매혹된 → 짜증 난
⑤ 즐거운 → 유죄의

구문 이해

1 Jenny **knew** she **would** win a prize at the science fair.
→ 주절의 동사가 knew로 과거형이므로 종속절의 동사도 will 대신 과거형인 would를 써서 주절과 종속절의 시제를 일치시켰다.
2 Jenny smiled and **began picking** up the cracked planets.
→ 동사 begin은 목적어 자리에 동명사와 to부정사 모두 올 수 있다.

FLOWCHART

1 win　　**2** cracked　　**3** (to) fix　　**4** chance

COMPREHENSION CHECK-UP

1 ④　　**2** ⑤　　**3** the model

1 urge는 '욕구, 충동'이라는 의미이므로 유의어인 ④ desire(욕구, 갈망)가 가장 적절하다.
① 평화
② 충고
③ 지지
⑤ 제안
2 But the model was heavier than Jenny expected.(하지만 모형은 Jenny가 예상했던 것보다 무거웠다.)를 다르게 표현한 문장이므로 expect의 유의어인 ⑤ anticipate(기대하다)라는 동사가 들어가는 것이 적절하다.
3 세 번째 줄 Suddenly, the model crashed to the ground.를 통해 the model임을 알 수 있다.

PARAPHRASING DRILL

rolled, down, split

TRANSLATION DRILL

1 그녀는 그녀의 모형을 만드는 데 3주를 보냈다.
2 그는 뒷마당에 있는 부서진 울타리를 고치는 데 4시간을 보냈다.

CHAPTER 2
20번대 문제 공략하기 Part 1

UNIT 03 주장, 요지 파악하기

예제 ❶ ③   예제 ❷ ⑤

❶ 예제
본문 p. 24

해설

삶에서 변화시키고 싶은 것이 있다면 그것에 대해서 써 보라고 하면서, 긍정적인 내용을 글로 쓰면 꿈을 이루는 데 동기를 부여할 수 있다고 주장하고 있으므로 정답은 ③이다.

해석

당신은 신데렐라처럼 요정 대모를 갖기를 소망해 본 적이 있는가? 동화 속에서, 당신은 지팡이를 튕기거나 마법 주문으로 원하는 것을 얻을 수 있다. 하지만, 마법은 존재하지 않는다. 현실에서, 펜은 지팡이만큼 강력할 수 있다. 만약 당신의 삶에 대해 바꾸고 싶은 것이 있다면, 그것에 대해 써 보라. 그러나 당신의 부정적인 감정에 집중하지 마라. 무력감을 느끼는 것에 집착하지 마라. 오히려, 긍정적인 것에 집중하도록 노력하라. 문제가 해결되었을 때의 당신의 삶을 마음속으로 그려 보려고 노력하라. 당신이 이루기 원하는 모든 목표를 목록으로 만들라. 예를 들어, 당신은 "나는 올해 축구팀을 만들 것이다."라고 쓸지도 모른다. 당신은 또한 "나는 모든 시험을 통과할 것이다."라고 쓸지도 모른다. 이러한 진술들은 당신이 꿈을 이루도록 동기를 부여할 것이다.

구문 이해

1 In reality, a pen may be **as powerful as** a wand.
→ 「as + 원급 + as」는 동등 비교의 형태로 as와 as 사이에 비교급 형태가 아닌 형용사나 부사의 원급이 오며, '~만큼 …하다'로 해석한다.

2 These statements will **motivate** you **to make** your dreams come true.
→ motivate는 5형식 동사로 목적격 보어 자리에 「to + 동사원형」 형태의 to부정사가 온다.

👁 지문 한눈에 보기

1 주문   **2** 바꾸고 싶은   **3** 긍정적인   **4** 동기

🎯 정답 적중하기

1 what
2 powerful
3 writing

---

❷ 예제
본문 p. 25

해설

발명가들은 세상에 필요한 것이 무엇인지 알아내고, 오랜 기간 인내하며 테스트하고 개선하는 과정을 통해 아이디어를 완성하여 세상을 바꾼다는 것이 글의 요지이므로 정답은 ⑤이다.

해석

자동차, 전구, 비행기 그리고 볼펜. 이것들은 인간이 사는 방식을 바꾼 발명품들 중 몇 가지에 불과하다. 발명가들은 어떻게 발명품을 생각해 낼까? 대부분의 경우, 그들은 필요성을 찾아낸다. 예를 들어, 과거에, 여행은 제한적이고 시간이 많이 걸렸다. 사람들은 돌아다닐 수 있는 더 빠르고 효율적인 방법이 필요했고, 자동차가 그것을 제공했다. 이와 같이, 발명가들은 끊임없이 주변의 세상을 바라보고 문제점들을 찾아내야만 한다. 그러고 나서, 그들은 이러한 문제들을 해결할 아이디어를 생각해 내야 한다. 하지만, 이것은 긴 과정이다. 대부분의 초기 아이디어들이 그렇게 유용한 것은 아니며, 발명가들은 많은 테스트와 개선을 필요로 한다. 어떤 경우에는, 이것은 몇 년 혹은 수십 년이 걸릴 수도 있다. 하지만 그 인내심으로, 발명가들은 세상을 바꾸는 것을 도울 수 있다.

구문 이해

1 These are just a few of the inventions that have changed **the way** humans live.
→ the way는 관계부사 how와 같은 표현으로 쓰였고, '~하는 방법'으로 해석한다. 단, the way와 how는 함께 쓰일 수 없다.

2 Then, they must come up with ideas **that** solve these problems.
→ ideas가 선행사이고, that이 주격 관계대명사인 문장이다. 주격 관계대명사 뒤에는 주어가 없는 불완전한 문장이 오며 주격 관계대명사는 단독으로 생략할 수 없다.

👁 지문 한눈에 보기

1 필요   **2** 효율적인   **3** 문제점   **4** 인내심

🎯 정답 적중하기

1 come up with
2 identify
3 help change

① ⑤   ② ④

❶
연습문제
본문 p. 26

해설

눈 앞에 보이지 않는 쓰레기 문제에 대해서 인식하고, 이를 환경 캠페인을 통해 해결할 수 있다는 것이 글쓴이의 주장이므로 정답은 ⑤이다.

해석

"눈에서 멀어지면, 마음에서도 멀어진다." 당신은 이 문구를 들어본 적이 있는가? 이것은 많은 사람들이 보이지 않는 문제에 대해 생각하지 않으려 한다

는 사실을 의미한다. 이것은 그들이 자신에게 직접적으로 영향을 미치는 것들에 대해서만 생각한다는 것을 의미한다. 이것은 또한 우리 행성에 관해서도 사실이다. 매년 인간들은 수십억 톤의 쓰레기를 만든다. 이 쓰레기는 우리의 땅과 물을 오염시킨다. 그러나, 대부분의 사람들은 매일 이 쓰레기를 보지 못한다. 따라서, 그들은 그것을 큰 문제로 여기지 않는다. 그들은 그들의 방식을 바꾸기 위한 조치도 취하지 않는다. 실제로, 많은 사람들은 같은 양의 쓰레기를 계속 생산한다. 그러나, 환경 캠페인들은 인식을 높이기 위해 많은 것을 해왔다. 이것들은 사람들을 사실과 이미지에 노출함으로써 작동한다. 결국, 그들은 더 이상 그 문제를 무시할 수 없다.

구문 이해

1 **Have** you **ever heard** this phrase?
➜ 「have + 과거분사(p.p)」는 현재완료로 부사 ever가 같이 오면 과거부터 현재까지의 경험을 나타낸다.
2 This is true **when it comes to** our planet, too.
➜ when it comes to에서 to는 전치사이므로 뒤에 명사나 동명사가 와야 하며 '~에 관한 한'으로 해석한다.

1 보이지 않는   **2** 오염시킴   **3** 생산함   **4** 무시할 수 없음

COMPREHENSION CHECK-UP

1 ⑤   **2** ③   **3** ①

1 affect는 '영향을 미치다'라는 의미로 ⑤ influence(영향을 주다)가 유의어이다. ① 맹세하다 ③ 받아들이다 ③ 제안하다 ④ 경고하다
2 In fact, many people continue to produce the same amount of trash.(사실, 많은 사람들은 같은 양의 쓰레기를 계속 생산한다.)를 다르게 표현한 문장으로 ③ keep producing(계속 생산하다)이 빈칸에 적절하다.
3 보이지 않기 때문에 문제로 여기지 않는 쓰레기 문제에 대한 내용이므로 ① The Invisible Problem: Trash Pollution(눈에 보이지 않는 문제: 쓰레기 오염)이 제목으로 적절하다.
② 재활용: 더 깨끗한 지구를 위한 해결책
③ 폐기물 저감을 위한 기술 혁신
④ 환경 운동의 역사
⑤ 쓰레기가 해양 생물에 미치는 영향

PARAPHRASING DRILL

1 Nevertheless
2 encounter
3 every day

TRANSLATION DRILL

1 이것들은 사람들을 사실과 이미지에 노출함으로써 작동한다.
2 그녀는 매일 연습함으로써 그녀의 기술을 향상시켰다.

②
연습문제

본문 p. 28

해설

역사는 단순히 사건의 나열이 아니라 유기적으로 연결되어 있고, 현재의 사회를 이해하기 위해서는 역사를 이해하는 것이 중요하다는 내용이 글의 요지이므로 정답은 ④이다.

해석

그것이 고대 그리스이든 단지 100년 전이든, 대부분의 사람들은 역사와 단절되어 있다고 느낀다. 그 시대의 사건들이 지금 일어나고 있다고 상상하는 것은 어렵다. 그런 사건들을 겪으며 살았던 사람들이 오늘날 사람들과 똑같았다고 상상하는 것은 훨씬 더 어렵다. 그러나, 작가 William Faulkner는 "역사는 있었던 일이 아니라 지금 있는 것이다."라고 말했다. 그에게, 역사는 단지 사건들의 기록이 아니다. 오히려, 이런 사건들이 우리가 오늘날 살고 있는 세상을 형성해 왔다. 많은 방식으로, 그것들은 우리가 아직 살고 있는 사건들의 연쇄적인 반응을 유발해 왔다. 그래서 그것들은 우리의 세상을 형성하는 것을 계속하고 있는 것이다. 현재의 사회를 이해하기 위해, 역사를 이해하는 것은 중요하다. 과거의 실수들은 반복될 수 있으며 그것이 다시 일어나는 것을 막을 수 있는 것은 바로 우리들이다.

구문 이해

1 **Whether** it is ancient Greece **or** merely 100 years ago, most people feel disconnected from history.
➜ whether가 양보를 나타내는 부사절 접속사로 쓰인 문장으로, '~이든 아니든'으로 해석한다. 여기서는 '그것이 고대 그리스이든 단지 100년 전이든'으로 해석한다.
2 **It**'s hard **to imagine** the events of those times happening now.
➜ 가주어 it과 진주어 to부정사가 쓰인 구문으로, 주어가 긴 경우에 가주어 it을 앞에 쓸 수 있다. 단, 가주어 it은 해석하지 않는다.

1 past   **2** imagine   **3** shape   **4** mistakes

COMPREHENSION CHECK-UP

1 ②   **2** chain reaction   **3** ③

1 prevent A from B(A가 B하는 것을 막다)를 대신해서 stop A from B를 쓸 수 있다.
① 동의하다 ③ 무시하다 ④ 게시하다 ⑤ 반복하다
2 과거의 사건들이 지금 우리가 살고 있는 세상을 형성했다는 것을 의미하는 단어는 chain reaction(연쇄 반응)이다.
3 The mistakes of the past can be repeated and it is up to us to prevent them from happening again.(과거의 실수들은 반복될 수 있으며 그것이 다시 일어나는 것을 막을 수 있는 것은 바로 우리이다.)라는 내용을 통해 ③ '역사를 이해하는 것은 이전의 실수를 반복하지 않는 데 도움이 된다'가 일치하는 내용임을 알 수 있다.
① 대부분의 사람들은 역사적 사건으로부터 연결되어 있음을 느낀다.
② 역사는 오늘날 우리가 살고 있는 세계를 형성하는 데 거의 영향을 미치지 않는다.
④ William Faulkner는 역사가 단순히 과거 사건들의 목록이라고 믿었다.
⑤ 오늘날 사람들은 고대에 살았던 사람들에 공감하는 것이 쉽다고 생각한다.

PARAPHRASING DRILL

1 difficult, occurring, present
2 various, domino, effect

UNIT 04 주제, 제목 파악하기

예제 **1** ③   예제 **2** ①

1 예제

본문 p. 30

해설

농작물 순환은 해마다 같은 밭에 다른 종류의 농작물을 심어 토양의 영양소를 보호하고 건강을 유지하기 위한 중요한 농업 방식이라는 내용의 글이므로, 글의 주제로 가장 적절한 것은 ③ '토양 보존에 있어 농작물 순환(윤작)의 필요성'이다.

해석

많은 농부들이 농작물 순환(윤작)을 실행한다. 이것은 주어진 밭에서 어떤 작물이 자라는지를 바꾸는 과정이다. 예를 들어, 한 농부는 그의 밭들 중 하나에 옥수수를 심을 수 있다. 다음 해에, 그는 다른 종류의 농작물을 심을 것이다. 그 다음 해에, 그는 또 다른 농작물을 심을 것이다. 만약 농부가 밭을 여러 개 가지고 있다면, 그는 매년 단순히 그의 옥수수 농작물을 다른 밭으로 옮길 수도 있다. 그는 다른 종류의 농작물에 대해서도 똑같이 해야 한다. 이 과정은 토양의 건강을 보호하기 때문에 중요하다. 서로 다른 농작물들은 토양에 여러 가지 영양소를 추가한다. 하지만, 같은 농작물을 계속해서 심는 것은 다른 중요한 영양소들을 없앨 수 있다. 시간이 지나면서, 이것은 토양의 품질을 상하게 한다. 수년이 지나면, 그 토양에서 어떤 것도 재배하기 어려울지도 모른다.
① 작물을 적기에 심지 않는 것의 위험
② 어떤 작물을 심을지 선택하는 가장 좋은 방법
④ 해마다 옥수수를 재배하는 것의 부정적인 영향
⑤ 농작물 생산에 대한 정부의 영향

구문 이해

1 **If** a farmer **has** multiple fields, he may simply move his corn crop to a different field each year.
➜ 조건의 if 부사절에서는 미래에 일어날 일이더라도 현재시제를 씀에 유의해야 한다.
2 After many years, **it** may be difficult **to grow** anything at all in that soil.
➜ 주어가 긴 경우 가주어 it을 활용하여 긴 주어를 뒤로 보낼 수 있다. 가주어 it은 해석하지 않고, 진주어 to grow(재배하는 것) 이하만 해석한다.

👁 지문 한눈에 보기

1 농작물   **2** 다른   **3** 여러 개   **4** 영양소

🎯 정답 적중하기

1 rotation
2 protects
3 same

2 예제

본문 p. 31

해설

집을 장식할 때 색상과 패턴을 적절하게 추가해야 개성을 반영할 수 있다는 내용의 글이므로, 글의 제목으로 가장 적절한 것은 ① '집 장식: 당신의 개성을 빛나게 하라'이다.

해석

당신의 집을 장식할 때, 어느 정도가 과한 것인지를 결정하는 것은 어려울 수 있다. 요즘에는 많은 집주인들은 안전하게 행동하는 것을 선호한다. 과거의 대담한 색상과 복잡한 패턴 대신에, 그들은 더 중립적인 색상을 선택한다. 베이지색, 흰색, 그리고 회색은 미니멀리스트의 집에서 흔히 볼 수 있다. 그러나, 어떤 사람들은 색상이 부족하면 집이 지루하게 느껴질 수 있다고 주장할 것이다. 패턴의 부족은 집이 인간미가 없다고 느껴지게 할 수 있다. 많은 디자이너들은 이제 "집을 꾸미는 것은 재미있는 모험이 되어야 합니다. 색상을 추가하는 것을 두려워하지 마세요."라고 말한다. 여전히, 많은 집주인들은 색상을 너무 많이 추가하는 것에 대해 신중하다. 디자이너들은 작게 시작하는 것을 추천한다. 문에 페인트를 칠해 보라. 벽 몇 면에만 벽지를 추가해 보라. 식물 화분과 작은 예술 작품을 들여놓아라. 어느새, 당신의 집은 당신의 개성을 반영할 것이다.
② 디자인 영감을 찾는 다섯 가지 방법
③ 과도한 장식을 피하고 미니멀리즘을 선택하라
④ 모든 것을 칠하라: 색이 많을수록 더 좋다
⑤ 집주인 되기: 해야 할 일과 하지 말아야 할 일

구문 이해

1 However, some would argue **that** a lack of color can leave a home feeling boring.
➜ 여기서 that은 명사절을 이끄는 접속사로 that절 이후 문장이 동사 argue의 목적어로 쓰였다. 이때 that은 생략할 수 있다.
2 Designers recommend **starting** small.
➜ 동사 recommend(~을 추천하다)는 3형식 동사로 쓸 때, 목적어로 동명사가 와야 한다. to부정사 형태인 to start로 쓰지 않음에 유의한다.

👁 지문 한눈에 보기

1 중립적인   **2** 부족   **3** 모험   **4** 개성

🎯 정답 적중하기

1 boring
2 impersonal
3 reflect

연습문제

① ⑤   ② ②

1 연습문제

본문 p. 32

해설

바이러스는 자가 복제가 되지 않으므로 숙주 세포를 통해 단백질을 만들어 새로운 바이러스를 만들어낸다는 과정과 이유를 설명하는 글이므로, 글의 주제로 가장 적절한 것은 ⑤ '바이러스가 그들 자신의 복제품을 생산하는 방법과 이유'이다.

해석

바이러스는 스스로 복제할 수 없다. 그래서 그들은 그렇게 할 숙주 세포를 찾는다. 바이러스가 몸 안으로 들어오면, 그것은 숙주 세포에 달라붙는다. 그런 다음 바이러스의 유전 물질 중 일부가 세포 안으로 들어간다. 이 유전 물질이 세포의 작동을 장악한다. 그것은 세포에게 특정 단백질을 만들도록 지시를 내린다. 이 단백질들은 새로운 바이러스를 만들기 위해 사용된다. 일단 이 단백질들이 모이면, 바이러스 세포는 숙주 세포를 떠난다. 이것은 숙주 세포를 심각하게 손상시키거나 심지어 죽인다. 그런 다음 이 바이러스들은 근처의 다른 숙주 세포에 붙는다. 이 과정이 반복되고, 매번 더 많은 숙주 세포가 파괴된다. 숙주의 면역 체계는 바이러스 세포들을 찾기 위해 열심히 일하는데 왜냐하면 이 세포들을 죽여야 하기 때문이다. 그렇지 않으면, 그 바이러스가 숙주에게 너무 많은 손상을 입힐 수 있다.
① 역사상 가장 치명적인 바이러스
② 약한 면역 체계의 증상들
③ 좋은 숙주가 되는 것의 중요성
④ 병후 치유의 어려움

구문 이해

1 When a virus enters the body, it attaches **itself** to a host cell.
→ 주어와 목적어가 가리키는 대상이 같을 때는 목적어 자리에 재귀대명사를 쓴다. 여기서도 주절의 주어와 목적어가 모두 virus를 가리키므로 재귀대명사 itself가 왔다.
2 These proteins are used **to create** new viruses.
→ to create가 to부정사의 부사적 용법 중 '목적'을 나타내는 의미로 쓰였으며, '~하기 위해서'로 해석한다.

FLOWCHART

1 복제	**2** 숙주	**3** 단백질	**4** 파괴	**5** 면역

COMPREHENSION CHECK-UP

1 ①　　　**2** genetic material　　　**3** ⑤

1 replicate는 '복제하다'의 의미로 ① make a copy of(~을 베끼다, 복사하다)로 바꿔 쓸 수 있다.
　② ~을 대신하다
　③ ~을 채우다
　④ ~을 펼치다
　⑤ ~와 관계가 있다
2 앞 문장에 나온 genetic material(유전 물질)을 가리키는 대명사다.
3 A host's immune system works hard to find viral cells ~(숙주의 면역 체계는 바이러스 세포들을 찾기 위해 열심히 일한다 ~)라고 했으므로 ⑤ '숙주의 면역 체계는 바이러스 세포를 찾을 필요가 없다'라는 내용은 일치하지 않는다.
　① 바이러스는 복제하기 위해 숙주 세포를 찾는다.
　② 유전 물질은 세포의 작동을 통제한다.
　③ 새로운 바이러스는 단백질에 의해 생성된다.
　④ 바이러스 세포가 떠나면 숙주 세포가 손상될 수 있다.

PARAPHRASING DRILL

1 seriously, harms, gets rid of
2 If not, result in, severe

TRANSLATION DRILL

1 그것은 세포에게 특정 단백질을 만들도록 지시를 내린다.
2 나는 너에게 자기 전에 읽을 재미있는 이야기를 보낼 것이다.

② 연습문제

해설

외로움이라는 감정은 인간이 관계를 맺고, 서로 돕고, 무리를 형성하게 하여 오히려 생존에 유리하게 한다는 내용의 글이므로, 글의 제목으로 가장 적절한 것은 ② '외로움: 인간 생존에서의 또 다른 역할'이다.

해석

대부분의 사람들은 외로움을 부정적인 감정으로 생각한다. 하지만, 이 감정은 인간의 생존에 중요한 역할을 했다. 이론들은 외로움이 사람들로 하여금 다른 사람들과 친밀한 관계를 형성하도록 강요한다는 것을 시사한다. 이러한 관계들을 통해, 사람들은 그들이 필요한 시기에 반드시 다른 사람들로부터 도움을 받는 것을 보장한다. 과거에, 외로움은 야생에서의 생존 수단이었을 수도 있다. 그것은 인간들이 무리를 형성하도록 격려했다. 각 무리의 구성원들은 야생 동물들로부터 서로를 보호했다. 그들은 또한 경쟁 집단과 악천후로부터 서로를 보호했다. 마찬가지로, 그들은 사냥하고, 식량을 재배하고, 아이들을 기르기 위해 함께 일했다. 그러므로, 개인들은 무리에 속해 있을 때 생존할 수 있는 가능성이 훨씬 더 높았다. 오늘날 인간들은 동일한 위험들에 직면하지 않을지도 모른다. 하지만 무리를 형성하는 것은 여전히 그들이 안전하고 행복하게 지낼 수 있도록 도와준다.
① 인간이 집단으로 아이들을 키우는 것을 선호하는 이유
③ 인간의 뇌는 시간이 지남에 따라 어떻게 진화했는가
④ 생존: 환경은 어떻게 적응하는가
⑤ 혼자 지내는 것의 단점

구문 이해

1 Theories **suggest** that loneliness **pushes** people to form close relationships with others.
→ suggest는 '~을 제안하다'와 '~을 암시[시사]하다'의 의미로 쓰일 수 있는데, '제안하다'의 의미일 때는 뒤에 나오는 that절의 동사를 원형으로 쓴다. 여기서는 문맥상 '이론들이 ~한 내용을 암시[시사]하다'라는 의미로 쓰여서 that 이하의 문장에 동사가 원형으로 오지 않고 주어와 수를 일치시켜 pushes로 썼다.
2 But forming groups still helps them **stay** safe and happy.
→ (준)사역동사 help의 경우에는 목적격 보어 자리에 동사원형이나 to부정사를 모두 쓸 수 있다. 여기에서는 동사원형 stay가 왔다.

BREAKDOWN

1 survival	**2** Forming	**3** Helping	**4** Protecting	**5** chances

COMPREHENSION CHECK-UP

1 ②　　　**2** wild animals, rival group, the elements　　　**3** ⑤

1 ensure는 '반드시 ~하게 하다, 보장하다'의 의미로 유의어는 ② guarantee(보장하다, 약속하다)이다.
　① 의지하다
　③ 거부하다
　④ 깨닫다
　⑤ 받아들이다
2 5행부터 7행까지 The members ~ from wild animals. They ~ from rival groups and the elements.를 통해 야생 동물, 경쟁 집단, 그리고 악천후가 위험들임을 알 수 있다.

3 Thus, individuals had a much better chance of surviving in a group.(그러므로, 개인들은 무리에 속해 있을 때 생존할 수 있는 가능성이 훨씬 더 높았다.)라는 내용으로 보아 ⑤ '모이는 것은 인간이 안전하고 행복하게 지낼 수 있도록 도와준다'는 내용이 일치한다.
① 대부분의 사람들은 외로움을 긍정적인 감정으로 여긴다.
② 외로움은 야생에서 살아남을 수 있는 기회를 약화시켰다.
③ 외로움은 인간이 집단을 형성하는 것을 단념시켰다.
④ 개인은 현재에도 과거와 동일한 위험을 가지고 있다.

PARAPHRASING DRILL

Almost, see, refers to

TRANSLATION DRILL

1 그것은 사람들이 무리를 형성하도록 격려했다.
2 책을 읽는 것은 아이들이 새로운 아이디어를 탐구하도록 격려한다.

CHAPTER 3
20번대 문제 공략하기 Part 2

UNIT 05 함축 의미 파악하기

예제 ❶ ③   예제 ❷ ⑤

본문 p. 38

해설

고대 이집트인들과 독일 시인 Goethe 모두 색이 사람의 내부 감정을 바꾸고 행동에 영향을 줄 수 있다고 믿었다는 내용 뒤에 이어지는 문장이므로 밑줄 친 부분이 글에서 의미하는 바로 가장 적절한 것은 ③ '색은 우리 마음속에 숨겨진 것들을 이해하는 데 도움을 줄 수 있다'이다.

해석

당신은 파란색 방에 있다가 슬퍼진 적이 있는가? 아마도 당신은 빨간색에 둘러싸여 있을 때 화가 난 적이 있을 것이다. 색채 심리학은 이 흥미로운 효과를 연구한다. 많은 사람들은 색이 사람의 기분을 바꿀 수 있다고 믿는다. 색은 또한 사람들의 행동에 영향을 줄 수 있다. 오래전, 고대 사람들은 색이 감정적인 효과를 지닌다고 믿었다. 고대 이집트인들은 병을 치료하기 위해 여러 가지 색을 사용했다. 그들은 방을 특정한 색으로 칠함으로써 이렇게 했다. 그들은 또한 수정을 통해 빛을 비췄다. 훨씬 나중에, 독일 시인 Goethe는 색에 대해 썼다. 그는 색이 인간의 감정을 반영할 수 있다고 믿었다. 유명한 심리학자인 Carl Jung은 이 생각을 한 단계 더 발전시켰다. 그는 "색은 잠재의식의 모국어다."라고 주장했다. 그는 색이 사람들이 나쁜 경험에서 회복하도록 도울 수 있다고 믿었다.
① 질병은 우리의 생각을 진찰함으로써 치료될 수 없다.
② 한 사람의 모국어는 그 사람의 정체성을 형성한다.
④ 색채 심리학은 해석 오류로 인해 바뀌어왔다.
⑤ 인간의 행동은 항상 하나 이상의 밝은색과 연관되어 있다.

구문 이해

1 They did this by **painting** a room a certain color.
➜ 「by + 동명사」는 '~함으로써'로 해석한다. by가 전치사이므로 뒤에 오는 목적어는 명사의 형태인 동명사로 쓰였다.
2 Colors are the mother tongue **of** the subconscious.
➜ 무생물의 소유격을 나타낼 때는 전치사 of를 쓰며 소유의 대상이 of 앞에 온다. 우리말과 어순이 다르므로 해석할 때 주의해야 한다.

지문 한눈에 보기

1 기분   **2** 감정적인   **3** 반영   **4** 잠재의식

정답 적중하기

1 change
2 affect
3 effect

본문 p. 39

해설

인간이 시각, 청각, 촉각, 미각, 후각을 가지고 있는 것과 달리, 일부 동물들은 이 중 일부 감각이 발달하지 않아 특별한 감각으로 이를 대신함으로써 환경에 적응한다는 내용이므로 밑줄 친 부분이 글에서 의미하는 바로 가장 적절한 것은 ⑤ '동물은 야생에서 살아남기 위한 그들만의 방식을 갖고 있다'이다.

해석

인간은 다섯 가지 주요 감각: 시각, 청각, 촉각, 미각, 그리고 후각을 가지고 있다. 이러한 감각은 우리가 세상을 안전하게 항해할 수 있도록 도와준다. 예를 들면, 후각은 우리가 위험한 화학 물질을 피할 수 있도록 도와준다. 시각은 우리가 부상 없이 이곳저곳으로 이동할 수 있도록 도와준다. 하지만, 어떤 동물들은 최상의 시력을 가지고 있지는 않다. 그들은 보기 위해 다른 특별한 감각에 의존해야 한다. 예를 들면, 오리너구리는 부리에 많은 센서를 가지고 있다. 이러한 센서는 전기 자극을 감지한다. 이것은 오리너구리가 깊은 물에서 먹이를 찾을 수 있도록 도와준다. 박쥐 또한 흥미로운 보는 방식을 가지고 있다. 그들은 근처의 물체에 소리를 반사시킨다. 이것은 그들이 먹이를 찾고 위험을 피할 수 있도록 도와준다. 어떤 동물들은 전통적인 인간의 감각을 가지고 있지 않기는 하지만, 그들은 자신들의 환경에 적응하는 데 있어 결코 덜 갖춰져 있지 않다.
① 생명체의 주변 환경이 그것의 수명을 결정한다
② 대부분의 동물들은 보고 사냥하는 독특한 방법을 가지고 있다
③ 박쥐를 연구하기 위해서는 특수 장비가 필요할 수 있다
④ 박쥐와 오리너구리 모두 같은 방법으로 사냥을 한다

구문 이해

1 They must **rely on** other special senses to see.
➜ rely on은 '~에 의존하다'라는 뜻을 가진 구문으로 depend on, count on 등과 비슷한 의미로 쓰인다.
2 **While** some animals may not have traditional human senses, they are no less equipped for their surroundings.
➜ 접속사 while은 '~하는 동안에'라는 뜻으로 많이 쓰이지만 여기서는 '반면에'의 의미로 although 또는 even though로 바꿔 쓸 수 있다.

지문 한눈에 보기

1 안전하게   **2** 의존   **3** 전기 자극   **4** 주변 환경

1 eyesight
2 see
3 avoid

 연습문제

  ① ④   ② ②

 ①
연습문제

본문 p. 40

해설

인공지능이 정말로 위험한 것은 그 유능함 때문이고, 인공지능이 인간을 해충처럼 취급할 수 있다는 내용이므로, 밑줄 친 부분이 글에서 의미하는 바로 가장 적절한 것은 ④ '인류를 해충의 지위로 격하하다'이다.

해석

많은 공상 과학 소설 작가들은 인공지능의 시대를 두려워했다. 그들의 이야기에서, 그들은 초현대적인 세계를 묘사했다. 이러한 세계들은 발전된 기술을 바탕으로 운영되었다. 그러나 그것이 반드시 긍정적인 것은 아니었다. 실제로, 많은 작가들은 인간과 인공지능 사이의 갈등을 묘사했다. 인공지능이 발전함에 따라, 많은 과학자들은 위험이 없다고 주장한다. 대신에, 인공지능은 단지 인간을 돕는 도구일 뿐이다. 하지만 Stephen Hawking은 완전히 동의하지는 않았다. 그는 "인공지능의 진짜 위험은 악의가 아니라 능숙함이다."라고 말했다. 그는 인공지능이 목표를 달성하는 데 매우 능숙할 미래에 대해 경고했다. 이 인공지능은 반드시 인간을 싫어하지는 않을 것이다. 오히려, 그것은 인류를 해충처럼 취급할 것이다. 인간은 우리가 개미를 보듯이 여겨질 것이다. "인간을 그 개미들의 위치에 두지 말자."라고 Hawking은 조언했다.
① 개미 군집 위에 우리의 집을 짓다
② 개미와 소통할 수 있는 인공지능을 개발하다
③ 작가들의 충고성 이야기를 믿다
⑤ 그들이 인공지능을 개발할 때 과학자들의 말을 듣다

구문 이해

1 Indeed, many writers depicted conflicts **between** humans **and** AI.
→ 상관접속사 between *A* and *B*는 '*A*와 *B* 사이에'라고 해석한다. 이 문장의 between humans and AI는 '인간과 AI 사이에'라고 해석한다.
2 Humans **would be viewed** the way we view ants.
→ 조동사 would 다음에 수동태 「be + 과거분사(p.p)」가 와서 '~하게 여겨질 것이다'의 의미로 쓰였다. 조동사 다음에는 항상 동사의 원형이 와야 하므로 be동사가 원형으로 왔다.

 BREAKDOWN

1 초현대적인   2 갈등   3 과학자들   4 경고   5 해충

COMPREHENSION CHECK-UP

  1 ④   2 AI   3 ③

1 depict는 '~을 그림으로 그리다, 묘사하다'라는 의미의 동사로 ④ describe (묘사하다, 기술하다)와 의미가 유사하다.
① 암시하다
② 주장하다
③ 전진하다
⑤ 완료하다

2 it은 앞 문장에 나온 This AI를 가리킨다. 한 단어로 쓰라고 했으므로 AI가 정답이다.

3 As AI advances, many scientists claim that there is no danger. ~ However, Stephen Hawking did not completely agree.(인공지능이 발전함에 따라, 많은 과학자들은 위험이 없다고 주장한다. ~ 하지만 Stephen Hawking은 완전히 동의하지는 않았다.)라는 내용으로 보아 ③ 'Stephen Hawking이 과학자들의 의견에 전적으로 동의했다'는 것은 글의 내용과 일치하지 않는다.
① 많은 작가들이 AI와 인간 사이의 갈등에 대해 걱정했다.
② AI가 발전함에 따라 많은 과학자들은 AI가 해롭지 않다고 믿는다.
④ Stephen Hawking은 인공지능의 진짜 위험은 능숙함이라고 주장했다.
⑤ Stephen Hawking은 인간이 해충으로 간주되는 것을 원하지 않았다.

PARAPHRASING DRILL

1 evolves, a lot of, threat
2 about, skilled, aims

TRANSLATION DRILL

1 그러나 그것이 반드시 긍정적인 것은 아니었다.
2 학식 있는 사람이 반드시 현명한 것은 아니다.

 ②
연습문제

본문 p. 42

해설

진로 선택에 있어서 무엇보다 중요한 것은 자신이 좋아하는 일을 선택해야 하는 것이며, 그럴 때 일은 더 이상 일이 되지 않는다는 의미의 공자의 말을 인용했으므로 ② '당신이 즐기는 직업은 일처럼 느껴지지 않는다'가 가장 적절하다.

해석

올바른 진로를 선택하는 것은 벅찬 일일 수 있다. 많은 젊은이들이 부모님이 자랑스러워하시게 만들어야 한다는 부담감을 느낀다. 그들의 부모님은 또한 그들의 아들이나 딸이 재정적인 안정성을 주는 직업을 선택하기를 원한다. 그러나, 돈이 모든 행복의 근원은 아니다. 때때로 가장 보수가 좋은 직업조차도 사람을 비참하게 만들 수 있다. 직업을 위해 좋은 교육을 받기 위해서는 오랜 시간이 걸린다. 따라서, 당신이 즐기지 않는 길을 선택했다는 것을 알게 되는 것은 충격적일 수 있다. 공자는 "당신이 좋아하는 직업을 택하라. 그러면 당신은 평생 하루도 일하지 않아도 될 것이다."라고 말했다. 진로를 선택할 때가 되면, 돈에 대해서만 생각하지 마라. 당신이 진정으로 즐기는 것들에 대해 생각하라. 그러고 나서, 그것을 안정적인 직업으로 바꾸는 방법들에 대해 생각하라.
① 어떤 직업은 업무를 회피하는 것을 가능하게 한다.
③ 직업을 선택하는 것은 완수하기에 어려운 일이다.
④ 직업을 선택할 때 돈이 요인이 되어서는 안 된다.
⑤ 올바른 진로는 재정적 안정을 가져다줄 것이다.

구문 이해

1 Their parents also want them **to choose** a job that will give their son or daughter financial stability.

→ 동사 want는 5형식 동사로, 목적어 뒤에는 to부정사가 목적격 보어로 온다.

2 **It** takes a long time **to get** a good education for a job.

→ It이 가주어, to부정사 이하가 진주어인 구문이다. 날씨, 시각, 요일, 날짜, 거리, 명암 등을 나타낼 때 사용하는 비인칭 주어 it과 혼동하지 않도록 한다.

MAPPING

1 pressured　　**2** stability　　**3** miserable　　**4** enjoy

COMPREHENSION CHECK-UP

1 ③　　**2** ①　　**3** ⑤

1 stable은 '안정적인'이라는 의미로 ③ secure(안전한, 확실한)가 유의어로 적절하다.
① 옳은
② 빈번한
④ 진품의
⑤ 성공한

2 돈보다는 자신이 좋아하는 일을 통해 안정적인 커리어를 개발하라는 내용이므로, From ① Passion to Profession: Creating a Stable Career (열정에서 전문성으로: 안정적인 직업 만들기)가 적절하다.

3 So, it can be devastating to find out that you've chosen a path you don't enjoy.(따라서 당신이 즐기지 않는 길을 선택했다는 것을 알게 되는 것은 충격적일 수 있다.)를 통해 ⑤ '선택한 직업을 즐기지 않는다는 것을 깨닫는 것은 충격적일 수 있다'가 일치하는 내용임을 알 수 있다.
① 진로를 선택하는 것은 젊은이들에게 쉬운 일이다.
② 젊은이들은 재정적 안정성에만 신경을 쓴다.
③ 돈은 모든 행복에 필수적이다.
④ 좋은 교육을 받는 데는 짧은 시간이 걸린다.

PARAPHRASING DRILL

ensure, under, satisfied

TRANSLATION DRILL

1 올바른 진로를 선택하는 것은 벅찬 일일 수 있다.
2 맛있는 음식을 요리하는 것은 나에게 기쁨을 가져다준다.

CHAPTER 4
20번대 문제 공략하기 Part 3

UNIT 06 도표 내용 파악하기

예제 ① ⑤　　예제 ② ⑤

본문 p. 46

해설

오른쪽 그래프에서 중국의 인구 성장률을 나타내는 막대가 아래쪽을 향하고 있고 중국의 인구 성장률이 마이너스(-)임을 알 수 있으므로 ⑤는 도표의 내용과 일치하지 않는다.

해석

위 도표들은 세계에서 가장 인구가 많은 두 국가인 인도와 중국에 초점을 맞추어, 나머지 나라들까지 세 곳의 인구 비율을 나타낸다. ① 인도와 중국 두 나라 모두 각각 세계 인구의 18%를 차지한다. ② 이는 두 국가가 합쳐서 36%를 차지한다는 것을 의미한다. ③ 이는 전 세계 인구의 64%가 다른 국가들에 분포되어 있음을 나타낸다. ④ 오른쪽에 있는 도표는 인도와 중국의 인구 성장률을 강조하고 있다. ⑤ 인도의 인구는 0.92%의 비율로 꾸준히 증가하는 반면, 중국의 성장률은 단지 0.03%에 불과하여, 향후 중국 인구에 큰 변화가 있을 가능성을 나타낸다.

구문 이해

1 **Both** India **and** China each account for 18 percent of the world's population.

→ both A and B는 'A와 B 둘 다'의 의미로 쓰는 상관접속사이다. 상관접속사는 함께 쓰여서 의미를 가지는 접속사들이다.

2 China's growth rate is just 0.03 percent, **indicating** that significant changes in China's population are likely in the future.

→ indicating 이하는 앞 문장의 사실이 어떤 결과를 암시하거나 시사하는지를 설명하는 분사구문으로 사용되었다.

 지문 한눈에 보기

1 성장률　　**2** 중국　　**3** -0.03　　**4** 중국 인구

 정답 적중하기

1 population
2 account for
3 growth rate

본문 p. 47

해설

그래프에서 20-30대의 10%가 캠핑장을 선호하며 스키 리조트 방문은 20%이므로, 선호도가 가장 낮다는 ⑤는 도표의 내용과 일치하지 않는다.

해석

위의 그래프는 20세에서 40세 사이의 사람들의 휴가지 선호도를 보여준다. ① 20세에서 30세 사이의 사람들 중 60%는 해변 리조트에 가는 것을 선호하지만, 나이가 더 많은 연령대의 경우에는 30%만 선호한다. ② 더 젊은 연령층의 10%만이 캠핑장에 가는 것을 선호하지만, 30세에서 40세 사이의 사람들 중 50%는 캠핑을 선호하는 것으로 나타난다. ③ 20대와 30대의 사람들 중 50%는 해외여행을 선호한다. ④ 30세에서 40세 사이의 사람들에게 가장 인기 있는 선택은 해외여행이며, 70%가 이를 선호한다. ⑤ 스키 리조트를 방문하는 것은 모든 연령대에서 가장 인기가 없는 선택지이다.

1 60 percent of people aged 20 to 30 **prefer going** to beach resorts, but only 30 percent of the older age group do.
➔ prefer는 목적어로 동명사와 to부정사가 모두 올 수 있으나, 주로 비교하는 상황에서는 동명사를 쓰는 것이 일반적이다.

2 Visiting a ski resort is **the least** popular option for all age groups.
➔ the least는 less와 little의 최상급 표현으로 쓰인다. 여기서 the least popular는 '가장 인기 없는'이라는 의미다.

 지문 한눈에 보기

1 선호　　**2** 해변 리조트　　**3** 캠핑장　　**4** 스키

 정답 적중하기

1 vacation
2 Only, while
3 popular

연습문제
① ①　　　② ④

 **①**
연습문제　　　　　　　　　　　　　　　　　　　본문 p. 48

해설

졸업장이 없는 주민은 10%이므로 90%가 졸업장이 있다는 것을 알 수 있다. 따라서 98%가 졸업장을 받았다는 ①은 도표의 내용과 일치하지 않는다.

해석

위의 그래프는 West Beach에 살고 있는 사람들의 교육 수준을 보여준다. ① 주민의 98%가 어떤 종류의 졸업장을 받았고 28%의 사람들이 고등학교를 마쳤다. ② 고등학교를 졸업한 사람들의 다수는 대학 학위를 취득하기 위해 진학했고 그 비율은 고등학교만 졸업한 사람들의 비율보다 16% 더 높다. ③ 특히, 주민의 44%는 학사 학위를 받았고 그들 중 일부는 또한 대학원에 입학했다. ④ 주민들 중 18%는 대학원 과정을 마쳤고 또 다른 학위를 받았다. ⑤ West Beach에 사는 사람들 중 10%는 고등학교를 졸업하지 않았고 그들은 어떤 종류의 졸업장도 가지고 있지 않다.

구문 이해

1 98 percent of **residents have** received a diploma of some kind.
➔ 「부분을 나타내는 표현 + of + 명사」의 경우 of 뒤의 명사에 동사의 수를 일치시킨다. 여기서는 residents가 복수 명사이므로 복수 동사 have가 적절하다.

2 They do not have **any** diplomas.
➔ any는 여기에서 부정문에 사용되어 '전혀'라는 의미를 전달하며, 특정 수량이나 종류가 없음을 강조한다.

 BREAKDOWN

1 Education　**2** high school　**3** a graduate degree　**4** graduate

---

 COMPREHENSION CHECK-UP

1 ④　　　**2** 10 percent of people in West Beach　　　**3** ②

1 complete는 '완료하다, 완수하다'의 의미로 여기에서는 ④ achieve(성취하다, 해내다)가 대신 쓰기 적절하다.
① 시도하다
② 참석하다
③ 남다
⑤ 변경하다

2 앞 문장에 나온 10 percent of people in West Beach를 받는 대명사이다.

3 28%의 사람들이 고등학교까지 마치고 대학에 가지 않았으므로, ②는 일치하지 않는다.

PARAPHRASING DRILL

1 residents, graduated, from
2 individuals, complete, no

TRANSLATION DRILL

1 이들의 비율은 고등학교만 졸업한 사람들의 비율보다 16% 더 높다.
2 이용자의 비율이 최근 증가했다.

②
연습문제　　　　　　　　　　　　　　　　　　　본문 p. 50

해설

그래프상으로는 이탈리아가 청정에너지에 투자한 금액은 2,000억 달러에 조금 못 미치는 수준으로 프랑스보다 조금 더 많다. 따라서 프랑스가 이탈리아보다 조금 더 투자했다는 ④는 도표의 내용과 일치하지 않는다.

해석

위의 도표는 5개국의 청정에너지 투자를 보여준다. 그래프에 나열된 국가는 스페인, 프랑스, 이탈리아, 독일, 미국이다. 이들의 투자는 2020년부터 2023년까지 이루어졌다. 미국은 청정에너지에 가장 많은 돈을 투자했다. ① (미국) 정부는 청정에너지에 5,000억 달러 이상을 썼다. ② 독일은 가장 많은 투자를 한 국가 중 2위를 차지했고, 그들의 투자 금액은 3,000억 달러 이상이었다. ③ 이탈리아와 프랑스는 모두 1,000억 달러 이상을 투자했다. ④ 그러나 프랑스는 이탈리아보다 약간 앞섰고 투자를 더 했다. ⑤ 스페인 정부는 청정에너지에 거의 1,000억 달러를 투자했는데 이는 다른 나라들과 비교해서 가장 적은 금액이다.

구문 이해

1 The countries **listed** are Spain, France, Italy, Germany, and the United States.
➔ listed 앞에는 주격 관계대명사와 be동사, that are가 생략되어 있으며, 문맥상 불필요하거나 의미가 명확할 때 「주격 관계대명사 + be동사」는 생략이 가능하다.

2 However, France **came** out slightly ahead of Italy **and invested** more.
➔ 등위접속사 and 앞뒤로 동사의 형태를 일치시켜야 한다. 앞에 나온 동사 came의 시제에 일치시켜 and 뒤에도 과거 동사 invested가 왔다.

BREAKDOWN

1 Investments   **2** largest   **3** less   **4** least

COMPREHENSION CHECK-UP

1 ④   **2** ②   **3** ⑤

1 slightly는 '약간, 다소'의 의미로 ④ clearly(분명하게)는 유의어가 아니다. ① a bit, ⑤ somewhat은 '약간, 다소'의 의미로 ② barely, ③ nearly는 '거의'의 의미로 쓰인다.

2 ② in terms of는 '~에 관해서'라는 의미의 관용표현이다.

3 스페인은 거의 1,000억 달러, 즉 1,000억 달러에 살짝 못 미치는 금액을 투자하고 있으므로 ⑤ '스페인은 1,000억 달러 미만을 썼다'가 그래프 및 글의 내용과 일치한다.

① 청정에너지에 투자한 국가는 4개국에 불과했다.
② 독일이 가장 많은 금액을 투자했다.
③ 이탈리아와 프랑스는 동일한 금액을 투자했다.
④ 프랑스는 2,000억 달러 이상을 투자했다.

PARAPHRASING DRILL

occurred, until, made

TRANSLATION DRILL

1 독일은 가장 많은 투자를 한 국가 중 <u>2위</u>를 차지했다.
2 그녀는 그녀의 첫 마라톤에서 <u>3위를 차지했다</u>.

07 내용 일치/불일치 파악하기

 ④   ④

본문 p. 52

해설

Marie Curie가 노벨상을 수상한 첫 번째 여성이라고 했으므로 ④는 글의 내용과 일치하지 않는다.

해석

Marie Curie는 1867년 폴란드에서 태어났다. 그녀의 일생 동안, Marie는 과학에 매료되었다. 이는 그녀의 아버지가 그녀에게 수학과 물리학을 가르쳤다는 사실 때문일 것이다. 하지만 그 지역 대학은 여자들이 그곳에서 공부하는 것을 허용하지 않았다. 그래서, Marie는 물리학을 공부하기 위해 프랑스로 이주했다. 1895년, 그녀는 Pierre Curie와 결혼했다. 그들은 함께 일했고 두 가지 새로운 원소를 발견했다. 이후, 그들은 노벨상을 수상했다. 이것으로 Marie는 노벨상을 수상한 첫 번째 여성이 되었다. 1911년 Marie는 화학 분야에서의 업적으로 두 번째 노벨상을 수상했다. 그녀는 두 개의 노벨상을 수상한 첫 번째 사람이다. 그녀의 업적 덕분에, 엑스레이 기계가 개선되었다. 그것들은 이제 더 정확한 이미지를 찍을 수 있다.

구문 이해

1 Throughout her life, Marie was **fascinated** by science.
→ 감정을 나타내는 동사는 사람이 감정을 느낄 경우에는 과거분사의 형태로 쓴다. 여기서는 Marie가 매료된 감정을 느낀 것이므로 fascinated가 왔다.

2 They **are** now **able to** take more accurate images.
→ 「be able + to부정사」는 조동사 can을 대신해서 '가능'을 나타내는 표현이다. 이때 be동사는 주어의 인칭과 시제에 따라 바꿔 써야 한다.

 **지문 한눈에 보기**

1 과학   **2** 프랑스   **3** 원소   **4** 여성   **5** 엑스레이

정답 적중하기

1 moved
2 discovered
3 win

본문 p. 53

해설

안내문 하단의 프로그램 포함 사항에 낚싯대 대여(fishing rod rentals)가 있으므로 ④가 글의 내용과 일치한다.

해석

Blue Lake 청소년 여름 캠프

당신은 야외 활동을 좋아하나요? 재미있고 안전한 환경에서 기본적인 생존 기술을 배우고 싶나요? 그러면 매년 열리는 저희 청소년 여름 캠프에 등록하세요. 아름다운 Blue Lake에서 3주를 보내세요. 보트 타기, 낚시, 캠프파이어, 그리고 다른 많은 것들을 즐기세요!

일시: 7월 8일 월요일~7월 29일 월요일
연령: 11~16세 청소년 대상
프로그램 비용: 1인당 375달러
프로그램 포함 사항: 공용 오두막집, 식사, 보트 대여, 수영 강습, 낚싯대 대여, 자연 투어, 캠프 유니폼 2벌, 벌레 스프레이 등!

등록하시려면, 저희 웹사이트 www.bluelakeyouthsummercamp.com/signup을 방문해 주세요.

구문 이해

1 **Spend** three weeks at the gorgeous Blue Lake.
→ 명령문은 문장 맨 앞에 동사원형이 오므로 여기서도 spend가 원형 그대로 왔다. 명령문은 주어 you가 생략된 형태라는 것도 알아두자.

2 Enjoy **boating, fishing, campfires, and many more**!
→ 셋 이상을 나열할 때는 각각의 단어를 쉼표(,)로 연결하고 마지막 단어 앞에는 and를 사용하는 것이 일반적이다.

지문 한눈에 보기

1 야외 활동   **2** 등록(신청)   **3** 포함   **4** 방문

정답 적중하기

1 survival
2 sign up
3 visit

①
본문 p. 54

해설

Lewis가 많은 이야기를 출판했지만 어린이책인 《The Lion, the Witch, and the Wardrobe(사자와 마녀와 옷장)》만큼 유명한 것이 없다고 했으므로 ④ '출판된 모든 이야기책이 유명해졌다'는 글의 내용과 일치하지 않는다.

해석

1898년 아일랜드에서 태어난 C.S. Lewis는 어린 시절에 자주 아팠다. 그럼에도 불구하고, 그는 세계에서 가장 유명한 작가 중 한 명이 되었다. 작가가 되기 전에, Lewis는 공부하기 위해 영국으로 갔다. 그는 1차 세계대전에서 군인으로서 싸웠다. 후에, 그는 선생님이 되었고 소설을 쓰기 시작했다. Lewis는 많은 이야기들을 출판했다. 하지만 그 어떤 것도 그의 어린이책인 《The Lion, the Witch, and the Wardrobe(사자와 마녀와 옷장)》만큼 유명하지 않았다. 그것은 《The Chronicles of Narnia(나니아 연대기)》 시리즈의 첫 번째였다. Lewis는 마법의 세계인 Narnia에서의 네 형제자매의 모험을 자세히 묘사한 7권의 책을 썼다. C.S. Lewis는 1963년에 교직에서 은퇴했다. 그는 얼마 지나지 않아 세상을 떠났다. 그의 이야기는 오늘날까지 책과 영화로 여전히 사랑받는다.

구문 이해

1 Despite this, he became one of the most celebrated writers in the world.

→ despite는 전치사로 '~에도 불구하고'로 해석되고 in spite of와 같은 뜻으로 쓰인다. 같은 뜻을 가진 접속사로는 although, (even) though가 있다. 이 문장에서는 뒤에 (대)명사가 왔기 때문에 전치사인 despite가 쓰였다.

2 C.S. Lewis retired **from teaching** in 1963.

→ 전치사 뒤에는 (대)명사 또는 동명사가 와야 하기 때문에 동사 teach가 동명사 형태로 왔다.

FLOWCHART

1 영국   **2** 소설   **3** 출판   **4** 모험

COMPREHENSION CHECK-UP

1 ⑤   **2** are   **3** ③

1 celebrated는 형용사로 '유명한'이라는 뜻이다. 유의어로 가장 적합한 것은 ⑤ admired(존경받는)이다.
① 비판받은
② 능숙한
③ 은퇴한
④ 훌륭한

2 그의 이야기는 오늘날까지 책과 영화로 여전히 즐겨지므로 수동태가 적절하다. 주어가 복수(His stories)이므로, to this day(오늘날까지)에 맞는 현재시제로 적절한 be동사는 are이다.

3 《나니아 연대기》의 작가인 C.S. Lewis에 대한 일대기이므로, ③ '병약했던 소년이 세계적인 작가가 되다'가 적절한 제목이다.

① C.S. Lewis의 어린 시절과 교육
② 제1차 세계대전의 참전 작가, C.S. Lewis
④ 《나니아 연대기》: C.S. Lewis의 걸작
⑤ 《나니아 연대기》의 모험과 마법

PARAPHRASING DRILL

1 spite, well-known, over
2 published, describing, sisters

TRANSLATION DRILL

1 작가가 되기 전에, Lewis는 <u>공부하기 위해</u> 영국으로 갔다.
2 그는 이탈리아 음식을 만드는 법을 <u>배우기 위해</u> 요리 수업을 들었다.

②
본문 p. 56

해설

제출 기간은 5월 13일 월요일부터 5월 17일 금요일까지 5일간이라고 했으므로 4일간이라는 ②는 글의 내용과 일치하지 않는다.

해석

New Poets Magazine 신인 콘테스트

당신은 시를 좋아하나요? 연 2회 열리는 《New Poets Magazine》의 콘테스트에 참가해 보는 건 어떠세요? 당신은 《New Poets Magazine》의 다음 호에서 특집이 될 기회를 얻을 수 있습니다!

제출 기간: 5월 13일 월요일~5월 17일 금요일
형식: 500단어 미만의 시 또는 소네트
수상자 발표: 5월 31일 금요일
수상 시 상품:
· 1등상 - 《New Poets Magazine》 7월 호에 글을 실을 자리
· 2등상 - 《New Poets Magazine》 1년 구독권
· 3등상 - Abbot's 서점 50달러 상품권

구문 이해

1 Do you love poetry?
→ 일반동사가 있는 문장의 의문문을 만들 때는 주어와 시제에 맞춰 Do, Does, Did를 이용한다. 주어 뒤에는 동사원형을 쓰는 것이 규칙이다.

2 You **could** win a chance to be featured in the next issue of *New Poets Magazine*!
→ could는 can의 과거형으로 많이 알고 있지만, 미래의 가능성을 나타낼 때도 쓸 수 있다.

MAPPING

1 Contest   **2** Purpose   **3** Period   **4** Requirements

COMPREHENSION CHECK-UP

1 ②   **2** July   **3** ⑤

1 지문에서 chance는 '기회, 가능성'이라는 뜻으로 쓰였으므로 ② opportunity(기회)가 적절한 유의어이다.

① 선택지
③ 선택 가능한 것, 선택된 것
④ 공정성
⑤ 노력

2 내용상 《New Poets Magazine》의 다음 호(the next issue)에 실릴 수 있다고 했고, 지문 하단 1등상 상품 내역에서 7월(July) 호에 실릴 기회를 준다고 했으므로 next가 July를 가리키는 것을 알 수 있다.

3 ⑤ '3등 당첨자는 Abbot's 서점에서 쓸 수 있는 50달러의 상품권을 받게 된다'가 일치하는 내용이다.
① 《New Poets Magazine》 신인 콘테스트는 매년 열리는 것은 아니다.
② 5월 13일부터 6월 17일까지 제출해야 한다.
③ 500단어 이상의 시만 공모전에 허용된다.
④ 대회의 수상자는 5월 30일에 발표된다.

PARAPHRASING DRILL

obtain, included, possibility

TRANSLATION DRILL

1 연 2회 열리는 《New Poets Magazine》의 콘테스트에 참가하는 건 어때요?

2 여가 시간에 새로운 취미를 탐구하는 건 어때요?

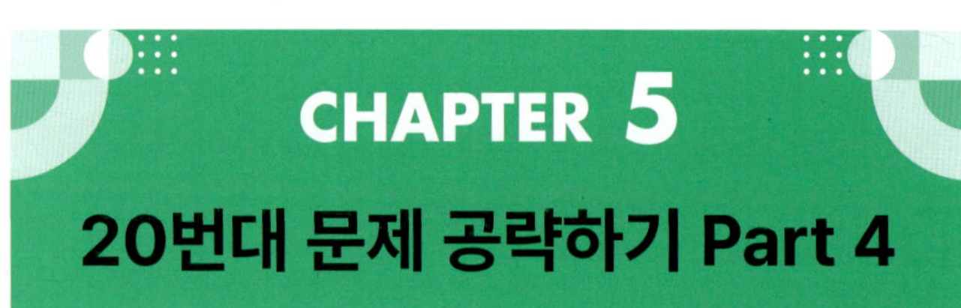

CHAPTER 5

20번대 문제 공략하기 Part 4

UNIT 08 어법 적합성 판단하기

 ①  ④

① 예제

본문 p. 60

해설

문장의 주어 many employers 뒤에 동사가 없으므로 ① to count를 count로 고쳐야 한다. 여기서 count는 '~을 간주하다'의 의미로 쓰였다.

해석

대부분의 산업화된 국가에서, 좋은 직업 윤리를 가지는(열심히 일하는) 것은 무엇보다도 중요하다. 많은 고용주들은 장시간의 근무를 생산성의 표시로 간주한다. 그러나 연구들은 휴식 기간이 실제로 한 사람의 생산성과 창의성을 향상시킬 수 있다는 것을 보여주었다. Alex Soojung-Kim Pang은 그의 책 《Why You Get More Done When You Work Less(당신은 왜 일을 덜 할 때 더 많은 것을 해내는가)》에서, 휴식하는 것은 많은 이점이 있다는 것을 보여주었다. 연구하는 동안, Pang은 매우 창의적이고 성공한 사람들의 삶을 관찰했다. 그는 그들이 극도로 생산적이지만, 종종 짧은 시간 동안만 일한다

는 것을 알아냈다. 한가한 시간에, 그들은 다른 활동에 참여했다. 이러한 활동들은 취미, 운동, 그리고 휴가를 포함했다. 이런 종류의 휴식은 그들의 뇌를 자극했다. 이는 그들이 맑고 상쾌한 정신으로 그들의 일에 다시 접근하는 것을 가능하게 했다.

구문 이해

1 In most industrialized countries, **having** a good work ethic **is** prized above all else.

➜ having은 동명사 주어로 '~하는 것'으로 해석하고 단수 취급하므로 be동사로 is가 왔다.

2 It **allowed** them **to approach** their work again with clear, refreshed minds.

➜ allow는 to부정사를 목적격 보어로 갖는 5형식 동사이므로 to approach가 왔다.

 **지문 한눈에 보기**

1 생산성   **2** 휴식   **3** 이점   **4** 짧은

 **정답 적중하기**

1 improve

2 productive

3 stimulated

② 예제

본문 p. 61

해설

(A) 영화, 장난감 및 테마파크 모두 사람에 의해 만들어져 온 것이므로 현재완료 다음에 수동의 의미를 가진 과거분사(created)가 와야 한다.

(B) 의미상 이야기들이 '말로' 전해진 것이므로 부사형(verbally)이 적절하다.

(C) 문장의 주어는 복수 명사 the tales이므로 be동사 are가 와야 한다.

따라서, 정답은 ④이다.

해석

어린이들에게 상품을 판매하는 것에 관한 한, 디즈니는 가장 성공적인 회사 중 하나다. 영화, 장난감, 그리고 심지어 테마파크도 디즈니의 많은 상징적인 만화 캐릭터들을 기념하고 홍보하기 위해 만들어졌다. 하지만, 이런 캐릭터들 중 많은 것들이 디즈니 작가들의 생각에서 비롯된 것은 아니다. 사실, 어떤 동화 캐릭터들은 수백 년 된 것이다. 1700년대에, 두 명의 독일 형제가 동화 이야기들을 모으기 시작했다. 그 당시에, 이런 이야기들은 구두로 전해졌다. 그 형제는 이야기들을 엮어서 출판했다. Grimm 형제에 의해 쓰여진 이야기들은 종종 어둡고 잔인하며 결말이 무섭다. 일반적으로, 디즈니의 전략은 이런 캐릭터들을 더 행복하고 장난기 많게 처리하는 것이다. 이 전략은 이런 오래된 캐릭터들이 오늘날의 어린이들 사이에서 사랑받게 하는 데 성공적이었다.

구문 이해

1 In fact, some fairy tale characters are **hundreds of** years old.

➜ hundred나 thousand 같은 수의 단위를 나타내는 말 뒤에 -s를 붙여 hundreds of, thousands of로 표현하면 '수백의', '수천의'라는 의미가 된다.

2 In the 1700s, two German brothers **began collecting** fairy tale stories.

→ 동사 begin은 '~을 시작하다'라는 의미로 뒤에 목적어로 to부정사(to collect)와 동명사(collecting)가 모두 올 수 있다.

1 성공적인   **2** 기념   **3** 결말   **4** 전략

1 successful
2 treatment
3 children

① ②   ② ②

연습문제

본문 p. 62

해설

3번째 줄 that 이하는 선행사 photos and videos를 수식하는 관계대명사절이다. that절 안의 동사 make는 사역동사로 '~을 …하게 만들다'라는 의미로 쓰이며, 이때 「사역동사 + 목적어 + 목적격 보어」의 어순을 취한다. 따라서 ② their은 목적격 대명사인 them(most influencers)이 되어야 한다.

해석

많은 사람들이 좋지 못한 신체 이미지로 고통받는다. 소셜 미디어의 증가와 함께, 신체 이미지 문제가 꾸준히 증가하고 있다. 이는 소셜 미디어의 선별된 스타일 때문일 가능성이 있다. 대부분의 인플루언서는 그들이 틀에 박힌 듯이 더 매력적으로 보이도록 고도로 편집된 사진과 영상을 게시한다. 더 많은 사용자가 이러한 종류의 콘텐츠에 관심을 가질수록, 그들 자신의 신체에 대한 이미지는 더욱 급락한다. 심리학자들은 좋지 못한 신체 이미지가 많은 부정적인 결과를 초래할 수 있다고 말한다. 영향받기 쉬운 젊은이들은 섭식 장애가 나타날 수 있다. 다른 사람들은 형편없는 자존감이 생길 수도 있다. 이것은 삶에 대한 그들의 자신감에 영향을 미칠 수 있고 그것은 심지어 학교와 직장에서 그들의 성과를 감소시킬 수 있다. 이것을 줄이기 위해, 전문가들은 젊은이들에게 미디어 리터러시(미디어 정보 해독력)를 가르치는 것을 제안한다. 이것은 그들이 노출되는 콘텐츠가 진정 진짜인지를 알아내는 데 도움을 줄 수 있다.

구문 이해

1 **The more** users engage with this sort of content, **the more** their own body image plummets.

→ 「the + 비교급, the + 비교급」 구문은 '~하면 할수록, …하다'라는 뜻으로 쓰인다. 이 문장에서는 The more ~, the more ~ 형태로 쓰였다.

2 To reduce this, experts suggest **teaching** young people media literacy.

→ suggest는 '~을 제안하다'라는 뜻을 가진 동사로 동명사구(teaching young people media literacy)가 목적어로 왔다.

1 증가   **2** 매력적으로   **3** 부정적인   **4** 감소

---

1 ③   **2** young people   **3** ①

1 attractive는 '매력적인'이라는 뜻이므로 ③ good-looking(잘생긴, 보기 좋은)이 유의어이다.
① 공격적인
② 수동적인
④ 정상적인
⑤ 활동적인

2 앞 문장 To reduce this, experts suggest teaching young people media literacy.(이것을 줄이기 위해, 전문가들은 젊은이들에게 미디어 리터러시를 가르치는 것을 제안한다.)를 통해 them이 '젊은이들(young people)'을 가리킴을 알 수 있다.

3 도입부에서 소셜 미디어의 증가로 신체 이미지 문제가 꾸준히 증가하고 있다고 언급했으므로 ①이 일치하지 않는다.

PARAPHRASING DRILL

1 upload, significantly, modified
2 figure, out, whether

TRANSLATION DRILL

1 소셜 미디어의 증가와 함께, 신체 이미지 문제가 꾸준히 증가하고 있다.
2 재택근무의 증가와 함께, 유연한 일정이 더 일반화되고 있다.

연습문제

본문 p. 64

해설

(A) 동사 agree의 목적어로 완전한 문장이 왔으므로 명사절 접속사 that이 적절하다. if가 명사절을 이끌 때는 '~인지 아닌지'의 의미이다.
(B) be동사 다음에는 보어 역할을 하는 형용사가 와야 하므로 형용사 dependent가 적절하다.
(C) 적절한 관계대명사를 고르는 문제다. 선행사가 those(사람들)이고 관계대명사 뒤에 동사 drive가 왔으므로 주격 관계대명사 who가 적절하다. 「Those who ~」는 '~하는 사람들'이라는 의미이다. 따라서, 정답은 ②이다.

해석

탄소 발자국은 어떤 활동이나 제품이 공기 중으로 방출하는 온실가스의 양이다. 대부분의 전문가들은 개인의 탄소 발자국을 줄이는 것이 중요하다는 것에 동의한다. 그러나, 많은 사람들은 어디서부터 시작해야 할지에 관해 확신하지 못한다. 그들 생활의 많은 부분이 환경을 오염시키는 기술에 의존하는 것을 중심으로 돌아간다. 그럼에도 불구하고, 현재 과학자들이 추천하는 몇 가지가 있다. 첫 번째로, 개인들은 더 깨끗한 교통수단을 선택할 수 있다. 만약 그들이 도시에 산다면, 대중교통은 좋은 선택이다. 운전하는 사람들은 연료 효율이 좋은 자동차를 구입할 수 있다. 전문가들은 또한 가능하다면 비행기로 여행하는 것을 줄일 것을 추천한다. 개인들은 가정에서도 역시 배출을 줄일 수 있다. 이것은 조명과 가전제품을 더 효율적인 모델로 업그레이드함으로써 할 수 있다. 집에 태양 전지판을 설치하는 것 또한 개인의 탄소 발자국을 줄일 수 있다.

구문 이해

1 A carbon footprint is the amount of greenhouse gases **that** an activity or product releases into the air.

→ that 뒤에 동사 releases의 목적어가 없는 불완전한 문장이 왔으므로 that은 목적격 관계대명사인 것을 알 수 있다. 선행사는 greenhouse gases이며, the amount of는 이를 수식하는 표현이다.

2 Nevertheless, **there are** a few things scientists now recommend.

→ 「there + be동사」 구문은 '~이 있다'라는 뜻으로 쓰이고, be동사의 수는 뒤에 오는 명사의 수에 일치시킨다. 여기서는 복수 형태의 주어 a few things에 맞춰 there are가 쓰였다.

MAPPING

1 transportation **2** fuel-efficient **3** Reducing **4** Installing

COMPREHENSION CHECK-UP

1 ⑤   **2** ⑤   **3** ③

1 opt for는 '~을 선택하다'의 의미로 ⑤ choose로 바꿔 쓸 수 있다.
① 거절하다
② 무시하다
③ 설명하다
④ 조사하다

2 탄소 발자국(carbon footprint)에 대해 소개하고, 개인이 온실가스를 줄일 수 있는 방법을 안내하는 글이므로 ⑤ '작은 변화, 큰 영향: 탄소 발자국 줄이기'가 제목으로 적절하다.
① 기술에 의존하는 생활 방식 수용
② 왜 탄소 발자국을 줄이는 것이 중요하지 않은가
③ 출발점: 탄소 발자국을 늘리는 방법들
④ 항공 여행 증가가 환경에 주는 혜택

3 Firstly, individuals can opt for cleaner transportation.(첫 번째로, 개인들은 더 깨끗한 교통수단을 선택할 수 있다.)을 통해 ③ '대중교통을 선택하면 탄소 발자국을 줄일 수 있다'가 일치하는 내용임을 알 수 있다.
① 탄소 발자국을 줄이는 것이 항상 중요한 것은 아니다.
② 많은 사람들이 탄소 배출을 줄이는 방법을 알고 있다.
④ 전문가들은 가능하다면 비행기로 여행할 것을 강력히 제안한다.
⑤ 태양 전지판을 설치하는 것은 탄소 발자국을 줄이는 데 도움이 될 수 없다.

PARAPHRASING DRILL

plenty of, begin, Yet

TRANSLATION DRILL

1 이것은 조명과 가전제품을 더 효율적인 모델로 <u>업그레이드함으로써</u> 할 수 있다.

2 친환경 차량을 <u>이용함으로써</u>, 우리는 환경을 보호하는 것을 도울 수 있다.

CHAPTER 6
30번대 문제 공략하기 Part 1

UNIT 09 어휘 적합성 판단하기

예제 ① ④   예제 ② ④

본문 p. 68

해설

서양에서는 아이들이 대략 오후 7시 30분이나 8시에 잠자리에 든다고 (This may be around 7:30 or 8:00 p.m.) 한 반면, 동양에서는 아이들이 10시나 11시 또는 더 늦게까지 깨어 있다고(children stay up until 10:00, 11:00, or even later) 했다. 즉, 서양 국가의 아이들이 일찍(early) 잠자리에 든다는 맥락이므로 ④ late를 early로 바꿔야 한다.

해석

부모들마다 아이들을 어떻게 키워야 하는지에 관해 다른 생각을 가지고 있다. 육아 방식은 지역과 문화에 따라 완전히 다를 수 있다. 예를 들어, 많은 사람들은 겨울에 그들의 아기를 야외에 둘 생각을 전혀 하지 못할 것이다. 하지만, 북유럽 부모들은 종종 아기를 유모차에 태워 밖에서 낮잠을 재운다. 그들은 심지어 시원한 공기가 아기를 바이러스로부터 보호할 수 있다고 믿는다. 또 다른 흔한 쟁점은 취침 시간이다. 많은 서양 국가들에서, 아이들은 꽤 늦게(→일찍) 잠자리에 든다. 이것은 오후 7시 30분이나 8시경이 될 것이다. 하지만, 많은 동양 국가들에서, 아이들은 10시, 11시, 또는 훨씬 더 늦게까지 깨어 있다. 그럼에도 불구하고, 육아에 접근하는 유일한 올바른 방법은 없다. 세계 모든 지역의 아이들은 안정적이고 건강한 어른으로 자란다.

구문 이해

1 However, Nordic parents often **let** their babies **nap** outside in their strollers.

→ let은 사역동사로 목적격 보어 자리에는 동사원형이 와야 한다. 여기는 nap이 동사원형으로 왔다.

2 Regardless, there is no single right way **to approach** parenting.

→ to부정사 형태인 to approach는 앞에 온 명사 way를 수식하는 형용사적 용법으로 쓰여 '접근하는 방법'으로 해석한다.

 지문 한눈에 보기

1 육아   **2** 밖에서   **3** 일찍   **4** 유일한

정답 적중하기

1 different
2 approach
3 grow up

 **2 예제**

해설

(A) 사용하지 않는 물건들을 제거(get rid of)해야 집안의 잡동사니를 처리할 수 있다. gather around는 '~의 주변에 모이다'라는 의미이다.

(B) 잡동사니가 가득한 집은 사람들을 스트레스 받게 하거나 불안하게(anxious) 만들 수 있다.

(C) 잡동사니를 정리하면 더 빠르고 효율적으로 일하거나 공부할 수 있다고 했으므로 생산성을 감소(decrease)시키는 것이 아니라 증가(increase)시키는 것이 옳다. 따라서, 정답은 ④이다.

해석

잡동사니는 집에 보기 흉한 난장판을 유발하며 빠르게 쌓인다. 만약 당신의 집이 너무 어수선해 보인다면, 지금은 사용하지 않는 물건들을 버릴 때일지도 모른다. 잡동사니 정리는 확실히 당신의 집의 모습을 개선시켜줄 것이지만, 그것이 전부가 아니다. 잡동사니 정리는 당신에게 다른 많은 방법으로 혜택을 줄 수 있다. 예를 들어, 잡동사니는 종종 사람들이 스트레스를 받거나 불안하게 느끼게 한다. 반면에, 잡동사니가 정리된 집은 당신의 기분을 좋아지게 하고 당신 자신에 대해 더 좋게 느끼도록 도와줄 수 있다. 그것은 당신의 생산성을 증가시킬 수 있어서, 당신은 더 빠르고 효율적으로 일하거나 공부할 수 있다. 마지막으로, 잡동사니가 정리된 집은 휴식의 감정을 증가시킬 것이다. 이것은 하루 종일 진정되는 효과를 만들고 당신은 밤에 잠을 더 잘 잔다는 것을 깨닫게 될 수도 있다.

구문 이해

1 **If** your home seems too cluttered, it **may** be time to get rid of unused items.

→ 단순 조건절의 if는 '~하면 …할 것이다'라는 의미로 현재나 미래에 실제로 일어날 수 있는 상황이나 조건을 나타낸다는 점에서 불가능한 일에 대해 이야기하는 가정법과는 다르다. 주로 「If + 주어 + 동사 현재시제, 주어 + 조동사 현재형 + 동사원형~」의 형태로 쓴다.

2 For example, clutter often **makes** people **feel** stressed out or anxious.

→ make가 사역동사로 목적어가 '~하도록 시키다'라는 의미가 될 경우 목적격 보어 자리에 동사원형이 와야 한다. 사역동사에는 make 이외에도 have, let 등이 있다.

지문 한눈에 보기

1 혜택　　**2** 증진　　**3** 생산성　　**4** 진정되는

정답 적중하기

1 improve

2 numerous

3 efficiently

연습문제

 ① ②　　② ③

 **1 연습문제**

해설

모든 감각 중 시각이 가장 중요하다고 생각하는 사람들이 있다는 문장 뒤에는 시각이 중요한 이유에 대한 내용이 이어지는 것이 적합하다. 따라서 ② blocks는 helps와 같은 표현으로 바꿔 시각은 사람들이 주변 세계를 완전히 경험하는 것을 돕는다는 의미가 되도록 해야 한다.

해석

다섯 가지 감각 중 어떤 것이 인간의 경험에 가장 중요한지 결정하는 것은 불가능하다. 어떤 사람들은 시각이 모든 감각들 중에서 가장 중요하다고 말할지도 모른다. 시각은 사람들이 그들 주변 세계를 완전히 경험하는 것을 막는다(→돕는다). 그것은 그들에게 위험에 대해 경고를 하는 동시에 그들이 주변 환경과 예술에 관여하도록 돕는다. 그러나, 다른 사람들은 촉각이 훨씬 더 유익하다고 말할지도 모른다. 그것이 없다면, 사람들은 매우 쉽게 다칠 수 있고, 세계를 항해하는 것이 어려울 것이다. 그럼에도 불구하고, 우리가 주변 세계를 경험할 때 많은 감각들이 함께 작용한다. 예를 들어, 우리는 먹는 것에 관한 한 미각만이 유일하게 관여하는 감각이라고 생각할 수 있다. 하지만 후각 또한 우리가 경험하는 맛에 관여한다.

구문 이해

1 **It** is impossible **to determine** which of the five senses is most important to the human experience.

→ it은 가주어로 쓰였으므로 따로 해석하지 않는다. 진짜 주어는 to determine 이하에 해당한다.

2 **Regardless**, many of the senses work together as we experience the world around us.

→ regardless는 '그럼에도 불구하고'라는 뜻을 가진 접속부사로 앞의 문장과 상반되는 내용이 나올 때 주로 사용한다.

 **BREAKDOWN**

1 불가능(함)　　**2** 경고　　**3** 다칠 수 있고　　**4** 맛

COMPREHENSION CHECK-UP

1 ⑤　　**2** Sight　　**3** ④

1 engaged는 '관련된, 연동된'의 의미로 쓰였으므로 ⑤ participated (관여된)가 유의어로 적절하다.

2 It은 앞 문장에 나온 Sight(시각)를 가리키며, 위험에 대해 경고하고 주변 환경과 예술에 관여하도록 돕는다는 점을 이어서 부연 설명하고 있다.

3 이 글은 시각, 촉각, 후각 같은 인간의 감각이 하는 역할에 대한 내용이므로 ④ '인간의 경험에서 감각의 역할'이 제목으로 적절하다.
　① 다중 감각이 예술 감상에 미치는 영향
　② 새로운 세계를 탐험하는 데 있어 촉감의 역할
　③ 미각과 후각의 관계
　⑤ 사람들이 관계를 맺는데 감각이 주는 도움

PARAPHRASING DRILL

1 interact, environment, warning

2 Nonetheless, contributes, perceive

② 연습문제

본문 p. 72

해설

(A) 생산되는 데(be produced) 오랜 시간이 걸린다는 의미가 되어야 적절하다. progress는 동사로 '진전을 보이다, 나아가다'라는 의미이다.
(B) 산업혁명의 긍정적인 측면에 대한 내용이 앞부분에 나오고 있으므로 positive(긍정적인)가 적절하다.
(C) 저임금과 열악한 노동 환경에 대해 언급했으므로 dangerous(위험한)가 오는 것이 자연스럽다. 따라서, ③이 정답이다.

해석

산업혁명은 인류 사회의 전환점을 나타내었다. 이 시기 이전에는, 상품들은 생산되는 데 오랜 시간이 걸렸다. 따라서, 상품들은 사기에 비쌌다. 산업혁명은 기계화된 공장들의 시작을 경험했다. 경제는 빠른 속도로 성장했고 취업 기회가 증가했다. 그 결과, 도시들은 빠르게 발전했다. 그러나, 산업혁명의 모든 영향이 긍정적인 것만은 아니었다. 그 당시, 공장들은 공기 중으로 엄청난 양의 이산화탄소를 방출했다. 마찬가지로, 오염 물질들이 물과 토양으로 유입되면서 환경 위기 증가에 일조했다. 노동자들은 이 시기 동안 훨씬 더 잘 지내지 못했다. 실제로, 그들은 낮은 임금을 받고 장시간 노동을 강요받았다. 공장 노동 환경은 종종 위험했고, 질병과 때때로 죽음으로까지 이어졌다.

구문 이해

1 Economies **grew** at a rapid pace **and** job opportunities **increased**.
→ and는 앞뒤 문장을 연결할 때 쓰는 등위접속사로 and 앞뒤의 동사의 형태나 시제가 일치해야 한다. 이 문장에서는 and 앞뒤 문장의 동사 grew와 increased의 시제가 과거로 일치한다.
2 Indeed, they **were forced to work** long hours for low wages.
→ force는 to부정사를 목적격 보어로 갖는 5형식 동사다. 이 문장에서는 수동으로 쓰여 be forced 뒤에 to work(목적격 보어)가 왔다.

MAPPING

1 growth　　2 development　　3 pollution　　4 long

COMPREHENSION CHECK-UP

1 ③　　**2** ④　　**3** ⑤

1 문맥상 fare는 '지내다' 또는 '살아가다'의 의미로 사용되어 ③ manage (어렵지만 해내다)와 가장 유사한 의미를 갖는다.
① 성공하다
② 기대하다
④ 성취하다, 이루다
⑤ 경쟁하다
2 산업혁명을 통한 성장의 장점도 있었지만 환경 오염과 노동 문제가 발생했음을 전달하고 있으므로 ④ '양날의 검: 산업혁명의 영향'이 제목으로 가장 적절하다.
① 느린 성장이 옳은 이유
② 산업혁명의 환경적 영향
③ 농업혁명: 결정적인 전환점
⑤ 산업화된 국가들의 환경 문제에 대한 해결책

---

3 산업 혁명 이후의 변화로 적절한 것은 ⑤ '노동자들은 더 적은 임금을 받았고 노동 환경도 나빠졌다'이다.
① 경제는 매우 느린 성장을 경험했다.
② 취업 기회는 감소했고 근로자들은 건강상의 위험에 직면하지 않았다.
③ 환경 안정성은 긍정적인 결과였다.
④ 오염 물질은 물과 토양에 유입되지 않았다.

PARAPHRASING DRILL

Similarly, leading, issue

TRANSLATION DRILL

1 이 시기 이전에는, 상품들은 생산되는 데 오랜 시간이 걸렸다.
2 우리는 여행을 계획하는 데 시간이 좀 필요하다.

CHAPTER 7
30번대 문제 공략하기 Part 2

UNIT 10　빈칸 추론하기

예제 ❶　④　　예제 ❷　①

① 예제

본문 p. 76

해설

도시를 벌집에, 시민을 벌에 비유하여 경제란 상인들이 재료를 가져오고, 상품을 만들고 고객에게 판매하는 체계적인 연결 시스템이라는 내용의 글이므로, 빈칸에 들어갈 말로 가장 적절한 것은 ④ systematically running (체계적으로 가동되는)이다.

해석

도시를 벌집이라고 상상해 보자. 벌집의 각 구역은 집이나 사업체이다. 각각의 벌은 하루 일과를 보내는 시민이다. 그러면 당신은 어디에서 경제를 찾을 수 있는가? 사실, 경제는 한 장소에 위치해 있는 것이 아니다. 그것은 한 번에 목격될 수 없다. 오히려, 경제는 네트워크다. 그것은 사업체, 고객, 그리고 그들 사이의 연결로 구성되어 있다. 벌집의 경우, 일벌들은 꽃가루를 가져온다. 도시에서, 상인들은 재료를 가져올 것이다. 그들은 그 후에 상품을 만들기 위해 이 재료들을 사용한다. 상품은 상점에서 고객들에게 판매된다. 그런 다음 돈은 상점을 통해 공장으로, 그리고 다시 상인들에게 흘러간다. 마치 벌집처럼, 이것은 체계적으로 가동되고 있다. 어떤 실수나 결함도 전체 시스템을 뒤엎을 수 있다.
① 침묵 속에서 작동하고 (있다)
② 힘을 잃고 (있다)
③ 여왕벌을 닮아 (있다)
⑤ 오직 고객을 응대하고 (있다)

구문 이해

1 **Each** bee is a citizen going about his or her day.

→ each는 '각각의'로 해석하는 한정사로 다음에 단수 명사가 온다. each of 뒤에는 복수 명사가 올 수 있다. 두 경우 모두 동사는 반드시 단수형으로 쓴다. 각각의 단일 요소를 강조한다고 보기 때문이다.

2 The goods **are sold** in stores to customers.

→ 수동태는 「be동사 + 과거분사(p.p)」로 쓰며 '~하게 되다, ~을 당하다'로 해석하며, 주어가 행위의 주체가 아니라 그 행위를 당하는 것을 나타낸다.

 **지문 한눈에 보기**

1 벌집　　**2** 네트워크　　**3** 상품　　**4** 체계적

정답 적중하기

1 honeycomb
2 network
3 connections

 **2** 예제

본문 p. 77

해설

빈칸 이후로 지식의 저주를 피할 수 있는 다양한 방법을 소개하고 있으므로 빈칸에 들어갈 말로 가장 적절한 것은 ① '그것을 피하는 몇 가지 방법이 있다'이다.

해석

누군가에게 무언가를 가르치는 데 어려움을 겪은 적이 있는가? 아마도 당신이 가르치고 있던 그 사람은 혼란스럽고 좌절감을 느꼈을 것이다. 이것은 지식의 저주의 예일지도 모른다. 지식의 저주는 다른 사람들이 당신이 가지고 있는 것과 같은 지식을 가지고 있다고 생각할 때 발생한다. 그것은 당신이 가르치고 있는 사람의 관점을 고려하지 않을 때 발생하는데, 이는 당신이 중요한 정보를 건너뛰도록 유발할 수 있다. 이것은 의사소통의 붕괴로 이어질 수 있다. 하지만, 그것을 피할 수 있는 몇 가지 방법이 있다. 예를 들어, 당신이 누군가에게 무언가를 가르칠 때 속도를 줄여 보아라. 그들의 관점을 고려하도록 노력하라. 그들이 어느 정도의 지식을 가지고 있는지 이해하라. 그런 다음 차분하고 상세한 방법으로 설명하는 것을 목표로 하라.
② 더 잘 배울 수 있는 방법을 찾을 수 있다
③ 느린 삶을 사는 것은 많은 이점이 있다
④ 지식의 저주는 흔하지 않다
⑤ 자신을 표현하는 것은 정신 건강을 증진시킨다

구문 이해

1 **Have you ever had** a difficult time teaching someone something?

→ 과거에 시작한 일이 현재까지 영향을 미칠 때 현재완료 시제를 쓰며 「have + 과거분사(p.p)」로 표현한다. ever는 경험을 강조하기 위해 쓰인 부사이다.

2 For example, slow down when you are **teaching someone something**.

→ teach는 4형식 동사로 가르쳐 '준다'는 점에서 수여동사라고도 한다. 수여동사 다음에는 간접목적어(~에게), 직접목적어(~을) 순으로 쓴다.

 **지문 한눈에 보기**

1 저주　　**2** 같은　　**3** 의사소통　　**4** 고려

정답 적중하기

1 curse
2 breakdown
3 perspective

① ⑤　　　② ④

 **1** 연습문제

본문 p. 78

해설

이 증후군은 자신의 몸과 주변을 인식할 때 오류를 일으키며, 주어진 문장의 앞에서 사물을 실제보다 더 작은 것으로(smaller) 인식할 수 있다고 했으므로, In other cases 이하에서는 반대로 ⑤ 너무 커 보이는 것(to be too large)으로 인식할 수 있음을 설명하는 것이 자연스럽다.

해석

Lewis Caroll의 유명한 소설 《이상한 나라의 앨리스》에서, 앨리스는 몇몇의 마법의 음식을 먹는다. 이 음식들 때문에, 앨리스의 몸은 크기가 바뀐다. 한 예시에서, 물약이 그녀를 아주 작은 크기로 줄어들게 한다. 다른 예시에서, 케이크가 그녀를 다시 커지게 만든다. 마법의 음식들은 소설의 소재이지만, 앨리스 이야기의 이 부분에서 이름을 따 지어진 신경 질환이 있다. 이상한 나라의 앨리스 증후군은 드문 질환이다. 그것은 이 질환을 겪는 사람들이 자신의 몸과 주변 세상을 인식할 때 오류를 일으킨다. 그들은 주변의 물체를 실제보다 더 작은 것으로 간주할 수 있다. 다른 경우에는, 이러한 똑같은 물체들이 너무 커 보일 수도 있다. 일부 물체들 또한 모양을 바꾸는 것처럼 보인다. 이러한 증상들은 영구적인 것이 아니라 시간이 지남에 따라 나타났다 사라졌다 한다.
① 건강한
② 작은 것
③ (몸의) 상태가 좋은
④ 통제하는 것

구문 이해

1 They may **view** the objects around them **as** smaller than they actually are.

→ 「view A as B」 구문은 'A를 B로 간주하다'라는 의미로 이때 view는 '관점'이라는 명사가 아닌 동사로 쓰였다.

2 Some objects **appear to change** their shapes as well.

→ 「appear + to부정사」는 '~하는 것처럼 보이다'라는 뜻으로 해석하며 이때 to부정사는 서술적으로 쓰인 형용사적 용법이다.

BREAKDOWN

1 크기　　**2** 드문(희귀한)　　**3** 오류　　**4** 작거나 크다고

COMPREHENSION CHECK-UP

1 ②　　**2** Alice in Wonderland Syndrome　　**3** ②

1 shrink는 '줄어들다'라는 의미의 동사로 같은 의미로 바꿔 쓸 수 있는 것은 ② shorten(짧아지다, 줄다)이다.
① 부수다
③ 확장하다
④ 조이다
⑤ 인식하다

2 증상에 대해 설명하고 있으므로 It은 앞 문장에 나온 Alice in Wonderland Syndrome(이상한 나라의 앨리스 증후군)을 가리킨다.

3 앨리스는 물약(portion)을 먹으면 몸의 크기가 줄어든다고 했다.

TRANSLATION DRILL

1 앨리스 이야기의 이 부분에서 <u>이름을 딴</u> 신경 질환이 있다.
2 식당 이름은 주인의 <u>딸의 이름을 따서 지어졌다.</u>

② 연습문제

본문 p. 80

해설

앞 문장에서 다시 일어서서 시도하는 한 실패해도 세상이 끝난 것이 아니라고 했고, 빈칸 바로 앞에 실패가 훌륭한 학습 경험이 될 수 있다는 내용이 온 것으로 보아 빈칸에는 이러한 것들이 가능한 이유에 해당하는 말이 오는 것이 적절하다. 따라서 ④ '우리는 무엇이 잘못되었는지 그리고 어떻게 개선해야 하는지를 파악할 수 있다'가 정답이다.
① 우리는 실패를 두려운 것으로 본다
② 우리는 실패보다 과정을 더 중요하게 생각해야 한다
③ 우리는 실패를 잊고 극복할 수 없다고 믿는다
⑤ 고집이 우리의 유전적인 특성이라는 의견이 있다

해석

어떤 사람들은 인간이 고집불통의 생명체라고 말할지도 모른다. 사실, 어떤 사람들은 포기하는 것이 더 쉽고 실용적일지라도 꿈이나 목표를 손에서 놓기를 어려워한다. 이러한 예는 성공한 사람들에게서 찾을 수 있다. 세상에서 가장 성공한 사람들은 종종 실패가 그들을 무너뜨리는 것을 거부한다. 대신, 그들은 실패를 교훈으로 여기며 당신도 그렇게 해야 한다. 우리가 실패할 때, 우리는 성공에 이르기 위한 대안을 찾도록 강요받는다. 이것은 우리의 창의력을 향상시키는 데 도움을 준다. 마찬가지로, 실패는 우리에게 더 탄력적이 되도록 가르친다. 우리가 다시 일어서서 시도하는 한, 실패해도 세상이 끝난 것은 아니다. <u>무엇이 잘못되었는지, 어떻게 개선해야 하는지를 파악할 수 있기</u> 때문에 실패는 훌륭한 학습 경험이 될 수도 있다. 우리는 또한 이 지식을 다른 사람들에게 전달할 수 있다.

구문 이해

1 In fact, some people **have a difficult time letting** go of dreams or goals even if it would be easier and more practical to give up.
→ 「have a difficult time + 동명사」 구문은 '~하는 데 어려움이 있다'라고 해석한다. time 뒤에는 in이 생략되어 있어 동사가 그대로 오지 못하고 동명사 형태를 취하는 것이다. 이 문장에서는 동명사 letting이 왔다.
2 Instead, they treat failure as a lesson and **so should you**.
→ 긍정적으로 동의할 때 쓰는 「so + (조)동사 + 주어」 도치 구문이다. 이 문장에서는 '여러분도 그래야만 한다'라는 의미를 나타내기 위해 so should you로 쓰였다.

MAPPING

1 difficult 2 lesson 3 boost 4 resilient

COMPREHENSION CHECK-UP

1 ⑤ 2 ② 3 ③

---

1 refuse는 '거절하다, 거부하다'라는 의미로 같은 표현으로는 ⑤ reject가 있다.
① 받아들이다
② 다시 시작하다
③ 삽입하다
④ 힘을 북돋우다
2 실패를 교훈 삼아 성공의 방법을 찾아가야 한다는 내용이므로 ② '성장과 성공에서 실패의 역할'이 제목으로 적절하다.
① 인생의 도전을 피하는 방법
③ 초기 계획을 따르는 것의 중요성
④ 어떤 대가를 치르더라도 실패를 피해야 하는 이유
⑤ 실패를 무시하는 것: 행복의 열쇠
3 This helps to boost our creativity. Likewise, failure teaches us to be more resilient.를 통해 ③ '실패는 우리가 더 창의적이게 되고 회복탄력성을 갖게 되도록 돕는다'가 일치함을 알 수 있다.
① 일부 사람들은 꿈을 포기하는 것을 쉽게 여긴다.
② 성공한 사람들은 결코 실패를 경험하지 않는다.
④ 인간은 목표를 쉽게 포기하는 존재로 묘사된다.
⑤ 가장 성공한 사람들은 실패로부터 배우는 것을 피한다.

PARAPHRASING DRILL

accomplished, individuals, frequently

TRANSLATION DRILL

1 우리가 다시 일어서서 <u>시도하는 한</u>, 실패해도 세상이 끝난 것은 아니다.
2 당신이 성실히 <u>공부하기만 한다면(공부하는 한)</u>, 시험에서 성공할 것이다.

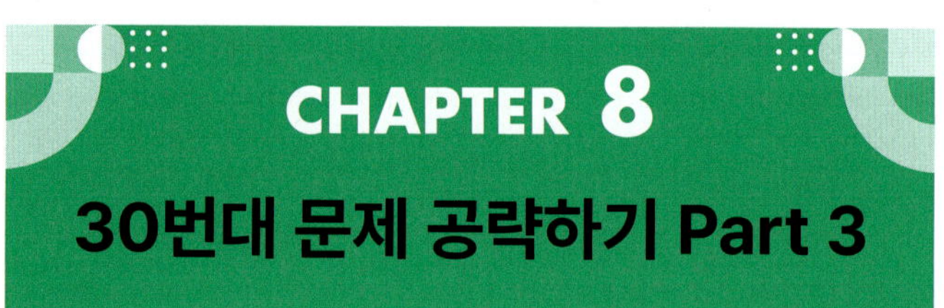

본문 p. 84

해설

동전과 복권을 예시로 들며 확률이 어떻게 활용되는지 설명하는 글이므로, 복권에 당첨되었을 때 나오는 5가지 결과에 대해 언급하고 있는 ③이 글의 전체 흐름과 관계가 없다.

해석

사건을 확실하게 예측하는 것은 어렵다. 그러나 확률은 어떤 것에 어느 정도의 가능성이 있는지 알아내는 데 도움을 줄 수 있다. 동전을 튕겨 올리는 것이 확률의 간단한 예다. 그것은 앞면이나 뒷면으로 떨어질 수 있다. 앞면으로 떨어질 확률이 50%이고 뒷면으로 떨어질 확률도 50%이다. 확률은 또한 복권에 당첨될 가능성을 결정하는 데도 사용될 수 있는데, 가장 쉬운 방법은 당첨 번호의 수를 (선택) 가능한 번호들의 수로 나누는 것이다. (복권에 당첨되면 5개 이상의 가능한 결과가 나온다.) 복권에 당첨될 가능성은 희박하고, 이것은 너무 많은 사람들이 한꺼번에 복권을 사기 때문이다. 어떤 경우에는, 당첨 가능성이 1,500만 분의 1이 될 수도 있고, 1억 5천만 분의 1이 될 수도 있다!

구문 이해

1 **It** is difficult **to predict events with certainty**.

→ 「it(가주어) ~ to부정사구(진주어)」 구문으로 가주어 it은 해석하지 않으며 이 문장의 진짜 주어는 to predict~certainty(예측하는 것)이다.

2 Probability can also **be used to determine** the odds of winning the lottery.

→ 「be used + to부정사」는 '~하기 위해 사용되다'라고 해석된다. 이 문장에서는 to determine이 와서 '결정하는 데 사용된다'로 해석한다.

 **지문 한눈에 보기**

1 가능성   **2** 50%   **3** 복권   **4** 희박

정답 적중하기

1 determine

2 probability

3 slim

예제   본문 p. 85

해설

대부분 이야기에서는 영웅적인 인물 중심으로 이야기가 전개되지만, 악당이 이야기의 중심이 되는 경우도 있다면서 뮤지컬 《위키드》를 예로 들고 있다. 따라서 만화책 속 악당을 동일시하는 팬들에 대해 언급한 ④가 글의 전체 흐름과 관계가 없다.

해석

대부분의 이야기에서는, 영웅이 주인공이다. 영웅의 눈을 통해, 우리는 세상과 사건들을 경험하고 자연스럽게 이 캐릭터에 대해 공감하고 응원한다. 하지만, 이 관점을 악당의 관점으로 바꾸는 것은 우리가 그 이야기에 대해 알고 있다고 생각했던 모든 것을 뒤집을 수 있다. L. Frank Baum의 《오즈의 마법사》에서는 여주인공인 도로시를 통해 이야기를 들려준다. 그녀의 관점을 통해, 독자는 이야기의 악당인 서쪽의 사악한 마녀를 두려워하고 싫어하게 된다. 하지만, 뮤지컬 《위키드》는 도로시의 이야기를 하지 않으며, 이야기가 중심을 두는 것은 악당이다. (만화책 속 악당들은 종종 팬들이 동질감을 느끼는 이들이다.) 그녀의 관점을 통해, 사람들은 그녀가 어떻게 악당이 되었는지를 이해하고 심지어 그녀의 이야기에 공감할 수도 있다.

구문 이해

1 However, shifting this point of view to a villain's may turn everything **(that)** we thought **(that)** we knew about the story upside down.

→ everything 다음에는 목적격 관계대명사 that이, thought 다음에는 명사절을 이끄는 접속사 that이 생략되어 있다.

2 Through her point of view, the reader **learns to fear and dislike** the story's villain, the Wicked Witch of the West.

→ learn은 목적어로 to부정사(to fear)를 취하는 동사이다. 등위접속사 and 뒤에는 (to)가 생략되어 동사원형 dislike가 왔다.

 **지문 한눈에 보기**

1 영웅   **2** 공감   **3** 악당   **4** 중심

 **정답 적중하기**

1 main

2 shifting

3 understand

연습문제

  ① ④   ② ④

연습문제   본문 p. 86

해설

신경 가소성은 성인이 되어서도 새로운 것을 배울 수 있게 해주는 우리 뇌의 특성이라는 것이 글의 요지이므로, 신경 가소성이 뇌 손상을 유발할 수 있다고 한 ④가 글의 전체 흐름과 관계가 없다.

해석

인간의 뇌는 25세까지 완전히 발달되는 것으로 생각되지만, 이것이 전적으로 사실인 것은 아니다. 사실, 뇌는 성인기에도 계속해서 잘 변화하고 있으며 이를 신경 가소성이라고 한다. 뇌는 수십억 개의 뉴런으로 구성되어 있고 이 뉴런들 사이의 경로 또는 연결을 확대시킨다. 이것은 우리가 주변의 것들을 경험하면서 발생하는데 이러한 연결은 우리가 배우고, 생각하고, 새로운 상황에 적응하도록 돕는다. 이러한 적응성은 우리가 어려움에 직면하고, 우리의 환경을 이해하도록 돕는다. 신경 가소성이 없다면, 무언가를 배우는 것이나 문제를 해결하는 것은 어려울 것이다. (신경 가소성은 또한 신경 연결 손상을 일으킬 수 있는 뇌졸중과 같은 다양한 형태의 뇌 손상을 유발할 수 있다.) 시간이 지남에 따라 뇌는 새로운 뉴런을 형성하고, 이것은 뇌졸중 환자와 같은 뇌 손상이 있는 사람이 말하고, 걷고, 문제를 해결하는 것을 다시 배우는 데 도움을 준다.

구문 이해

1 The human brain **is thought to be** fully developed by age twenty-five, but this is not entirely true.

→ 「be thought + to부정사」는 '~로 생각되다'로 해석한다. 이 문장에서는 to부정사 자리에 to be fully developed가 쓰여 '완전히 발달되는 것으로 생각된다'로 해석할 수 있다.

2 Over time, the brain forms new neurons, **which** help people with brain damage, such as stroke victims, relearn to speak, walk, and solve problems.

→ 선행사 new neurons 뒤에 콤마와 which가 온 것으로 보아 which가 계속적 용법의 관계대명사임을 알 수 있으며, 앞에 내용을 부연 설명하는 역할을 한다.

 **BREAKDOWN**

1 신경 가소성   **2** 성인기   **3** 뉴런   **4** 뇌졸중

1 ④　　**2** ④　　**3** ⑤

1 constantly는 형용사 constant(끊임없는, 지속적인)의 부사형으로 ④ continuously(지속적으로)가 유의어로 적절하다.
① 부분적으로
② 전적으로
③ 강하게
⑤ 동시에

2 인간의 뇌가 계속 발달할 수 있게 하고 뇌졸중 환자의 회복도 돕는 신경 가소성에 대한 내용이므로 ④ '인간의 뇌를 계속 성장시키는 것'이 제목으로 적절하다.
① 성인의 뇌질환 유형
② 뉴런: 생명을 위한 고정 연결
③ 변하지 않는 뇌의 구조
⑤ 성인의 뇌와 어린이의 뇌의 차이

3 Over time, the brain forms new neurons ~(시간이 지남에 따라 뇌는 새로운 뉴런을 형성한다)를 통해 ⑤의 내용이 일치하지 않음을 알 수 있다.

PARAPHRASING DRILL

1 consists of, develops, among
2 engage, enable, circumstances

TRANSLATION DRILL

1 이러한 적응성은 <u>우리가</u> 어려움에 직면하고, 우리의 환경을 <u>이해하도록 돕는다</u>.
2 그 소프트웨어는 <u>사용자들이</u> 더 효율적으로 작업을 <u>완료하도록 돕는다</u>.

2 연습문제

본문 p. 88

해설

음악이 인간의 정신에 영향을 미친다는 점에 착안하여 심리학자들이 음악 치료 관련 연구를 했다는 것이 이 글의 요지이므로, 사람들은 무리 지어 활동할 때 더 좋은 결과를 낸다고 한 ④가 글의 전체 흐름과 관계가 없다.

해석

당신이 몸이 좋지 않다고 상상해 보라. 당신이 가장 좋아하는 노래를 틀자, 갑자기 당신의 기분이 좋아진다. 만일 당신이 아플 때도 마찬가지일 수도 있다. 당신은 증상이 조금 덜해지는 것을 알게 될 수도 있다. 이것은 음악이 인간의 정신에 엄청난 영향을 미치기 때문이고, 그것이 몇몇 심리학자들이 음악 치료법으로 실험을 시작한 이유이다. 그들은 음악이 정신 질환에 미치는 영향을 실험하기 위한 연구를 했다. 이 연구 동안, 환자들은 함께 그룹으로 나뉘어져 노래를 불렀고 몇몇은 심지어 그들만의 독창적인 음악을 작곡했다. (사람들은 무리 지어 활동할 때 더 좋은 결과를 낸다.) 심리학자들은 이러한 활동들이 참가자들의 정신 건강을 크게 개선한다는 것을 발견했고, 몇몇 참가자들은 감정적인 혼란을 덜 느낀다고 보고했다.

구문 이해

1 The same might be true **if** you are feeling down.
→ 여기서 if절은 단순 조건으로, 불가능한 상황을 가정하는 가정법의 if절과는 쓰임이 다르다. 조건의 부사절에서는 현재 시제가 미래 시제를 대신한다.
2 They did a study **to test** the effects of music on mental illnesses.

→ '실험하기 위해서' 연구를 했다는 의미이므로 to test가 to부정사의 부사적 용법 중 '목적'을 나타내는 의미로 사용되었다. to test 대신 in order to test를 써서 목적의 의미를 강조할 수도 있다.

FLOWCHART

1 증상　　**2** 영향　　**3** 정신 질환　　**4** 혼란

COMPREHENSION CHECK-UP

1 ①　　**2** some psychologists　　**3** ④

1 profound는 '엄청난, 심오한'이라는 의미로, 여기에서는 명사 effect와 함께 '엄청난 영향'이라는 의미로 쓰였으므로 ① great(대단한)와 의미가 가장 유사하다.

2 They는 음악이 정신 질환에 미치는 영향을 실험하기 위해 연구를 실시한 주체이므로, 앞 문장에 나온 some psychologists(몇몇 심리학자들)를 가리킨다.

3 6행의 some even composed their own original music을 통해 환자들이 작곡도 했음을 알 수 있으므로 ④ '이 실험에서 작곡은 환자들에 의해 수행되지 않았다'가 일치하지 않는다.
① 좋아하는 노래를 듣는 것이 당산의 기분을 향상시킬 수 있다.
② 음악은 아플 때 증상을 완화시키는 효과가 있다.
③ 심리학자들은 음악이 인간의 정신에 영향을 끼친다는 것을 발견했다.
⑤ 참가자들은 음악 치료 후 감정적 혼란을 덜 느꼈다.

PARAPHRASING DRILL

Influence, motivates, investigate

TRANSLATION DRILL

1 <u>이 연구 동안</u>, 환자들은 그룹으로 나뉘어져 노래를 불렀고 몇몇은 심지어 그들만의 독창적인 음악을 작곡했다.
2 폭풍우 동안에, 나무들이 도로 위에 넘어졌다.

UNIT
12 글의 순서 파악하기

예제 **1** ②　　예제 **2** ③

1 예제

본문 p. 90

해설

대부분의 인기 스포츠가 공을 포함하지만 그 모양은 다르다는 주어진 내용 다음에 (B)를 통해 공 모양이 둥근 스포츠의 예를 제시하고, (A)에서는 반대로 둥글지 않은 공을 사용하는 스포츠의 예를 든 다음, (C)에서 공의 모양과 상관없이 스포츠마다 공에 대한 규칙이 있다는 내용으로 이어지는 흐름이 자연스러우므로 ②가 적절한 순서이다.

해석

가장 인기 있는 스포츠 중 많은 것이 공을 포함한다. 스포츠에 따라, 공은 매

우 다르게 생길 수 있다. (B) 어떤 스포츠는 작고 둥근 공을 필요로 한다. 예를 들어, 야구공은 타자가 치기 위해서 작고 둥글어야 한다. 야구공보다 축구공은 더 크고 더 부드럽다. 이것은 선수들이 그것들을 부상 없이 발로 차거나 머리로 들이받을 수 있게 해준다. 농구공은 둥글고, 공기로 가득 차 있다. 이것은 농구공들이 계속해서 튕기기에 완벽하게 만들어 준다. (A) 하지만, 어떤 스포츠는 둥글지 않은 공을 필요로 한다. 미식 축구공은 둥근 모양을 가지고 있지 않다. 오히려, 그것들은 양쪽 끝이 뾰족하다. 이것은 공이 던져질 때 회전할 수 있도록 해준다. 골프공은 외부에 전체적으로 움푹 파인 곳들이 있다. 이 움푹 파인 곳들은 바람의 저항을 줄여준다. 이것은 골프공들이 공기를 쉽게 통과해서 날아가는 것을 가능하게 해준다. (C) 모양에 상관없이 모든 스포츠에는 공에 관한 규칙들이 있다. 이 규칙들이 공의 무게와 부드러움을 결정한다. 또한 규칙들은 어떤 재료가 쓰일 수 있는지 결정한다. 이 규칙들은 경기를 공정하게 유지하는 데 도움이 된다.

구문 이해

1 That **allows** them **to fly** through the air easily.

→ allow는 5형식 동사로 목적격 보어 자리에 동사가 올 때 to부정사 형태를 취해서 목적어가 '~하는 것을 허락하다, ~하게 하다'의 의미로 쓰인다.

2 They also dictate **which materials** may be used.

→ which는 지시 형용사로 '어떤'이라는 의미로 다음에 온 명사를 꾸며주고 있다.

1 포함　　**2** 튕기기　　**3** 저항　　**4** 재료

1 popular
2 different
3 rules

본문 p. 91

해설

마찰력이 무엇인지 묻는 질문으로 시작했으므로 (B)를 통해 마찰력이 언제 발생하며 어떤 특징이 있는지 설명하고, (C)에서 포장도로와 눈 쌓인 언덕의 마찰력을 비교한 후, (A)에서 얼음의 마찰력과 스케이트의 관계를 설명하는 흐름이 적절하므로 ③이 정답이다.

해석

당신은 윤이 나도록 닦인 바닥에서 미끄러진 적이 있는가? 마찰력의 부족 때문에 이러한 일이 일어났는데, 마찰력이란 무엇일까? (B) 그것은 우리의 일상생활 어디에나 있고 두 표면이 맞닿아 미끄러질 때 발생한다. 이 표면은 서로 저항하는 경향이 있다. 울퉁불퉁한 표면은 저항이 많이 발생할 것이다. 더 부드러운 표면은 저항이 더 적을 것이다. (C) 당신이 어떤 포장도로에서 넘어졌다고 상상해 보라. 당신의 바지 무릎 부분이 찢어진다. 당신은 고통스러운 찰과상을 입는다. 이제 당신이 눈 덮인 언덕에서 넘어졌다고 상상해 보라. 당신의 바지는 찢어지지 않는다. 대신에, 당신은 언덕을 미끄러져 내려간다. 이것은 눈이 포장도로보다 덜 울퉁불퉁하기 때문이다. 그래서 마찰력이 더 적다. (A) 마찬가지로, 얼음은 마찰력이 매우 적다. 이것이 아이스 스케이팅을 가능하게 만드는 것이다. 당신의 스케이트 날은 얼음을 가로질러 미끄러지도록 설계되었다. 그것들은 또한 당신이 속도를 내고 회전하는 것을 돕기 위해 (얼음에) 파고들 수 있다. 피겨 스케이트 선수들은 최고 속도로 회전하기 위해 낮은 마찰력을 사용한다.

구문 이해

1 This is **what** makes ice skating possible.

→ 여기서 what은 '~하는 것'이라는 뜻을 가진 관계대명사로 선행사 the thing을 포함하고 있기 때문에 앞에 별도로 선행사가 필요하지 않다.

2 They can also dig in to **help you pick up** speed and turn.

→ help는 준사역동사로 목적격 보어 자리에 동사원형이나 to부정사가 올 수 있다. 반면에, 사역동사(make, have, let 등)는 목적격 보어 자리에 동사원형만 온다.

1 마찰력　　**2** 저항　　**3** 적은(낮은)　　**4** 속도

1 little
2 everywhere
3 bumpy

본문 p. 92

해설

주어진 글은 고대 사람들의 메시지 전달 방식이 오늘날과는 매우 다르다는 내용이다. 따라서 그 예로 잉카 사람들의 메시지 전달 방식을 설명한 (A)와 이들의 방식을 더욱 구체적으로 설명한 (C)가 차례대로 오고, 추가적으로 메시지의 주요 출처를 언급한 (B)가 이어지는 흐름이 가장 적절하므로 ②가 정답이다.

해석

오늘날, 우리는 메시지를 전달하는 수많은 방법들을 가지고 있지만, 이것들은 고대 사람들이 메시지를 보냈던 방법과는 많이 다르다. (A) 그 예로, 잉카 사람들은 효율적인 메시지 전달로 유명하다. 몇몇 문화와 달리, 그들은 말을 타고 메시지를 전달하지 않았다. 오히려, 그들은 걸어서 메시지를 전달했다. 전달자들은 잘 달리는 사람이어야만 했다. 그들은 주요 도로를 따라 위치한 오두막에서 살았다. (C) 매일, 전달자들은 주자들이 다니는 길을 지켜봤다. 주자가 다가오면, 그들은 메시지를 받기 위해 오두막에서 뛰쳐나왔다. 메시지는 종이를 사용하기보다는 구두로 전달되었다. 각 주자는 메시지를 외웠다. 그런 후에 그는 다음 주자에게 메시지를 전달했다. 이어달리기처럼, 메시지는 도로를 따라 수백 마일을 이동했다. (B) 보통, 그 메시지들은 왕이 보낸 것이었다. 그는 종종 이런 방식으로 다른 지역에 정보와 명령을 보냈다. 주자들 덕분에, 그의 메시지들은 겨우 며칠 만에 먼 거리를 이동할 수 있었다.

구문 이해

1 **Rather**, they delivered them on foot.

→ rather은 '대신에, 차라리'라는 뜻의 부사로 앞에 언급한 내용과 다른 내용을 전개할 때 쓰는 단어이다. 이외에도 '꽤, 약간'이라는 의미로도 쓸 수 있다.

2 He often **sent information and orders to other regions** this way.

→ 4형식에서 3형식으로 바꿀 때 send는 간접목적어 앞에 전치사 to가 오는 동사이다. 참고로, make, buy, cook, get, find는 전치사 for가, ask는 of가 온다.

1 걸어서(도보로) **2** 오두막 **3** 구두(말) **4** 왕

COMPREHENSION CHECK-UP

1 ⑤ **2** the message **3** ②

1 numerous는 '많은, 다수의'라는 의미로 ⑤ limited(제한된)로 바꿔 쓸 수 없다.
① 다양한
② 풍부한
③ 다양한
④ 셀 수 없이 많은
2 각각의 주자가 '그 메시지(the message)'를 외운 다음 '그것(it)'을 다음 주자에게 전달했다는 내용이므로 it은 the message를 가리킨다.
3 전달자들은 주요 도로를 따라 각각 오두막에서 생활했다고 했으므로 ②는 일치하지 않는다.

PARAPHRASING DRILL

1 famous, effective, passing
2 Due, cover, just

TRANSLATION DRILL

1 이어달리기처럼, 메시지는 도로를 따라 수백 마일을 이동했다.
2 시스템 덕분에, 그의 메시지는 며칠 만에 수백 명의 사람들에게 도달했다.

② 연습문제

본문 p. 94

해설

주어진 글은 과거 군주제에서는 한 명의 지도자가 장기간 통치했다는 내용으로, 그 뒤에는 왕 또는 여왕의 직위를 가지고 통치하다가 사망하면 왕위를 보통 큰아들이 이어받았다는 내용의 (C), 자녀가 없으면 다음 순서의 남자 친족이 왕위를 승계받았지만 여자가 물려받기도 했다면서 엘리자베스 1세를 언급한 (B), 엘리자베스 1세에 대해 추가로 설명한 (A) 순으로 글이 이어지는 것이 적절하므로 ⑤가 정답이다.

해석

과거에는, 군주제가 일반적인 정부의 형태였다. 이 정부들은 여러 해 동안 한 명의 지도자에 의해 이끌어졌다. (C) 많은 경우에, 이런 지도자는 그 혹은 그녀의 전 생애 동안 통치했다. 그 혹은 그녀는 보통 왕이나 여왕의 칭호를 가졌다. 그 혹은 그녀가 사망하면 왕위는 친족에게 돌아갔다. 보통, 이것은 가장 나이가 많은 아들이었다. (B) 그러나, 가끔은 자녀가 없을 때도 있었다. 따라서, 왕위는 다음 순서의 남자 친족에게 돌아갔다. 이것은 사촌이나 조카일 수 있었다. 어떤 경우에는, 여성이 대신 왕위에 앉혀졌다. 가장 강력했던 통치자 중 한 명은 엘리자베스 1세였다. (A) 엘리자베스 1세는 헨리 8세의 딸이었다. 그녀는 1558년부터 1603년까지 잉글랜드를 다스렸다. 자신의 지배권을 지키기 위해, 그녀는 결혼하는 것을 거부했다. 만약 그녀가 그랬더라면(결혼했다면) 그녀는 남편에게 권력을 잃었을 것이다. 대신, 그녀는 여왕과 왕 모두로서 통치했다.

구문 이해

1 If she **had done** so, she **would have lost** power to her husband.

→ 과거의 사실에 반대되는 상황을 가정하는 가정법 과거완료로 「If + 주어 + had + 과거분사(p.p) ~, 주어 + 조동사 과거형 + have + 과거분사(p.p)」의 형태로 쓴다.
2 **One** of the most powerful rulers **was** Queen Elizabeth I.
→ 「one of the + 복수 명사」 구문은 주어가 단수 명사 one이기 때문에 동사도 단수 형태로 써야 한다. 이 문장에서는 was가 왔다.

1 Monarchy **2** the eldest son **3** male relative **4** marry

COMPREHENSION CHECK-UP

1 ④ **2** ① **3** ⑤

1 preserve는 '지키다, 보호하다'의 의미로 ④ protect와 유의어 관계이다.
① 추정하다
② 예측하다
③ 생산하다
⑤ 항의하다
2 군주제에서의 왕위 계승 순서를 설명하는 글이므로 ① '군주제의 독특한 계승 규칙'이 제목으로 적절하다.
② 엘리자베스 1세의 생애와 시대
③ 엘리자베스 1세의 정치적 전략
④ 군주제의 문제점
⑤ 군주제의 역사
3 엘리자베스 1세는 결혼하는 대신 여왕과 왕 모두로서 통치하였다고 했으므로 ⑤ '엘리자베스 1세는 결혼하지 않았기 때문에 권력을 유지할 수 없었다'는 옳지 않다.
① 군주제는 과거에 일반적인 정부 형태였다.
② 한 지도자가 그 혹은 그녀의 군주제를 여러 해 동안 이끌었다.
③ 왕이나 여왕이 사망하면 왕위는 때때로 친족에게 주어졌다.
④ 엘리자베스 1세는 1558년부터 1603년까지 잉글랜드를 통치했다.

PARAPHRASING DRILL

keep, power, remained

TRANSLATION DRILL

1 그녀는 1558년부터 1603년까지 잉글랜드를 통치했다.
2 인구가 10년 동안 10,000명에서 50,000명으로 급증했다.

13 주어진 문장 위치 파악하기

예제 **1** ② 예제 **2** ③

본문 p. 96

해설

물이 담긴 컵 두 개 중 하나에 식초를 넣는다고 상상한 후에, 물만 남기고 컵

을 제거하는 상상을 하는 것이 글의 흐름에 자연스럽다. 뒤 문장에서도 컵을 제거한 후의 상황이 이어지고 있으므로 주어진 문장이 들어가기에 가장 적절한 곳은 ②이다.

해석

당신은 지구의 바다가 단순히 하나의 거대하고 균일한 수역(水域)이라고 생각할지도 모른다. 그러나, 바다는 사실 서로 다른 수역들로 구성되어 있고, 많은 곳에서 육지가 이들 수역을 분리하지 않는다. 이것은 물의 화학적인 구성과 온도 때문이다. ① 당신이 물 두 컵을 가지고 있고 그것들 중 하나에 약간의 식초를 추가한다고 상상해 보라. ② 이제, 물만 남기고 컵을 제거한다고 상상해 보라. 당신이 가진 물의 양은 총 2컵으로 변하지 않은 상태로 유지되지만, 식초 혼합물은 이제 다른 화학적 구성을 가지고 있다. ③ 그 두 종류의 물은 그들이 닿는 곳에서 약간 섞이겠지만, 그것들은 완전히 섞이지는 않을 것이고 이것은 바다에 대해서도 마찬가지이다. ④ 바다의 소금 함유량이 그것의 화학적 구성을 결정한다. ⑤ 그래서, 바다들이 만나는 곳에서는 서로 다른 소금 함유량들을 가지기 때문에, 완전히 섞이지 않는다.

구문 이해

1 You **may** think Earth's oceans are simply one large, uniform body of water.

→ 조동사 may는 허가(~해도 된다)의 의미와 추측(~일지 모른다)의 의미를 가지고 있다. 여기서는 '당신은 ~라고 생각할지 모른다'의 의미로 추측을 나타낸다.

2 So, oceans do not fully mix where they meet, **having** different salt contents.

→ having different salt contents는 다른 소금 함유량들을 가지고 있기 때문이라는 의미로 쓰인 분사구문이다.

1 (서로) 다른　**2** 온도　**3** 화학적　**4** 함유량(들)

1 separates
2 fully
3 salt contents

②

예제　　　본문 p. 97

해설

자신이 그린 그림이 원하는 이미지와 일치하지 않을지라도 그 그림을 따라 그리면서 실수를 정리하면 그림이 조금씩 나아지게 할 수 있다는 내용 뒤에 주어진 문장, 즉 '이 과정을 반복하면 놀라운 것을 발견할 수 있다'는 내용이 오고, 그 뒤에 이제 그림이 머릿속 이미지와 더 비슷해 보인다는 내용이 이어지는 것이 자연스러우므로 주어진 문장이 들어가기에 가장 적절한 곳은 ③이다.

해석

당신은 아름다운 이미지를 상상하고 그것을 그려 보려고 한 적이 있는가? 아마도 당신의 그림이 완전히 잘못 나와서 당신은 그것을 당신의 머릿속 이미지와 일치시킬 수 없었을 것이다. 이것은 꽤 흔한 상황이다. 심지어 경험이 많은 예술가들도 처음부터 어떤 이미지를 만들어 내는 데는 어려움을 겪을 수도 있다. ① 그러나, 당신의 작품을 버려서는 안 된다. ② 대신에, 당신의 그림을 따라 그려 보면 당신은 실수를 정리함에 따라 그것이 약간 개선되

는 것을 발견할 것이다. ③ 이 과정을 계속해서 반복하면, 당신은 놀라운 것을 발견할 수 있을 것이다. 당신의 그림은 이제 당신 마음속의 이미지와 훨씬 더 비슷해 보인다. ④ 이 기술은 여러 시대에 걸쳐 예술가들에 의해 사용되어 왔는데, 르네상스 예술가들은 종종 한 작품의 여러 버전을 만들었다. ⑤ 그들 중 많은 사람들 역시 고대 이집트, 그리스, 로마의 예술에 감탄했고 그들은 그들 자신의 예술적인 기술을 향상시키기 위해 이러한 유명한 작품들을 반복적으로 모방했다.

구문 이해

1 Even experienced artists may **have trouble creating** an image from scratch.

→ 「have trouble + 동명사(~ing)」는 '~하는 데 어려움을 겪다'라고 해석하고, trouble 다음에 전치사 in이 생략된 구조이므로 뒤에 동명사 형태가 와야 한다.

2 This technique **has been used** by artists throughout the ages.

→ 「have/has been + 과거분사(p.p.)」는 현재완료 수동태로 '~되어 왔다'라고 해석한다. 이 문장에서는 has been used가 쓰여서 '사용되어 왔다'로 해석한다.

1 일치　**2** 예술가　**3** 개선　**4** 유명한

1 creating
2 copying
3 amazing

①　③　　②　①

①

연습문제　　　본문 p. 98

해설

주어진 문장은 혀의 모든 부분에서 다양한 맛을 느낄 수 있다는 내용이므로 미뢰들이 부위로 분리될 수 없다는 문장 뒤에 오고, 그 뒤에 역접의 접속부사 however와 함께 혀의 각각 다른 부분이 혀의 나머지 부분보다 먼저 맛을 인식할 수는 있다는 내용이 이어지는 것이 적절하다. 따라서 정답은 ③이다.

해석

오래전, 과학자들은 혀에 특정한 맛을 느낄 수 있는 특정한 부위가 있다고 믿었다. 단맛은 혀의 끝부분에서, 신맛은 혀의 옆부분에서, 쓴맛은 구강 뒤쪽에서 맛이 느껴진다는 것이었다. 그러나 1980년대와 1990년대에, 연구원들은 미각 부위라는 개념이 완전히 잘못되었다는 것을 깨달았다. 그 잘못된 생각은 한 독일 연구의 번역에서 비롯되었는데, 불행히도 그 번역은 많은 오류를 포함했다. ① 오늘날, 연구자들은 미뢰(味蕾)에 대해 훨씬 더 많이 이해한다. ② 사실, 미뢰는 부위로 분리될 수 없다. ③ 실제로, 혀의 모든 부분에서 다양한 맛을 느낄 수 있다. 그러나, 혀의 각각 다른 부분들이 혀의 나머지 부분보다 먼저 맛을 인식할 수도 있다. ④ 예를 들어, 당신이 (맛이) 쓴 무언가를 먹고 있다고 상상해 보라. ⑤ 당신은 아마도 먼저 구강 뒤쪽에서 그 맛을 느낄 것이고, 이것은 혀의 단지 한 부분만이 주어진 맛을 느낄 수 있는 것처럼 보이는 이유이다.

1 Actually, **every** part of the tongue is capable of tasting a variety of flavors.

→ every 뒤에는 단수 명사를 쓰고, 따라오는 동사도 단수 형태로 써야 한다. '모두'를 모아 놓은 것은 '하나'로 인식하기 때문이다.

2 For example, imagine you are eating **something bitter**.

→ 대명사 something은 뒤에 형용사가 와서 수식하며 이것을 '후치수식'이라 부른다. 이 문장에서는 bitter(쓴)라는 형용사가 something을 뒤에서 수식하고 있으며 '(맛이) 쓴 무언가'로 해석한다.

1 부위　　**2** 미각 부위　　**3** 다양한　　**4** 먼저

COMPREHENSION CHECK-UP

1 ④　　**2** ⑤　　**3** ③

1 separated는 '분리된'이라는 뜻으로 ④ divided(나누어진)와 유의어 관계이다.
　① 완성된
　② 결합된
　③ 등록된
　⑤ 주어진

2 혀의 미각 부위에 대한 기존 개념이 잘못되었다고 한 후 새롭게 발견된 개념을 설명하고 있으므로 ⑤ '혀의 미각 부위에 대한 진실'이 제목으로 알맞다.
　① 맛을 보는 다양한 방법
　② 개인적 맛 선호도
　③ 혀의 다양한 역할들
　④ 혀의 기능 향상시키기

3 쓴맛은 구강 뒤쪽에서 느껴진다고 믿었지만 현재 밝혀진 사실에 따르면 혀의 모든 부위에서 여러 가지 맛을 느낄 수 있다고 했으므로 ③이 일치하지 않는 내용이다.

PARAPHRASING DRILL

1 discovered, idea, incorrect
2 probably, makes, particular

TRANSLATION DRILL

1 오늘날, 연구원들은 미뢰에 대해 **훨씬 더 많이** 이해한다.
2 최신 노트북 모델은 이전 것보다 **훨씬 더 가볍다.**

본문 p. 100

해설

주어진 문장의 these symbols가 가리키는 내용이 세 번째 문장 These views have become symbols in art, song, and literature.에서 언급되므로 주어진 문장이 이 문장 바로 뒤에 오고, 그 뒤에 구체적인 예가 이어지는 것이 글의 흐름에 적절하다. 따라서 주어진 문장이 들어가기에 가장 적절한 곳은 ①이다.

해석

역사를 통틀어, 인간은 자연 세계에서 자신들을 위한 장소를 만들어 왔다. 게다가, 서로 다른 문화들은 동물에 대한 서로 다른 관점을 발전시켜 왔다. 이러한 관점들은 예술, 노래, 그리고 문학에서 상징이 되었다. ① 그러나, 이러한 상징들은 문화들 사이에서 항상 공유되는 것은 아니다. 예를 들어, 소는 서양 국가들에서 주로 식량 공급원으로 여겨지고, 많은 경우에 그것들은 잔인하게 취급받는다. ② 그러나, 네팔에서 소는 신성한 동물이고 매우 좋게 취급을 받는다. ③ 마찬가지로, 많은 서양 문화들은 뱀을 싫어하는데, 뱀이 위험하거나 심지어 악과 연관되어 있다고 생각한다. ④ 반면에, 고대 이집트인들은 뱀을 숭배했고 그것들을 힘과 비옥함의 상징이라고 생각했다. ⑤ 특정 문화 내에서도 관점들은 또한 크게 다를 수 있는데, 비록 미국의 많은 사람들이 뱀을 싫어하지만, 어떤 사람들은 자신의 집에서 뱀을 반려동물로 기른다.

구문 이해

1 Throughout history, humans **have built** a place for themselves in the natural world.

→ 과거의 일이 현재까지 연관되어 있을 때 사용하는 현재완료는 「have + 과거분사(p.p)」 형태로 쓴다. 이 문장에서는 과거부터 현재까지 계속 '만들어 왔다'는 의미의 계속 용법으로 쓰였다.

2 For example, cows **are** mostly **seen** as a food source in Western countries, and in many cases, they **are treated** cruelly.

→ 주어인 cows가 '보여지고', '취급받는' 수동의 의미이므로 「be + 과거분사(p.p)」의 수동태로 쓰였다.

1 views　　**2** cultures　　**3** sacred　　**4** dangerous

COMPREHENSION CHECK-UP

1 ①　　**2** snakes　　**3** ⑤

1 sacred는 '신성한, 종교적인'의 의미로 ① holy(거룩한, 신성한)가 비슷한 의미를 가지고 있다.
　② 안전한
　③ 가혹한
　④ 고대의
　⑤ 근대의

2 미국 사람들의 다수가 뱀을 싫어하지만 일부 사람들은 '그것들'을 가정에서 반려동물로 키운다는 내용이므로 them이 가리키는 것은 snakes이다.

3 글의 마지막 부분으로 보아 ⑤ '미국의 몇몇 사람들은 광범위한 혐오에도 불구하고 뱀을 반려동물로 기른다'가 일치하는 내용이다.
　① 한 문화권 내에서 동물에 대한 관점은 획일적이다.
　② 서양 국가에서는 소를 신성한 동물로 취급한다.
　③ 고대 이집트인들은 뱀이 파괴의 상징이라고 믿었다.
　④ 뱀은 보편적으로 힘과 비옥함의 상징으로 숭배된다.

PARAPHRASING DRILL

mainly, regarded, unkind

TRANSLATION DRILL

1 그러나, 이러한 상징들은 문화들 사이에서 **항상 공유되는 것은 아니다.**
2 사람들이 다른 사람들에 대해 가지는 첫인상은 **항상 정확한 것은 아니다.**

CHAPTER 9
40번대 문제 공략하기 Part 1

UNIT 14 요약문 완성하기

예제 1 ② 예제 2 ①

예제 1 본문 p. 104

해설

최초의 휴대용 시계인 회중시계는 대중적이지 않았지만 이후에 일반적인 패션 액세서리가 되면서 유행을 따르는 패션 시계로 거듭났다는 내용의 글이다. 요약문의 (A)에는 '유행을 따르는'에 해당하는 stylish가 들어가고, (B)에는 '널리 보급된'이라는 의미의 widespread가 들어가서 현대 시계는 유행을 따르는 아이템이지만, 과거에는 휴대용 시계가 널리 보급되지 않았다는 내용이 되는 것이 적절하므로 정답은 ②이다.
① 단순한 - 유행에 민감한
③ 호의적인 - 주목할 만한
④ 유행을 따르는 - 비싼
⑤ 단순한 - 인기 있는

해석

시간의 흐름은 역사를 통틀어 인간에게 중요했다. 그것을 측정하기 위해, 사람들은 다양한 시계를 생각해 냈다. 회중시계는 최초의 휴대용 시계였다. 그것은 본래 16세기에 최초로 발명됐다. 이 작은 시계는 보통 체인에 붙어 있었다. 체인은 재킷이나 조끼에 고정됐다. 시계 문자판은 작은 주머니 안에 넣어져 있었다. 그러나, 이 초기 시계들은 무겁고 비쌌다. 그래서, 그것들은 백 년이 지나서야 비로소 일반적인 패션 액세서리가 됐다. 1810년, 최초의 손목시계가 나폴리 여왕을 위해 만들어졌다. 손목시계는 곧 인기를 얻었다. 시간이 지나면서, 그것들은 선호되는 패션으로서 회중시계를 대체했다. 다른 모든 액세서리들처럼, 그것들은 최근 생겨난 트렌드로 인해 외관이 크게 변했다. 오늘날, 수많은 시계 스타일과 브랜드가 있다. 각각은 특정한 메시지를 전달한다. 그러나 많은 면에서, 스마트워치가 전통적인 시계를 대체하기 시작했다.

⬇

현대 시계는 (A) 유행을 따르는 아이템으로 손목에 착용되는 반면, 최초의 휴대용 시계는 줄에 부착되어 호주머니에 보관되었으며, 과거에는 (B) 널리 보급되지 않았다.

구문 이해

1 Thus, **it was not until** a hundred years later that they became a common fashion accessory.
→ it was not until ~은 '~가 되어서야 비로소 …하게 되었다'의 의미를 가진 구문이다. 이 문장에서도 '백 년이 지나서야 비로소 일반적인 패션 액세서리가 되었다'라고 해석한다.

2 **Each one makes** a certain statement.
→ each는 뒤에는 단수 명사가 와야 하고, 동사도 단수형으로 수일치를 해

야 한다. 이 문장에서는 each one이 주어이므로 동사로 makes가 와서 수를 일치시켰다.

 **지문 한눈에 보기**

1 다양한   **2** 휴대용   **3** 무겁고   **4** 스마트워치

 **정답 적중하기**

1 portable
2 preferred
3 replace

예제 2 본문 p. 105

해설

한 연구에서 학생들을 세 그룹으로 나누어 실험을 했는데, 휴대전화를 가까이 둘수록 수행 능력이 떨어지는 결과를 얻었고, 학생들은 심지어 휴대전화가 부정적인 영향을 준 것을 알아차리지 못했다는 내용의 글이다. 따라서 요약문의 (A)에는 '부진한, 좋지 않은'에 해당하는 poor가 들어가고, (B)에는 '인식하다'에 해당하는 recognize가 들어가는 것이 가장 적절하므로 정답은 ①이다.
② 긍정적인 - 개선하다
③ 부진한 - 무시하다
④ 긍정적인 - 받다
⑤ 더 나은 - 인정하다

해석

당신은 휴대전화가 시야 안에 있는 상태에서 공부한 적이 있는가? 아마도 당신은 휴대전화를 확인하지 않았기 때문에 이것이 괜찮다고 느꼈을 것이다. 하지만 연구원들은 이것에는 눈에 보이는 것 이상의 것이 있을 수도 있다고 생각한다. 한 연구에서, 학생들은 세 그룹으로 나뉘었다. 한 그룹에서, 학생들은 책상 위에 휴대전화를 놓고 시험을 치르도록 요청받았다. 다른 그룹에서, 학생들이 가방에 휴대전화를 넣어두었다. 세 번째 그룹에서, 학생들이 휴대전화를 다른 방에 두었다. 압도적으로, "책상" 그룹이 가장 나쁜 점수를 받았다. 휴대전화를 다른 방에 두었던 학생들이 가장 잘했다. 이것은 휴대전화가 시야 내에 있지 않을 때 학생들이 훨씬 더 잘 수행한다는 것을 암시했다. 시험이 끝난 후, 학생들은 자신의 수행 능력을 평가하도록 요청받았다. 모든 학생들은 자신들이 휴대전화의 영향을 받지 않았다고 느꼈다. 휴대전화가 우리에게 부정적인 영향을 미칠 때 우리는 그것을 깨닫지조차 못할 수도 있기 때문에 이것은 주목할 만한 일이었다.

⬇

한 연구에서, 연구원들은 휴대전화의 존재가 학생들의 (A) 부진한 수행 능력으로 이어질 수 있고, 그들이 그것을 (B) 인식하지 못할 수도 있다는 것을 확인했다.

구문 이해

1 In one group, they **were asked to take** a test with their cell phones on their desks.
→ ask는 5형식 동사로 to부정사를 목적격 보어로 갖는다. 수동태로 바꾸면 「be asked + to부정사」 형태가 되며 '~하도록 요청받다'로 해석한다.

2 This **suggested that** students perform much better without their phones in sight.

→ 동사 suggest는 '~을 제안하다' 또는 '~을 암시하다'로 문맥에 따라 다르게 해석될 수 있다. 이 문장에서는 that 이하의 내용이 드러났다는 맥락이므로 '~을 암시하다'라고 해석한다.

지문 한눈에 보기

1 공부 **2** 세 그룹 **3** 나쁜(낮은) **4** 부정적

정답 적중하기

1 more
2 best
3 noteworthy

연습문제

 ① ④    ② ③

본문 p. 106

해설

전 세계적으로 화석 연료 의존도를 낮추고 무한한 재생 가능한 에너지의 사용을 늘리려는 시도를 하고 있다는 내용의 글이다. 따라서 요약문의 (A)에는 '의존'에 해당하는 reliance가 들어가고, (B)에는 '무제한'에 해당하는 unlimited가 들어가는 것이 적절하므로 ④가 정답이다.
① 효과 - 통제된
② 독립성 - 점검되지 않은
③ 독립성 - 제한된
⑤ 의존 - 점검된

해석

현재, 세계의 많은 부분이 여전히 화석 연료에 의존하고 있다. 화석 연료는 지구의 지각 아래 깊은 곳에서 발견된다. 그것들은 동물과 식물을 분해하는 것으로부터 만들어진다. 이 과정은 수백만 년이 걸린다. 몇몇 예는 석유, 석탄, 그리고 천연가스다. 이것들은 모두 재생 불가능한 에너지원이다. 이것은 그것들의 공급이 제한적이라는 것을 의미하며, 그리고 우리는 언젠가 그것들을 다 써버릴 것이다. 많은 나라들은 화석 연료에 대한 의존을 줄이기를 희망한다. 그러므로, 그들은 더 많은 재생 가능한 에너지를 사용하려고 시도하고 있다. 재생 가능한 에너지는 모든 무한한 에너지원이다. 이런 종류의 에너지를 모으는 것은 환경에 부정적인 방식으로 영향을 미치지 않는다. 바람과 태양 에너지는 가장 인기 있는 예시들 중에 두 가지이다. 바람과 햇빛의 공급은 풍부하기 때문에, 우리는 절대 이것들을 다 써버릴 수 없을 것이다. 연구자들은 또한 바이오매스로 실험을 하고 있다. 이것은 식물, 나무, 농작물, 해조류, 동물의 배설물 등과 같이 살아있는 생물체로부터 나오는 에너지다. 그것은 태워서 열을 얻거나 연료로 바꿀 수 있다.

많은 국가들이 재생 가능한 에너지를 지지하며 화석 연료에 대한 (A) 의존을 줄이는 것을 목표로 하는데 왜냐하면 그것은 (B) 무제한이고 환경에 안전하기 때문이다.

구문 이해

1 Renewable energy is **any** unlimited energy source.
→ any는 이 문장에서 '모든'에 가까운 의미로 사용되어, unlimited energy source라는 명사구를 수식하는 한정사로 재생 가능 에너지가 제한 없이

다양한 형태로 존재할 수 있음을 강조하는 역할을 한다.

2 Wind and solar energy are **two of the most popular examples**.
→ 전치사 of는 '~ 중에'라고 해석하기도 한다. 이 문장에서 two of the most popular examples는 '가장 유명한 예시 중에 두 가지'로 해석한다.

BREAKDOWN

1 화석 연료 **2** 제한적(임) **3** 재생 가능(한) **4** 무한한

COMPREHENSION CHECK-UP

1 ⑤   **2** Renewable energy   **3** ③

1 decomposing은 동사 decompose(분해하다)의 동명사형이다. decompose와 의미가 유사한 동사 decay(부패하다)의 동명사형인 ⑤ decaying이 정답이다.
2 앞 문장에 나온 재생 가능한 에너지(Renewable energy)를 가리킨다.
3 4행의 This means that there is a limited supply of them.(이것은 그것들의 공급이 제한적이라는 것을 의미한다.)을 통해 ③이 일치하지 않음을 알 수 있다.

PARAPHRASING DRILL

1 Nowadays, nations, relying
2 Therefore, trying, utilize

TRANSLATION DRILL

1 이런 종류의 에너지를 <u>모으는 것</u>은 환경에 부정적인 방식으로 영향을 미치지 않는다.
2 책을 <u>읽는 것</u>은 당신의 지식을 확장시킨다.

본문 p. 108

해설

블랙베리는 다른 식물과 달리 독성이 있는 망간을 이용하여 주변 식물을 죽이고 자신이 자랄 공간을 확보한다는 내용의 글이다. 따라서 요약문의 (A)에는 '운반하다'에 해당하는 transfers가 들어가고, (B)에는 '~로부터 이득을 보다'에 해당하는 benefits가 들어가는 것이 가장 적절하므로 정답은 ③이다.
① 운반하다 - 비롯되다
② 제거하다 - 보호하다
④ 제거하다 - 손상을 주다
⑤ 수집하다 - 사라지다

해석

망간은 많은 식물들에게 독성이 있다. 하지만 한 특별한 식물은 흥미로운 방식으로 망간을 이용한다. 망간에 의해 해를 입는 대신, 블랙베리 나무는 이 물질을 이용하고 옮길 수 있는 능력이 있다. 뿌리를 사용해서, 이 식물은 토양 속 깊은 곳에서 망간을 모은다. 그것은 그런 다음 망간을 위로 이동시킨다. 뿌리는 그것을 토양의 상층으로 방출한다. 이 행동은 블랙베리 나무에게 해를 끼치지 않는다. 사실, 이 식물은 심지어 이 망간의 일부를 흡수하는 능력까지 가지고 있다. 그것이 자라면서, 그것은 망간을 뿌리와 줄기 위로 끌어

올린다. 그것은 망간이 잎에 모이도록 한다. 결국, 이 잎들은 말라 버리고 주변 땅에 떨어진다. 잎이 썩으면서, 더 많은 망간이 토양으로 유입된다. 이 모든 망간은 근처의 식물들에게 독성이 있는 영향을 미친다. 이 식물들은 쉽게 죽어서 그 지역을 깨끗하게 한다. 이것은 블랙베리 나무가 자랄 수 있는 충분한 공간을 보장한다.

블랙베리 나무는 주변 토양으로 망간을 (A) 운반하는데 다른 식물들을 죽이고 그 결과로부터 (B) 이득을 보기 위해서이다.

구문 이해

1 In fact, the plant even has **the ability to absorb** some of this manganese.
→ to부정사가 앞에 오는 명사를 수식할 때 to부정사의 형용사적 용법이라고 하며 '~하는'으로 해석한다. 이 문장에서는 the ability를 to absorb가 수식하여 '흡수하는 능력'으로 해석한다.

2 It **lets** the manganese **collect** in its leaves.
→ 사역동사 let은 목적격 보어로 동사원형이 와서 '~가 …하도록 허락하다'로 해석한다. 사역동사에는 make, have, let이 있다.

FLOWCHART

1 독성   **2** 옮기는   **3** 말라 버림   **4** (떨어져) 썩으면서
5 충분한 공간

COMPREHENSION CHECK-UP

1 ②   **2** ④   **3** ②

1 toxic은 형용사로 '독성이 있는'이라는 뜻으로 ② poisonous(유독한)가 유의어로 적절하다.
2 망간의 독성을 이용하여 성장에 이득을 얻는 블랙베리 나무에 대한 내용이므로 ④ '블랙베리와 망간: 독성의 이점'이 제목으로 적절하다.
　① 블랙베리 나무를 생산적으로 재배하는 방법
　② 망간이 모든 식물의 생장에 미치는 영향
　③ 블랙베리 나무가 망간 독성을 피하는 방법
　⑤ 블랙베리 나무가 방출하는 대체 독소
3 It lets the manganese collect in its leaves.(그것은 망간이 잎에 모이도록 한다.)라고 하였으므로 ② '망간은 블랙베리 식물의 잎에 모인다'가 일치하는 내용이다.
　① 블랙베리 나무는 망간을 이용하고 옮길 수 없다.
　③ 블랙베리 나무는 흡수하는 망간에 의해 해를 입는다.
　④ 근처의 식물은 망간이 있는 곳에서 번성한다.
　⑤ 망간은 근처의 식물이 자라고 번성할 수 있도록 도와준다.

PARAPHRASING DRILL

Rather, utilize, transport

TRANSLATION DRILL

1 그것이 자라면서, 그것은 망간을 뿌리와 줄기 위로 끌어 올린다.
2 그녀가 나이가 들어감에 따라, 그녀는 점점 더 그녀의 어머니처럼 보였다.

CHAPTER 10
40번대 문제 공략하기 Part 2

UNIT 15 장문 독해

예제 ① ⑤ ② ④   예제 ③ ③ ④ ⑤ ⑤ ④

1~2 예제

본문 p. 112

해설

1 음성 언어로 시작한 인간의 언어가 지금의 복잡한 언어 체계로 발전하기까지의 과정을 담고 있는 글이므로, 글의 제목으로 가장 적절한 것은 ⑤ '언어의 진화: 인간의 의사소통 역사'이다.
　① 글의 발명: 주요 날짜와 사실
　② 인간의 진화와 발성 기관의 변화
　③ 인간의 발달: 7만 년 전부터의 유전적 변화
　④ 미래의 언어: 인공지능과의 대화
2 초기 인류는 복잡한 소리를 내는 능력이 없었고, 다음에 발성 기관이 발달했다는 내용이 나오므로 발성 기관이 완전히 발달하지 못했을 때는 다양한 범위의 소리를 내기가 어려웠다고 해야 문맥에 적합하다. 따라서 ④ (d)의 easy는 difficult 또는 hard가 되어야 한다.

해석

우리가 증거로 가지고 있는 가장 오래된 문자 체계들은 고대 수메르인, 이집트인, 아카드인이 사용하던 것들이다. 그 이전에는, 인간은 의사소통을 하기 위해 구어에 의존했다. 고대 문명은 복잡한 음성 언어를 사용했지만, 어떻게 이러한 언어들이 발달했을까? 일부 전문가들은 언어들이 다양한 소리와 몸짓으로부터 발달했다고 주장한다. 하지만 초기 인류는 복잡한 소리를 낼 수 있는 능력을 가지고 있지 않았다. 인간은 7만여 년 전에야 비로소 발화 유전자를 발달시켰다. 이 유전자는 뇌가 소리로부터 의미를 이해하도록 해주었다. 그 당시에는, 발성 기관이 아직 완전히 발달되지 않았다. 따라서, 인간이 다양한 범위의 소리를 내는 것은 쉬웠다(→어려웠다). 약 5만 년 전, 발성 기관이 발달을 마쳤다. 인간은 더 다양한 범위의 소리를 만들어 내기 시작했다. 수천 년 동안, 이러한 소리들은 더 복잡한 소리로 변형되었다. 그 소리들로부터, 단어들이 발달했고 문법 체계가 마침내 형성되었다. 전문가들은 복잡한 언어들이 2만 년 전부터 생겨나기 시작했다고 주장한다. 이러한 언어들을 통해, 사회가 형성되기 시작했다. 아이디어들이 공유되었고, 기술들이 발달했다.

구문 이해

1 It **wasn't until** around 70,000 years ago **that** humans developed a speech gene.
→ 「It wasn't until + (시점) + that + (일어난 일)」의 형태로, 특정 시점까지 어떤 일이 일어나지 않았음을 강조할 수 있다. 이 문장에서는 70,000년 전까지 인간이 발화 유전자를 발달시키지 않았음을 의미한다.
2 This gene **allowed** the brain **to get** meaning from sounds.
→ allow는 to부정사를 목적격 보어로 갖는 5형식 동사로 목적어가 무엇 하

는 것(목적격 보어)을 '가능하게 하다'라는 의미의 동사이다. 이 문장에서는 목적격 보어 자리에 to get이 왔다.

지문 한눈에 보기

1 구어 **2** 복잡한 **3** 발달 **4** 더 다양한 범위의 **5** 문법 체계

정답 적중하기

1 develop
2 vocal
3 wider

3~5 예제

본문 p. 114

해설

3 (A) 마을 시장에 나타난 녹색 괴물이 과일 가판대에 가서 먹을 것을 달라고 하자 (C) 상인들이 괴물에게 욕을 하고 돌을 던져 괴물을 더욱 화나게 했지만 (D) 군중 속에 있던 한 소년이 자신의 사과를 괴물에게 건네자 (B) 저주가 풀린 괴물이 왕자로 변해 소년에게 금을 주겠다고 했다는 내용이 되어야 자연스러우므로 ③이 정답이다.
4 ⑤ (e)는 어린 소년(the little boy)을, 나머지는 괴물(the monster)을 가리킨다.
5 괴물은 어린 소년에게 사과를 받았으므로(The monster took the shiny fruit from the boy's hand.) ④가 글에 관한 내용으로 적절하지 않다.

해석

(A)
한 아름다운 왕국의 한가운데에 평화로운 마을이 있었다. 어느 날 아침, 흉측한 괴물이 마을 시장으로 비틀거리며 들어왔다. 그 생물은 녹색이었고 끈적한 진흙으로 덮여 있었다. 그의 머리카락은 엉겨 붙어 있었고 그에게서는 늪 같은 냄새가 났다. 그는 과일 가판대를 향해 비틀거리며 가서는, "저에게 먹을 것을 주세요."라고 말했다.
(C)
상인은 뒷걸음질치며 "저리 가, 추한 생물아! 여기는 괴물이 있을 곳이 아니야!"라고 소리쳤다. 다른 마을 사람들도 동참하여 괴물에게 잔인한 욕을 했고, 그들 중 일부는 그에게 돌을 던졌다. 이것은 괴물을 화나게 했을 뿐이었고, 그는 더 커지기 시작했다. 그의 이빨은 커져서 날카롭고 치명적인 송곳니가 되었다.
(D)
한 가난한 소년이 군중 속에서 지켜보고 있었다. 다른 아이들은 여전히 그 괴물에게 돌을 던지고 있었다. 돌 대신에, 그 어린 소년은 그의 가방에서 하나뿐인 사과를 꺼냈다. 그것이 그가 가진 유일한 음식이었지만, 그는 군중을 헤치고 나가 성난 괴물을 향해 성큼성큼 걸어갔다. 부드럽게, 그는 그 괴물에게 자신의 사과를 권했다.
(B)
그 괴물은 소년의 손에서 반짝이는 과일을 잡았다. 갑자기, 그 괴물이 조금 더 작아 보였다. 그의 얼굴 생김새가 부드러워졌고, 그의 녹색 피부는 정상으로 변했다. 곧, 한 왕자가 그 어린 소년 앞에 서 있었다. "나를 저주에서 구해줘서 고마워."라고 그가 그 어린 소년에게 말했다. "친절만이 그렇게 할 수 있었어. 보답으로, 내가 너에게 금이 들어있는 자루 열 개를 줄게."

구문 이해

1 His features softened, and his green skin **turned normal**.
→ 동사 turned 뒤에 오는 normal은 주격 보어로, 그의 피부가 어떻게 변했는지를 설명하는 형용사이며 「주어 + 동사 + 주격 보어」로 이루어진 2형식이다.
2 Soon, a prince **was standing** before the little boy.
→ 「be + 현재분사(-ing)」는 진행형으로 '~하는 중이다'라고 해석한다. 이 문장에서는 was standing으로 과거진행형이 쓰였고, '서있었다' 정도로 해석한다.

지문 한눈에 보기

1 과일 가판대 **2** 송곳니 **3** 사과 **4** 금(금 열자루)

정답 적중하기

1 village
2 food
3 reward

1~2 연습문제

본문 p. 116

해설

1 일기를 쓰면 자신의 감정을 분석할 수 있고 부정적인 감정이 드는 것을 막아주는 등 불안감을 완화시켜주는 데 효과가 있다는 내용의 글이므로, 제목으로 가장 적절한 것은 ④ '일기 쓰기가 불안을 가진 사람들을 어떻게 도울 수 있는가'이다.
① 여행 일지를 시작하는 방법
② 베스트셀러 일기를 쓰는 방법
③ 일기를 쓴 유명한 작가들
⑤ 시대를 관통하는 일기의 역사
2 글의 흐름상 일기 쓰기가 부정적 생각을 해소하는 데 도움이 된다는 내용으로 연결되어야 하므로 연구 참가자의 불안감이 증가한 것이 아니라 감소했다고 해야 맥락에 맞다. 따라서 ② (b) increased(증가했다)는 decreased(감소했다)로 바뀌어야 한다.

해석

수년에 걸쳐, 일기 쓰기의 이점에 대한 수많은 연구가 수행되었다. 2018년, 70명의 성인 그룹이 일기를 쓰도록 요청받았다. 12주 과정 동안, 그들은 매일 일기를 썼다. 참가자 각각은 불안 장애 진단을 받았다. 연구가 끝날 때즈음, 참가자들의 불안 수준은 상당히 증가했다(→감소했다). 이것은 아마도 불안을 겪는 사람들이 종종 부정적인 생각에 집중하기 때문일 것이다. 일기 쓰기는 그들이 이러한 생각을 말로 표현하는 데 도움을 줄 수 있다. 이것은 그들이 그들의 감정을 분석하는 데 도움을 주고 이러한 감정들이 지배하는 것을 막는다. 2021년에 수행된 한 연구도 감사 일기를 쓰는 것의 이점에 역시 주목했다. 감사 일기는 많은 형태를 취할 수 있다. 그것은 당신이 매일 감사하는 것들의 목록이 될 수 있다. 그것은 또한 당신의 삶에서 일어나는 모든 좋은 일들을 자세히 설명하는 편지도 될 수 있다. 연구자들은 감사 일기를 쓰는 것이 일부 사람들이 우울감을 덜 느끼는 데 도움이 되었다는 것을 밝혀냈다. 그것은 우울증을 악화시키는 부정적인 생각 패턴을 깨는 데 도움을 주었다.

1 Journaling can **help** them **put** these thoughts into words.
→ 준사역동사 help는 목적격 보어로 to부정사 또는 동사원형이 올 수 있다. 이 문장에서는 put이 동사원형으로 왔다.

2 It helped to break the negative thought patterns **that** worsen depression.
→ 주격 관계대명사 that이 이끄는 절이 선행사(the negative thought patterns)를 수식하는 구조이다. 주격 관계대명사가 이끄는 절은 주어가 없는 불완전한 문장이다. 여기서도 that 뒤에 주어 없이 동사 worsen이 바로 왔다.

1 불안 장애　　**2** 부정적인　　**3** 분석　　**4** 우울(증)

COMPREHENSION CHECK-UP

1 ①　　**2** gratitude journal　　**3** ⑤

1 gratitude는 '감사'라는 의미의 명사로 ① appreciation이 유의어이다.
② 중요성
③ 개선
④ 참여
⑤ 분석

2 It은 앞 문장에 나온 '감사 일기(gratitude journal)'를 가리키는 대명사로, 매일 감사하는 것들의 목록도 감사 일기의 한 형태가 될 수 있다는 맥락이다.

3 A gratitude journal can take many forms.(감사 일기는 많은 형태를 취할 수 있다.)를 통해 감사 일기의 형태가 다양함을 알 수 있다. 따라서, 이 글의 내용과 일치하지 않는 것은 ⑤이다.

PARAPHRASING DRILL

1 Every, identified, condition
2 likely, individuals, concentrate

TRANSLATION DRILL

1 그것은 이러한 감정들이 지배하는 것을 막는다.
2 깊게 숨을 마시는 것은 분노가 나의 판단을 흐리는 것을 막는다.

3~5
연습문제

본문 p. 118

해설

3 Anna의 무용 발표회를 축하하기 위해 Anna를 데리고 멕시코 식당에 갔다는 내용으로 이야기를 시작했으므로 식당에 도착해서 인도에 누운 채 구걸을 하는 Fred를 보게 된 (C), Fred의 안타까운 사정에 대해 알게 된 (B), Anna가 먹을 것을 포장해서 Fred에게 가져다주고, 다음날 Fred를 위해 친구들과 모금 행사를 조직하는 (D) 순으로 이어지는 것이 흐름상 가장 적절하다. 따라서 ②가 정답이다.

4 ⑤ (e)는 식당 여종업원을 가리키고, 나머지는 Anna를 가리킨다.

5 Anna는 음식을 먹지 않고 포장을 해서 Fred에게 그 음식을 주었기에, ④가 글에 관한 내용으로 적절하지 않다.

(A)
지난주, 내 딸 Anna는 무용 발표회를 했다. 축하하기 위해, 나는 저녁을 먹으러 Anna를 데리고 그녀가 가장 좋아하는 멕시코 식당에 갔다. Anna는 항상 같은 것, 나초를 곁들인 치킨 부리토를 주문하곤 했다. "빨리 먹고 싶어요."라고 Anna가 차 안에서 배를 문지르며 말했다. "몹시 배고파요!"

(C)
우리는 식당에 도착해서 차를 주차했다. 우리가 식당으로 걸어갈 때, 그녀는 인도에 누워 있는 한 노인을 발견했다. 그는 지저분해 보였고 신발을 신고 있지 않았다. 안에 녹슨 동전 몇 개가 들어있는 작은 컵이 그의 발 앞에 놓여 있었다.

(B)
Anna는 나에게 "저 남자 집 있어요, 엄마?"라고 속삭이기 위해 몸을 가까이 기울였다. 나는 슬프게 고개를 흔들고 "그런 것 같지 않아."라고 대답했다. 그녀는 그 남자에게 인사하기 위해 멈췄다. 그의 이름은 Fred인 것으로 밝혀졌고 그는 심각한 자동차 사고를 당한 것이었다. 그는 다리를 다쳤고, 이것은 그가 더 이상 일을 할 수 없다는 것을 의미했으며 그래서 결국 그는 집을 잃었다.

(D)
그의 이야기를 들은 후, 우리는 작별 인사를 하고 식당 안으로 들어갔다. 음식이 나왔을 때, Anna는 창밖의 Fred를 응시하기만 했다. "저는 더 이상 그렇게 배가 고프지 않아요."라고 그녀가 말했고, 여종업원에게 음식을 포장 상자에 넣어달라고 부탁했다. Anna는 그녀에게 그 상자를 받고 나서, 음식을 가지고 Fred에게 가져다주었다. 다음 날, Anna는 모든 친구들을 불렀다. 그들은 함께 Fred를 돕기 위한 모금 행사를 조직했다. 나는 Anna가 보여준 동정심과 친절이 정말 자랑스러웠다!

구문 이해

1 "I can't wait to eat," Anna said in the car, **rubbing** her tummy. "I'm starving!".
→ 이 문장에서 rubbing은 동시 동작을 나타내는 분사구문으로 쓰였다. 즉, Anna가 말하면서 동시에 자신의 배를 문질렀음을 알 수 있다.

2 **I was so proud** of Anna's compassion and kindness!
→ be proud of는 '~을 자랑스러워하다'라는 뜻을 가진 표현으로 이 문장에서는 강조의 부사 so가 함께 쓰였으므로 '~을 매우 자랑스러워하다'로 해석한다.

1 누워 있는 것　　**2** 교통사고(자동차 사고)　　**3** 여종업원
4 모금 행사　　**5** 친절

COMPREHENSION CHECK-UP

1 ③　　**2** ⑤　　**3** ⑤

1 starving은 동사 starve(굶주리다)의 현재분사형으로 '배가 고픈'이라는 뜻의 ③ hungry가 유의어로 적절하다.
① 다친
② 불안한
④ 근면한
⑤ 무관심한

2 Anna가 Fred에게 음식을 나눠준 작은 친절이 Fred를 위한 모금 운동으로 발전하게 된 과정이 잘 반영된 ⑤ A Kind Heart: A Change That Started with One Shared Meal(친절한 마음: 공유된 한 끼로 시작된 변화)이 이야기의 주제와 잘 맞아떨어진다.

① 어느 저녁의 슬픈 경험
② 노숙자: 문제와 해결책
③ 유명한 멕시코 식당들과 그 유래
④ 노숙자를 만났을 때: 해야 할 것과 하지 말아야 할 것

3 "I'm not that hungry anymore," she said and asked the waitress to put her food into a to-go box.를 통해 ⑤가 일치함을 알 수 있다.

① Anna는 지난달에 무용 발표회를 했다.
② Anna는 항상 치즈를 곁들인 소고기 부리토를 주문했다.
③ Anna는 거리에 앉아 있는 어린 소년을 만났다.
④ Anna는 교통사고로 다친 남자와 이야기하지 않았다.

PARAPHRASING DRILL

injury, get, loss

TRANSLATION DRILL

1 그녀는 그 남자에게 인사하기 위해 멈췄다.
2 그는 가장 가까운 주유소 방향을 물어보기 위해 멈췄다.

수능 영어 독해 번호별 완벽 대비

수능 트레이닝 영어 독해 시리즈!